Strategic Conversations

Most organizations fail to take full advantage of their employees' knowledge, initiative, and imagination. In this accessible and practical book, J.-C. Spender and Bruce A. Strong provide a guide for building entrepreneurial workforces through carefully designed conversations between management and employees. These "strategic conversations" make employees partners in the strategy development process, engaging them to help shape the organization's future. The result is transformational: instead of strategy being a dry, periodic planning exercise for the few, it becomes a dynamic and continuous act of co-creation enriched by the many. Case studies illustrate how leading organizations have used strategic conversations to build sustained competitive advantage, create innovative business models, make better decisions under uncertainty, reduce the need for change management, and enhance employee engagement. The book will appeal to managers, entrepreneurs of all stripes, and teachers and students in schools of business and public administration.

J.-C. SPENDER is Research Professor at Kozminski University, Warsaw and Visiting Professor at Cranfield University and ESADE (Ramon Lull University). Before entering academic life he worked for Rolls-Royce, IBM as a large account manager and special products planner, in merchant banking, and was involved in several Silicon Valley start-ups. He was on the faculty at various universities, including UCLA and Rutgers. In 2003 he retired as Dean of the School of Technology & Business at SUNY/FIT, and between 2007 and 2008 he served as the Fulbright-Queen's Research Chair. His current research involves theorizing on firms and markets under conditions of Knightian uncertainty, with additional interests in, and publications about, the history of management and management education, strategy, and knowledge management.

BRUCE A. STRONG is a founding partner of Cambridge Partners and Associates Inc., a multidiscipline consulting company serving the US and international business communities. He is an entrepreneur, founding systems integration firm Context Integration (that did more than $250 million in sales), he is also a consultant to the senior management of global organizations such as PwC, the World Bank, and State Street Financial, and is a featured speaker and lecturer on knowledge and strategy. He has been written up in Fortune and Fast Company magazines for his knowledge management work, and has written both academic and business articles, including two for the Wall Street Journal, one on knowledge management and the other (with J.-C. Spender) on innovation.

"*Strategic Conversations* redirects our focus to the pent-up, under-utilized asset right in our own back yards: our people and the powerful ideas they are capable of generating. For leaders, the book provides a practical blueprint for what it will take to effectively design, motivate, and harvest this kind of employee engagement. It shows that successful strategies aren't the product of a regimented, top down process, but of passionate conversations constructed by leaders who know how to listen."

Sindri Anderson
Managing Partner, Enact Global Consulting

"In health care, innovation that makes a difference is rarely the product of a single individual – it takes a team. *Strategic Conversations* shows how to engage a range of stakeholders, from employees to external partners, to create business-model-enhancing change."

Naomi Fried
Chief Innovation Officer, Boston Children's Hospital

"The financial markets are increasingly complex and challenging. There is no room for slack in the system. We have to tap into our greatest asset – the intelligence of our employees – in a meaningful and engaging manner to shape our future optimally and responsibly. *Strategic Conversations* provides managers with a guide for engaging employees directly to become active contributors."

James Hardy
COO Global Markets, State Street

"The authors' notion that the purpose of strategy is to address knowledge absences is insightful. Their prescription for dealing with fundamentally irresolvable uncertainty is a unique contribution to the strategy literature."

Mary Lee Kennedy
Former Chief Knowledge Officer, Microsoft; Senior Associate Provost, Harvard University; Currently Chief Library Officer, New York Public Libraries

"It takes a few entrepreneurs to start a business. Sustained success needs many entrepreneurs. *Strategic Conversations* shows how great companies create and sustain a culture of employee entrepreneurship."

Tony Lent
Senior Managing Director, Wolfensohn

"The 'secret sauce' of an innovative company is ability to sustain a culture that is agile, fearless and in sync. *Strategic Conversations* demonstrates how to create engagement across your entire organization."

Michael Maddock
CEO, Maddock Douglas

"It's rare to read a strategy book that says something new, insightful, and useful. *Strategic Conversations* by J.-C. Spender and Bruce A. Strong does. They argue strategy calls for judgment as well as analysis, so senior management does well to call on the practical judgment of their colleagues inside and outside the business. Their book is a practical handbook for doing this and will help you think differently and creatively about both developing and executing strategy."

Professor Andy Neely
Founding Director, Cambridge Service Alliance

"In work and in life there is a higher return on invention. The authors understand this new value equation and extract many wonderful examples of how companies are accelerating their businesses by creatively engaging employees in re-imagining the future."

Lori Senecal
CEO, KBS+

"To innovate its business model, the World Bank is increasingly engaging its partners and clients in strategic conversations. This act of co-creation is imperative for keeping the Bank focused on achieving its goals and fulfilling its mission."

Klaus Tilmes
VP Financial and Private Sector Development, World Bank

Strategic Conversations
Creating and Directing the Entrepreneurial Workforce

J.-C. SPENDER

BRUCE A. STRONG

CAMBRIDGE
UNIVERSITY PRESS

CAMBRIDGE
UNIVERSITY PRESS

University Printing House, Cambridge CB2 8BS, United Kingdom

Cambridge University Press is part of the University of Cambridge.

It furthers the University's mission by disseminating knowledge in the pursuit of education, learning and research at the highest international levels of excellence.

www.cambridge.org
Information on this title: www.cambridge.org/9781107621176

© J.-C. Spender and Bruce A. Strong

First published 2014

Printed in the United Kingdom by Clays, St Ives plc

A catalogue record for this publication is available from the British Library

Library of Congress Cataloguing in Publication data
Spender, J.-C.
    Strategic conversations : creating and directing the entrepreneurial workforce / J.C. Spender, Bruce A. Strong.
        pages cm
Includes index.
ISBN 978-1-107-03619-2 (Hardback) – ISBN 978-1-107-62117-6 (Paperback)
1. Strategic planning.   2. Human capital–Management.   3. Knowledge management.   4. Organizational effectiveness.   5. Organizational behavior.
I. Strong, Bruce A.   II. Title.
HD30.28.S6385 2014
658.4'5–dc23   2013045298

ISBN 978-1-107-03619-2 Hardback
ISBN 978-1-107-62117-6 Paperback

Contents

List of figures   *page* ix

List of tables   xi

Acknowledgements   xii

Preface   xv

1 Introduction – what are strategic conversations?   1

2 The strategic conversations imperative   7

3 Strategic conversations in the wild   23

4 Engaging employees in management's agenda   48

5 Strategizing and the leaders' role   71

6 Putting strategic conversations into practice –
innovation communities   99

7 Conversation trumps structure – new norms for dialog   126

8 Strategic conversations across geographies, generations,
and the multitude   148

9 Engaging the world outside in the conversation   164

10 Creating a self-reinforcing innovation platform –
collateral benefits   182

11 Measuring the future   196

12 Epilogue – on managing   209

    Further reading   211
    Notes   212
    Index   228

Figures

Figure 2.1   Diagram of a hypothetical opportunity space   *page* 11

Figure 3.1   Based on the authors' observations, this figure
shows the typical level of engagement for different
types of "innovation days" participants.   25

Figure 3.2   Shows the typical level of engagement for the
different types of participants in "competitions"   27

Figure 3.3   Shows the typical level of engagement for the
different types of participants in "challenges"   29

Figure 3.4   Shows the typical level of engagement for the
different types of participants in "sensing and
operationalizing"   31

Figure 3.5   Shows the typical level of engagement for the
different types of participants in "T-shaped
management"   32

Figure 3.6   Shows the typical level of engagement for the
different types of participants in "employee
strategy reviews"   35

Figure 3.7   Shows the typical level of engagement for the
different types of participants in "chaordic
conversations"   37

Figure 3.8   Shows the typical level of engagement for the
different types of participants in "innovation
communities"   41

Figure 3.9   Graph showing typical levels of engagement of
primary stakeholders for all types of strategic
conversations   46

Figure 5.1   Diagram of a hypothetical opportunity space   83

Figure 5.2   Strategizing in an organization that fails to
engage employees in its strategizing process   94

Figure 5.3   Strategic conversations and the strategizing process 96

Figure 6.1   Physician drawing documenting extent of
retinopathy in one examination of a premature
infant. Lines are drawn freehand on a preprinted
template, provided courtesy of Boston Children's
Hospital   107

Figure 6.2   Screen capture from "Hyde," provided by and
used with permission of KBS+   112

Figure 6.3   Best Buy stock returns charted against the
Standard & Poor's Index, 2002–2013   118

Figure 7.1   Strategizing wheel   128

Figure 11.1   Innovation attention map   206

Tables

Table 3.1   Comparison of participant engagement levels by
strategic conversation types   *page* 43
Table 11.1 Strategic conversation contribution map   205

Acknowledgements

We were introduced by Larry Prusak, one of the few people we know who has as firm a grasp of academic theories that might be relevant to management practice as of the management practices that might be illuminated by academic theorizing. We are flattered by Larry's interest, and grateful for his correct intuition that we would find each other's work intriguing and expanding – even as he left us entirely to our own devices. We thank him warmly for the introduction, and hope he is not too disappointed by what he helped bring forth. At the same time we thank our commissioning editor at the Cambridge University Press, Paula Parish, for her great commitment to our project. We also thank Claire Poole of Cambridge University Press, who ushered our process along. Alexis Adair was invaluable in locating, and then convincing, our prestigious and very busy interviewees to take the time to talk with us. She was also instrumental in helping to edit the text. Finally, we extend our appreciation to Michelle Suazo who designed our graphics, and was always gracious and patient with our changing notions of what was needed.

Over the years, as we've ruminated on the subjects presented here, and wondered aloud whether there was a book to be written, we received guidance and encouragement from several fronts. Especially inspirational were Thomas Davenport, Brook Manville, and Herminia Ibarra, all masters of taking complicated ideas and research and rendering them useful to practicing managers. Friends and colleagues Ellen Kamp, Joshua Middleman, Joselyn DePetta, Patrick Moran, Linda A Smith, Rachel Newton Bellow, Marc Roudebush, Carlota Vollhardt, Sudhir Chadalavada, Tim Hargrave,

Pamela Mattsson, Al Jacobson, Charles Burck, and Mary Lee Kennedy provided substantial commentary on the text as it was developed.

This is a book about practice, and over the years we've had the privilege of working with some very talented leaders in organizations both large and small. Chris Cipriano and Corinna Snyder at PricewaterhouseCoopers, Ana-Maria Arriagada, Phyliss Pomerantz, Jan Weetjens, Klaus Tilmes, and Ani Dasgupta at the World Bank, Charles D'Antonio, James A. Hardy, Jee Chung, Julee Sanderson, Matt McKillop, Telly Theodopolous, Flora Sah, John Looney, David John Grady, Jesper Kornerup, Sanjeev Kumar, and Joe Salvatore at State Street, and Sarah Telford of the United Nations, have been sources of great inspiration.

Inspiration also comes in (organizationally) smaller packages. We've benefited from being exposed to the genius of entrepreneurs like Armond Cohen, Joe Chaisson, Brad Kain, T. C. Lau, Reagan Coleman, Abdou Touray, Sindri Anderson, Tony Lent, Ruth Reber Long, Owen Davis, Andreas Merkl, Jeffrey Rosenberg, and Michael Dunn.

Finally, we offer the usual disclaimer that none of the people acknowledged here should be implicated in any way as being culpable for any of the errors of commission or omission found in this book. For these the authors take full responsibility.

Chapter heading icons: illustration 2013 © Igor Kisselev

Preface

This book is the fruit of a mutually exploring and informing conversation that has lasted several years, kept going by our shared passion for the topic. Some people argue over baseball, others over astrophysics; this book's authors are hooked on managing – a strange hobby perhaps. Admittedly, we are an odd couple. Spender is a retired business school professor who had earlier careers as a nuclear engineer and consultant, Strong is a full-time management consultant with a new family. For more than forty years Spender has been working on ideas in the relatively recent field of knowledge management. In an earlier era Strong founded and helped manage an information technology services firm that did over $250 million worth of business before it was sold. Strong has been looking to underpin his intuitions about management practice with robust theory. Spender has lately been questioning the theories current in business schools, finding them increasingly rigorous but of declining relevance to real-world managers.

Our book is intended to offer actionable advice to managers on how to develop and execute superior strategies, and to do so more effectively and efficiently. We believe we offer managers techniques that will allow them to make better decisions under uncertainty, engage employees more fully, and deliver better results more quickly. Our conceit is that when leaders are able to harness the imagination of employees to the purposes of the firm, the result is valuable business model innovation. Our book shows managers how to make this rewarding connection.

Writing a book along these lines, offering practical advice rather than sketching a theory or design, demands a certain humility. Writing is one thing, managing is quite another. It helps that both of us have been managers at various times. We are abundantly aware that it is easy to suggest a new management aesthetic as we sit writing, it is quite another to carry it through in the press of the managerial life. So we hope our book captures and communicates our admiration for those engaged executives – especially those prominent in the cases we offer – whose work helps create new value in ways that neither our consulting advice nor our theorizing can claim to.

September 2013   *J.-C. Spender*
                                                                                  Bruce A. Strong

Introduction – what are strategic conversations?

> A great part of the machines ... were originally the invention of common workmen, who, being each of them employed in some very simple operation, naturally turned their thoughts towards finding out easier and readier methods of performing it. Whoever has been much accustomed to visit such manufactures, must frequently have been shewn very pretty machines, which were the inventions of such workmen, in order to facilitate and quicken their own particular part of the work.
>
> Adam Smith, *Wealth of nations*[1]

Many organizations are sitting on an untapped mother lode of sustainable competitive advantage and don't know it. We're talking about a massive amount of energy and imagination, informed by deep industry knowledge. It has the potential to help companies keep their business models fresh and vital. It's already paid for, but rarely deployed.

Where is this rich vein of untapped value? Right at hand, begging to be used: it's the business' own people. Many studies show employees want to make a difference.[2] They are eager to use their talents, domain knowledge, and energy to help grow their organizations. Too often, however, this potential is buried by management practices that stifle employee enthusiasm. Peter Drucker put it well, "So much of what we call management consists of making it difficult for people to work."[3] Most companies don't know how to ask employees to think about making the business stronger, don't have the processes to channel this energy, and don't know how to recognize and reward it. But just like Adam Smith's pin factory workers, today's employees have what Clay Shirky calls "cognitive surplus,"[4] time and mental space not tied directly to their day-to-day work lives. This uncommitted employee energy and imagination is available to the organizations, if only they knew how to harness it.

Wasting this talent is unacceptable today. In the world of globalization and cheap, near-instantaneous information flows, where the business landscape changes almost daily, companies need all hands on deck working constantly to renew their competitive advantage. They can no longer expect to grow and prosper with employees who just take orders. Engagement is an absolute requirement for staff as well: global competition does not treat withdrawn employees kindly. When their employers go out of business, disengaged employees find themselves on the street with atrophied skills and tarnished reputations.

Our book is a guide for leaders who want to develop an engaged and entrepreneurial workforce dedicated to creating value for the organization. It shows how what we call 'strategic conversations' – carefully designed dialogs between management and employees that engage the workforce to explore opportunities for, and constraints to, company growth – can unleash this employee energy. Through strategic conversations employees can contribute substantively to strategy development and business model innovation, activities that used to be the exclusive purview of the C-suite, and in so doing create substantial competitive advantage.

The promise of strategic conversations is already being realized by many leading organizations. These organizations have been able to:

1. strengthen decision-making under uncertainty;
2. develop and promote an entrepreneurial workforce; and
3. accelerate business growth.

As we'll see, they have done this at low or no incremental cost.

While there are ample examples of how to achieve the benefits of strategic conversation, there is no formula. Modern business is complicated – managerially, competitively, legally, technologically, and emotionally – for most people really do care about what they do at work. There is no clearly structured business model that identifies the resources, skills, and arrangements that make competitive success certain. The complexity of modern business also means senior management cannot have all the answers or achieve total control. Like us all, they depend on the advice and support of others with specific skills and connections.

The business teachers and financial press all too easily brush these inconvenient truths under the carpet as they watch from the sidelines and presume that business and managing can be reduced to a quantitative science. Managers know different. So our book is about how to share the burdens of business leadership practically between those with authority and those with important knowledge about how the business might best proceed. We argue that talk, respectful conversation between managers and engaged knowledgeable people, is the key to business success. From this point of view strategy and direction are not developed in isolation and delivered to the business as tablets of truth. They are best developed collaboratively, combining administrative needs with the facts of best practice.

While there is no single path for achieving the benefits of strategic conversations, both experience and theory provide clear guidance on key success factors as well as pitfalls. Our book's goal is to smooth your path to achieving the benefits of strategic conversations by giving you a solid understanding of what works and what doesn't. Because of the uncertainties of real business situations and processes, we know there is no single approach to strategizing, or to a business model, or its innovation. In the absence of such theory-claims we argue for respectful conversation – democratic dialog – between those that are engaged; the objective is to get many different contributions from many different people and turn them into collaborative practice.

Chapter 2, The strategic conversations imperative, explains why developing and implementing strategy and business model innovation is so difficult in today's environment, and why effective employee engagement gives the business a leg up. It also works to debunk many of the common objections to bringing employees to the strategy-making table. Given that strategic conversations are themselves a creative act of business model innovation, it's not surprising that they are employed in many different ways. Chapter 3, Strategic conversations in the wild, helps show that there are plenty of examples around already. We provide an overview of the myriad forms we have observed – often in combination – and analyze their relative effectiveness.

Starting with Chapter 4, Engaging employees in management's agenda, we move from describing strategic conversations to explaining how to put them into practice, sometimes by showing what they are not. Many organizations have used variations of the suggestion box to gather employees' views, and many corporate intranets have been created to do just this. But they have a poor track record. Understanding how strategic conversations operate helps clarify why they always beat trying to implement a theory. Contrary to what many assert, there are no theoretical bases for a successful business model or for optimal strategizing.[5] The image of the off-site brainstorming session that seeks such 'silver bullets' is burned into most executives' minds. Understanding strategic conversations helps explain why these seldom produce useful results. Chapter 4 provides techniques and guidance for leaders so that they can shape the conversation to ensure that it is grounded in the organization's goals and realities.

If there is no science or theory here, what is a strategy and how is it decided? We argue it only exists as real-world practice, a collaborative imaginative activity that adds value by engaging the business situation's uncertainties. Good strategy adds value, bad does not. The practice does not get 'designed' or 'decided' as much as it gets built, through dialog among people who know what they are talking about, as a matter of successful practice. Of course, it is meetings all over again – and why meetings are both inevitable and necessary, and sometimes productive. Leaders must learn how to set up and run productive meetings, especially about how to act when the facts are unclear and information about them is not widely shared. Increasingly effective communications mean these conversations can be 'real' or 'virtual.' At best, though, technologies merely facilitate what people choose to do. Chapter 5, Strategizing and the leaders' role, tackles these thorny questions and explores leadership's and employees' responsibilities to each other. It asserts that strategizing is continuously guiding practice rather than a discrete formalized decision process. And it's an activity that is uniquely human, fired by imagination, informed by personal and organizational values, and, by its very nature, ethically burdened.

Chapter 6 drills down on a particular mechanism for having a strategic conversation, what we call innovation communities. Showcasing this particularly rich type of strategic conversation will help deepen the reader's understanding of strategic conversations as a workable corporate practice. Strategic conversations are just that, conversations. How organizations carry on these conversations matters. Chapter 7 talks about the speech etiquette required for conversational success and why the way organizations hold conversations is much more important than the organization's structure.

Conversation is a dialog between two or more people that, to be effective, needs to be direct, meaningful, and have an impact on behavior. But how to have such conversations in large, global organizations? Cynics will insist large organizations are marred by infighting, turf wars, willful interference and other dysfunctions. Everyone has these stories to tell; but it is like a glass half empty. There is the complementary story of people helping each other without requiring or receiving benefit, for a business is not a perfect market in which everything has a price. The business only persists because it is a community. In practice, organizations function because people collaborate beyond what their instructions demand and so become members of a community, sometimes grudgingly and complaining, but a community nonetheless, like a family. Strategic conversations treat these aspects of organizational life as absolutely crucial and help bring them to higher fruition.

Chapter 8, Strategic conversations across geographies, generations, and the multitude shows how organizations can overcome these challenges and manage to have rich conversations, even under difficult circumstances.

Strategy needs to be influenced by an organization's internal resources and capabilities, as well as by external market forces. This means that effective strategic conversations involve the outside world as well. Chapter 9, Engaging the outside world in the firm's strategic conversation, shows how organizations can bring outsiders into the conversation to enrich the organization's understanding of the outside world, strengthen strategy, and stimulate business model innovation.

The benefits of strategic conversations don't stop with better strategy and more business model innovation. Chapter 10, Creating a self-reinforcing innovation platform – collateral benefits, shows how strategic conversations strengthen employee engagement, talent development, organizational learning, change management, and branding. It will show how new leaders joining the organization can use effective management of strategic conversations to supercharge their transition.

How do you know if strategic conversations are providing value? Chapter 11, Measuring the future, illustrates the various ways organizations have measured the impact of strategic conversations and offers suggestions for creating a simple but effective measurement regimen that will help instrument your strategy and business model innovation creation process.

Strategic conversations bring new requirements and responsibilities for leaders. The concluding chapter, Epilogue – on managing, explains how strategic conversations create deep human relationships that replace the more transactional ones found in command and control environments, and how, when managing is effective, many hands are brought to the pumps. This chapter explores how strategic conversations are morally freighted in ways that we're just beginning to understand.

2 The strategic conversations imperative

> Global businesses, from GM to PwC, are facing increasingly complex problems. We need to expand the sources of solutions for everything from capital "P" problems like where do we find that next $100 million line of business to little "p" problems like how do we satisfy a particular client. Big or small, all these issues are amenable to engaging the diverse source of intelligence available from employees.
>
> Sheldon Laube, Chief Innovation Officer at PricewaterhouseCoopers (retired)[1]

Often when we introduce the notion of employees having an important place at the table of strategy development and business model innovation, we are met with incredulity. "Wouldn't that just introduce chaos?" "You'll have the inmates running the asylum." "Employees just want to be heads down in their own jobs – they don't have time or interest for thinking about the organization as a whole."

Until recently, these types of responses would have been typical. But today we're at an inflection point. Organizational leaders have become acutely aware that the old ways of managing just aren't working. The digital revolution of ever cheaper information is changing the rules of the game. Since the 1960s, several related long-term trends, independent of economic cycle, have come to dominate the business world:

- The pace of innovation has increased.
- Competition has radically intensified, as reflected in both a reduction in the concentration of industries (meaning there are more competitors in a given market space) and an increase in topple rates (companies in the Fortune 100 are less likely to still be there five years hence).

- Overall, corporate returns on both assets and equity have steadily declined. On the demand side, with more information about pricing and quality, consumers are able to make better decisions that cut into margins once protected by brand. On the supply side, knowledge workers better understand their worth and are taking advantage of greater career mobility. The result: winners are barely holding on to what they had and laggards are taking it on the chin.[2]

For reasons we'll explore fully in this chapter, leading organizations are addressing these very problems by increasingly giving employees a seat at the strategy table – and often in unexpected places. PricewaterhouseCoopers (PwC), a huge, global partnership in a highly regulated industry with roots going back to the nineteenth century, would seem an unlikely candidate for this type of employee engagement, and yet even here thousands of employees have been involved in helping to architect the business. If strategic conversations can work here, they can work anywhere.

We'll return to PwC's story soon, but first we need to set the stage as to *why* organizations need to move strategy and business model innovation out of the C-suite and open it up to employees too. In order to do this, we'll need to carefully define what we mean by 'business model' and 'strategy.'[3]

First we'll look at the notion of the business model. The term has come into general usage only quite recently. It is now used regularly on the financial pages and in finance discussion on TV and among executives. Yet it has been difficult to know exactly what is meant. A great deal has been written on it. The core thought is that every business needs a business model, and the quality or potential of its model has a huge impact on the business' possibilities. According to economist David Teece:

> a business model describes the design or architecture of the value creation, delivery, and capture mechanisms it employs. The essence of a business model is in defining the manner by which the enterprise delivers value, entices customers [or donors] to pay for

value, and converts those payments to profit [or public goods].
It thus reflects management's hypothesis about what customers
want, how they want it, and how the enterprise can organize to best
meet those needs, get paid for doing so, and [achieve its mission].
Whenever a business enterprise is established, it either explicitly
or implicitly employs a business model.[4]

A business model embraces factors such as the supply chain, how
products are marketed, how interactions with customers are managed, intellectual property policies, and the company's posture
towards government and its regulations. It also includes internal
factors such as hiring, business processes, outsourcing practices, and
plant, office, and distribution locations.

Business models come in all shapes and sizes and it makes no
sense to say there is some fundamental formula that all must follow.
Our society and economy offers those who wish to be entrepreneurs
an amazing variety of alternative ways of doing business and making
a profit. This openness is one of our most treasured political achievements. It makes choosing precisely how to do business both interesting and demanding. Those who suggest that business models
must have some common architecture miss the point. It is precisely
because our economy is so open that choosing how to proceed is so
tricky and demands such attention to detail. The essence of the
business model lies in these details. This also means that the business model is the very opposite of the 'helicopter view,' some bland
generalization about the business. The business model guides the
attention of everyone involved on what details matter and which
do not. It is a profoundly practical and empirical notion, the very
opposite of any general theory about firms. Since so much of the
detail is tied up with effective practice, it is probably impossible for
anyone to appreciate the business model's essence unless they have
worked in the firm's specific situation – as the academics say,
'inhabited' it. This is exactly why involving employees in the creation of the business model through strategic conversations is so

vital; no one inhabits the business model more than the employees who work within its constraints.[5]

Nonetheless, we can make some general comments about business models and the choices made as they are constructed. The effectiveness of these choices is shaped by two factors: the organization's ability to execute on the business model and the business model's suitability to the business environment. The combination of the business model, the organization's ability to execute upon it, and the detailed structure and process of the external environment defines what we can call the organization's 'opportunity space.' These factors are never exactly the same for any two companies, so each business model is unique, and this is why managers sense their firms are different. Everything in this equation is dynamic and constantly changing, and so with it the business model.

The opportunity space is the company's market potential given its environment, including such factors as the demand for its products, the cost and availability of inputs, and the legal and legislative climate. In Figure 2.1, the opportunity space is represented by the space inside the solid lines. The different lines represent the constraints on the business model coming from multiple directions. Financial constraints are in one dimension, the firm's culture lies in another, while the status of its body of technical knowledge suggests a third. Empirical research shows most private sector opportunity spaces can be pretty well framed using around a dozen dimensions. Many of these are characteristic of an industry, though some will be reflections of the firm's own specific nature, founders, and history.[6]

Often, a business model doesn't fully exploit its opportunity space. For instance, without changing its business model at all a business might have the opportunity to expand into a geographic region – say Ikea into Beijing – to meet unfilled demand.

A company's opportunity space is constantly shifting and is often under attack from competitors as well as other forces, such as laws and regulations that might be imposed by governments. At the same time, the business may be able to shift some of the relevant

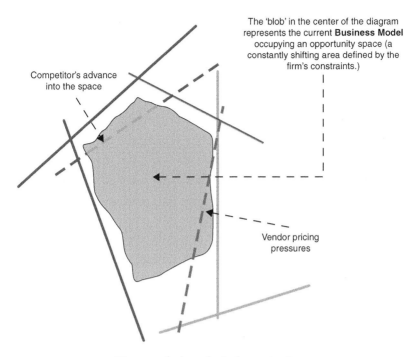

The 'blob' in the center of the diagram represents the current **Business Model** occupying an opportunity space (a constantly shifting area defined by the firm's constraints.)

Competitor's advance into the space

Vendor pricing pressures

FIGURE 2.1 Diagram of a hypothetical opportunity space

constraints – R&D progress might have some impact on the firm's methods of production, changing its price and delivery options. Alternatively, negotiations with suppliers might have some impact on the firm's price and delivery schedules. Businesses are also able to shift their emphasis and products and services to move into different market segments; banks move into mortgages, firms move from supplying hardware into services and franchising.

While a business model isn't completely malleable – a fast food chain will probably never become an aerospace company – there is considerable freedom to create new opportunity or to push back on constraints. For instance, Best Buy reacted to the threat of online sales – which are often more convenient and don't involve sales tax – from the likes of Amazon by introducing services like those offered by the Geek Squad, which Amazon would be hard-pressed to duplicate. They have tested the option of designing their own products to push back on supplier power and to draw closer to their customers. And they are working to shape the environment in which they compete by lobbying for online retailers to collect sales tax.

Business models are useful because they are just that, models of how the organization actually works. They are thought exercises that can be used to explore what the organization is and could be. In that regard, the diagram above is actually a representation of the human thinking process. Business models do not 'exist,' on the contrary they are simply artifacts people make. They comprise data we gather, the meanings we attach to the data, and the practices that we have created to link them to our situation.

Business models provide value in two complementary ways. First, they allow us to run thought exercises to tease out the parts of the business that provide competitive advantage or that might be under attack. Variations on the model can be imagined, and experiments made (for instance, Apple's introduction of their retail stores). Patterns become apparent that can then be turned into recipes for replication elsewhere.[7] The act of creating a business model is an exercise in imagining a specific constructible future that doesn't yet exist. It becomes the mental model for how the organization will help shape the world to create new opportunity spaces and possibilities.

Business models are also crucial devices for learning. As they are put into effect, assumptions in the model are confirmed or repudiated (e.g., people will stop pirating songs if they can buy them conveniently and can access them seamlessly across a variety of devices; Netflix users will accept one level of service for ordering DVDs by mail and another for streaming video). Because they are subjective versions of reality, not only is every business model unique, each person's interpretation of a business model will likely be different. Herein lies a tension: if people's understanding of the business model is too homogeneous then groupthink can sap organizational vitality. Conversely, if everyone's idea of the business model is too divergent (or too vague), then fruitful alignment is difficult to achieve. When a workable balance is achieved, organizational learning is optimized because the business model frames people's thinking about the world enough for sense-making and communication. Rich business models facilitate rich conversations that propel organizational learning.

By this point it is hopefully clear what business models have to do with strategic conversations: they are the mechanism for informing leadership's decisions on how to change the business model. *In our view, leadership's primary function is to be accountable for expanding and exploiting the company's opportunity space by constantly adapting the business model to opportunities and threats.* But which opportunities or threats? There's the rub. Figure 2.1 is a grossly simplified representation of a business' situation.

In a competitive, fast-changing, and global economy, senior management can't possibly have all the facts or intuitions about the future and how to shape it. Their appreciation of the business model is conditioned by, and viewed through, the prism of their own experiences and the particular scope of their own skilled practices. For example, the senior management in an engineering company may well be able to assess the risks of pushing into a new line of business – moving into chain saws from being a manufacturer of small high-performance gas engines, or of setting up a branch operation in a new country such as Kenya or Argentina. But these executives are not likely to be able to assess the engineering risks of changing technology – for instance of using a novel lithium battery in a new aircraft, or using carbon fiber in lieu of aluminum – that became major issues for the Boeing 787 Dreamliner. And the design engineers who can assess these risks seldom know the risks that have to be managed on an ongoing basis by ground crew and maintenance operatives. The general point is that the division of labor that promotes and exploits specialization, with hugely positive consequences, also has a major downside: the resulting difficulty of communicating richly across functional areas and organizational hierarchies. This is where strategic conversations become imperative. They are self-energized practices that ameliorate and manage the downside of the rising professionalization and specialization that marks modern business.

With this background on business models and leadership's accountability for them in place, it's time that we introduce our Five Iron Laws of Value Creation. They are the foundation on which the strategic conversation concept is built.

1. **Innovating the business model is a company's primary source of sustainable growth and profit.** There is a substantial body of data that shows that business model innovation always trumps technical innovation when it comes to generating profits.[8] One classic case of a triumphant business model innovation is XEROX and the 914 Copier. The first copiers were prohibitively expensive. Firms like IBM, Kodak, and GE had access to the technology but decided against marketing it because they calculated that only the government and a handful of other large organizations would ever be able to afford them. By changing the revenue stream from being purchase-based to lease-based, Haloid (soon renamed XEROX) created a huge new market. This business model innovation allowed Haloid to define, create, and then target new customer segments with limited budgets: corporate departments and medium-sized businesses. Departmental bosses could authorize the revenue stream of a lease payment where they could not authorize the capital cost of outright purchase. And the relationships with their customers were altered: Haloid still owned the machines so their technicians were always available to baby the finicky technology and bring the company up the learning curve.[9] A more modern example is the iPod. MP3 players were largely a commodity by the time Apple introduced its product. But because of a legal business model innovation – Apple had negotiated with the music companies to sell songs for 99 cents each – buyers' music became inextricably bound to Apple's iTunes store. Apple is now the largest music distributor in the world.[10]

2. **All business models require a leap of faith.** Back in 1921 economist Frank Knight introduced the idea that in competitive markets, economic rents (above average returns on investment) only exist if

there is uncertainty. If all the relevant facts are known, then there is no room for competitive advantage and above average profitability. Of course, rigorous strategists do their best to address what we call "knowledge absences," but in any business there will be uncertainty. Calculating the future is impossible, even with the biggest computer running the most sophisticated algorithms.[11] Creating business models is an act of imagination, and deciding which ones would be the best to implement requires judgment. There is no formula.[12]

3. **Companies must continually update their business models, so management must be perpetually entrepreneurial.** While business models are generally more enduring than technical innovations, even innovative ones are vulnerable to attack and obsolescence.[13] For this reason, simply managing existing processes towards incremental improvement is not enough; managers must work actively to innovate their firm's business model. Staying competitive means that managers, just like start-up artists, must be comfortable making decisions under a great deal of uncertainty. For years, IBM dominated its market by selling mainframe hardware and software used for running large commercial applications. Then competitors like Sun Microsystems and Microsoft muscled in on its market share by offering software (and in Sun's case, hardware) that would allow customers to replace IBM mainframes with smaller, cheaper servers. IBM was so far behind in developing this type of software that even if it had spent billions of dollars playing catch-up success was, at best, uncertain. Using a new business model, it adopted the Linux operating system piggybacking on the open source movement – a radical proposition for a proud company that was used to leading with proprietary products. It sold open solutions software at rock bottom prices while aggressively growing its services. This model enabled it to enter the new market at a fraction of the investment a homegrown solution would have required. Today, IBM's Global Business Services group is its highest grossing division.[14]

4. **The better the knowledge flows and the more that relevant perspectives are brought to bear on the strategizing process, the more opportunity there is for innovation**. Business models are affected by many factors: technical, legal, financial, organizational, market, and cultural to name a few. C-level managers, strategic planning departments, and those in R&D also know all kinds of things, but they can't possibly identify all the salient risks and opportunities that the business model needs to take into account. Once again, a key activity for strategists is to remove as many relevant knowledge absences as possible. They need as much help as they can get.[15]

5. **The benefits of business model innovation can best be realized when the innovation is done internally**. Hiring consultants to change the business model doesn't work well – the business' employees must ultimately make the changes, for they are the ones who breathe life into it with their everyday actions. Once the model incorporates their collective knowledge and experience, it becomes a difficult-to-copy source of enduring value and sustainable advantage. In the 1980s Toyota developed the Toyota Production System, making its employees partners with management in creating continuous improvement. This strategy provided the company with two decades of competitive advantage. Toyota officials were so confident of this relationship that they would invite GM managers to visit their plants, knowing full well that the Americans – with their high walls between management and labor – would be hard-pressed to duplicate their approach. The Toyota employees understood, supported, and implemented their firm's business model in a way outsiders never could because they were the ones that helped create it.

These Five Iron Laws reveal why many traditional management practices aren't very successful at promoting business-sustaining innovation – and why leaders in the firms we focus on have moved beyond them.

Some businesses rely heavily on R&D for new products and technologies that can then drive their business model innovation. But research shows a weak correlation between R&D spending and profitability.[16] Innovation poster-child Apple, for example, has one of its industry's lowest ratios of R&D spending to revenues. The reason is that R&D focuses on technical, rather than business model innovation (Law 1) and draws in too few of the business model's necessary perspectives (Law 4). Purely technical innovations rarely create substantial value because they are often easy to duplicate and improve upon, leaving first-movers shouldering most of the costs of the innovation while garnering few of the benefits.[17]

Companies often try to buy innovations, but here again the research – by McKinsey and others – doesn't suggest good outcomes. Indeed, acquiring innovative capacity through an M&A strategy is more likely to destroy value than to create it.[18] Business model innovation in highly competitive markets is a necessary core competency that must be owned by management (Law 3) and implemented through collaboration with employees (Law 5). Organizations that offer only cash and infrastructure to the businesses they acquire often inadvertently destroy value. Nor do organizations have much luck when they try to rent innovative capacity from consultants and other outside experts. Strong innovators rarely, if ever, use outsiders to improve their business models. How can they know the strengths, weaknesses, and possibilities of the business better than the business' own people? Innovation is outsourced at an organization's peril.

Still other companies recruit star-quality top leaders (white knights) to generate the ideas and options that will transform the firm's future. But this model – where fewer than 1 percent of the people are called upon to imagine how the business will grow – leaves most of the organization's potential value on the table (Laws 4 and 5).

Both the managers and employees of successful companies intuitively understand the Iron Laws of Value Creation and the strategic conversation techniques required to create the entrepreneurial workforce. The benefits of using these techniques are great and their cost is near zero. Companies that use strategic conversations to power the improvement of their business model don't need to hire more people to do the work – rather they deepen their employees' engagement so they become willing and able to devote the extra effort required.

Strategic conversations solve the riddle posed by management's imperative to devise company strategy – one that will position it to take advantage of new opportunities – when it is impossible to know which decisions will result in the optimal outcome. They define a management aesthetic; a way of thinking about leadership that creates a rewarding, dynamic, and harmonious relationship between managers and employees. It is a mindset that derives satisfaction from co-creation and risk-taking rather than control. It cherishes relationships with staff based on dialog and persuasion rather than on commands or instructions. It favors managers secure enough to embrace surprise when staff improve upon their ideas. In this collaborative world leaders emerge because they have followers based on the merits of their ideas and their ability to implement them, not because they are ordained from above. It's an aesthetic that takes many managers outside of their comfort zone but, when adopted, relieves them of the burden of believing that they are the only ones tasked with sustaining and growing the firm. They relish discovering that these burdens can be shared without eroding their authority.

So what is strategy and how does it relate to business models? In our view they are part and parcel of each other. Strategizing indicates the creative process of engaging a business context marked by uncertainties or knowledge absences that have the possibility of being translated into profit opportunities by the firm's leadership. The process leads to the development and selection of the business model, and choosing how and to what extent to fund it. The result puts the firm into action. As we mentioned earlier, business models are just that, models that can be built, tinkered with, replicated, and tested in markets both large and small. Organizations can also operate multiple business models simultaneously when they are synergistic and mutually support, rather than interfere with, each other. For instance, most banks now operate both retail banking and wealth management business models. Blockbuster movies or art museum exhibits come with increasingly extensive tie-in merchandising programs.

As we've spoken to friends and colleagues over the past year, we've heard a series of arguments against involving employees in strategy development and business model innovation. Of course, the strongest argument in favor is the direct evidence of it actually happening in the wild. (The next chapter will be a review of several of the different ways in which organizations are doing this today.) Nonetheless, addressing specific objections is instructive since it helps illustrate some of the issues currently inhibiting strategic conversations – issues that must be addressed before strategic conversations can be implemented successfully.

The objection: Strategic conversations will introduce small thinking at best, chaos at worst. One objection is that having employees involved in the strategic processes of business model innovation will merely introduce chaos. Those who make this argument say that employees aren't equipped to contribute; they don't have the background or temperament. Expecting employee participation, they say, is just encouraging people to do things they aren't capable of doing. At best, employees will only come up with small-bore ideas that won't materially affect the business' performance.

Experience shows that on those occasions when this seems to be borne out in practice, it is less a question of potential than one of the employees not being given the knowledge to innovate successfully. Employees can only contribute to improving the business model if they understand the current one. Numerous studies show that between 60 percent and 85 percent of most firms' employees don't know or understand their organization's strategy.[19] So, organizations can make a choice – have employees blithely unaware of how the organization plans to succeed – or truly give them the knowledge. And with that knowledge, and the proper training to act upon it, strategic conversations contribute to alignment, the opposite of chaos. As to the impact of openness and engaging employees, the proof is in the pudding. Employees may well come up with many small-scale ideas, but they have on occasion been responsible for opening billion-dollar markets precisely tailored to customer needs because of the employees' proximity to those who use the organization's products and services (we'll document one such example in Chapter 6). Nor should small ideas be dismissed as unworthy – we'll address further in Chapter 5 how it can be impossible to know which actions will prove most strategic, and how seemingly small ideas can sometimes turn into major business model innovations.

The objection: It's not employees' role to help devise strategy. Another objection is that while employee participation is all well and good, we all have our jobs to do. Senior management takes the long view, thinking of a strategy that will take the organization forward in the next five years or so. Executives in the middle manage the strategy with a timeframe of a year or two. Employees should focus on the here and now to execute the strategy day to day.[20]

This division of labor has somehow become accepted wisdom, but it wasn't always so. Adam Smith, the economist who popularized the notion of division of labor back in 1776 with his publication of the *Wealth of nations*, never advocated that workers should turn off their brains. Rather, he observed that the time saved through creating a division of labor was, in part, used by workers to further innovate, creating a virtuous cycle.

Modern systems theory supports this thinking. It is generally understood that optimizing parts of a system without an understanding of the system as a whole generally results in sub-optimization.[21] Employees can only do their best work when they understand the whole. But we argue that the knowledge gaps are reciprocal: executives only do their best work when informed by the knowledge of employees and the sub-systems for which they are responsible.

The objection: Strategic conversations are expensive and slow. Some object that even if employees can contribute, the time and effort involved in informing them about the organization's direction, soliciting their ideas, and sorting through them is too expensive, time-consuming, and anyway almost impossible in large global organizations. In response to this we would ask, "What's the opportunity cost of not using the employees' ideas and energy to grow?" The knowledge and abilities of its employees are the firm's most fundamental resource. What's more, as we'll see in later chapters, social media and the power of modern analytics have made the process of communicating and aggregating ideas affordable for mid-sized and large organizations alike.

The objection: Strategic conversations will reveal organizational secrets. Another concern we've heard is that sharing strategy with employees could risk exposing that strategy to potential competitors, thus giving them a leg up. This objection cannot be lightly swept aside. Sometimes first-mover advantage really does depend upon surprise. Apple is a case in point, given Jobs' legendary anxieties and efforts to keep things secret. Perhaps Apple's competition could have had a better chance of blocking the introduction of iTunes if they had had advanced knowledge of Apple's negotiations with music distributors. But we would argue this is not generally the case: business model innovation is often difficult to copy. Even when prototype iPhones fell into the hands of competitors, did that really change Apple's situation? Southwest Airlines' short-hop, no-hub, one plane-model strategy was not hard for competitors to divine because it was on display every flight they flew. But as with Toyota, copying it turned out to be nearly impossible for others in the airline business. Once again, the proof is in the pudding; as we'll see, most companies in competitive fast-moving industries like high tech expose their strategy to employees (and to some extent competitors) all the time. They may be judicious in protecting some secrets, but overall we suggest the value of employee involvement far outweighs the risks because employees who are deeply involved with their firm's business model achieve a sense of intellectual ownership and are keen to keep the firm's secrets secure.

The objection: Strategic conversations are too demanding of corporate cultures. Finally, some argue that strategic conversations are all well and good, but in organizations that tend towards command and control, and internal competition rather than collaboration, they would require a virtually impossible-to-achieve culture change that, even if possible, would take many years to accomplish. But, as we'll see, using strategic conversations releases employee energy that already – in some cases desperately – wants to be used. Once the dam of management attitudes that has been preventing employees from contributing is breached, massive cultural change is possible in quick time. Smaller organizations can see effects within months – even huge global firms (the storage and big data software firm EMC is a prime example) have experienced substantial cultural improvements within two to three years.

One objection we expected to hear, but haven't, is that facilitating greater employee involvement will disturb the rhythm of the strategy development process. We suspect the reason is that today's business people sense that yearly strategy meetings aren't enough in an increasingly volatile world; organizations need to be able to modify, abandon, or develop new strategies continuously to parry challenges and seize fleeting advantage. In this environment, a lot more information needs to be circulated and vetted, and a lot more brainpower applied to synthesizing this information into informed action. As Jim Whitehurst, CEO of Red Hat Software told us, "All strategy problems are shallow given enough eyeballs."[22] This is why, in spite of the objections, leading businesses are adopting strategic conversations. With strategic conversations, strategy and business model innovation are ingrained into everyday work for every member of an organization. With everyone involved, the organization is awake to the dangers and opportunities facing it in a way it wasn't before, more ready than ever to shape its future in the world, and more nimble in execution of its chosen vision.

3 Strategic conversations in the wild

Change what works and change everything else.

Tweet from Lori Senecal, CEO of KBS+[1]

So far we've been discussing strategic conversations in the abstract – now it's time to see what they look like in action. Not surprisingly, given that strategic conversations are about engendering business model innovation, they themselves have benefited from innovation and come in a variety of forms. Our strategic conversations typology attempts to categorize the phenomenon to help make sense of what is happening in organizations around the world. This chapter provides an overview, describing eight styles of strategic conversations we have observed being practiced in organizations today. This chapter will also provide some guidance on which types of strategic conversations are most valuable under which circumstances and in what combinations. Subsequent chapters will delve more deeply into how strategic conversations work and how to derive the maximum benefit from them.

In the wild, we have observed eight distinct types of strategic conversations:

1. Innovation days
2. Competitions
3. Challenges
4. Sensing and operationalizing platforms
5. T-shaped
6. Strategy reviews
7. Chaordic
8. Innovation communities

A description of each is given here.

Suggestion boxes

While the classic suggestion box may at first blush seem like a way to engage employees and capitalize on their ideas and feedback, you'll notice that it is missing from our list. That's because the iconic suggestion box isn't a strategic conversation – in fact, it's a sort of anti-strategic conversation. Recall that in Chapter 1 we defined a strategic conversation as a "carefully designed *dialog* between management and employees that engages the workforce to explore opportunities for, and constraints to, company growth." Throwing suggestions into a box (be it physical or electronic) and then waiting for a response from the box's (often faceless) attendant isn't a conversation. Without a dialog, the ideas being proffered may not relate to issues of interest to management, because management hasn't made an effort to shape the conversation. And valuable ideas may go unrecognized, if they are written in a language not familiar to the executive reader, or the idea isn't developed enough to recommend particular action. Creating or innovating a new business model requires that everyone involved have skin in the game. It becomes an act of inspiration that requires encouragement, exploration, challenges, and the passion to engage risks. The suggestion box offers none of these. The result is that mutual learning is virtually non-existent; we have come across no cases where an organization's ability to grow has been positively affected by a suggestion box. None.

Innovation days. An innovation day – the first type of strategic conversation we'll illustrate – provides a focal point for promoting innovation, involving either a physical or virtual event, often on a yearly schedule. They are generally available to all employees, and may involve clients and partners. This strategic conversation comes in two very different flavors: ideation and celebration.

Ideation-type innovation days provide a forum for generating discussion around strategy and business model innovation. Senior management may raise key issues they'd like addressed to provide

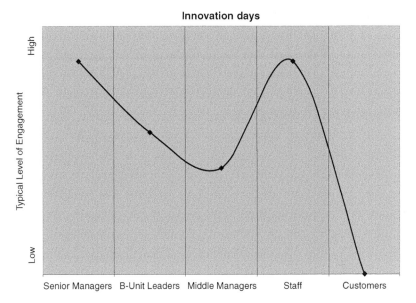

FIGURE 3.1 Based on the authors' observations, this figure shows the typical level of engagement for different types of "innovation days" participants.

focus. IBM Innovation Jams are among the best-known example. Hundreds of thousands of employees participate simultaneously in a "massively paralleled online conference" designed to answer specific questions posed by senior management, like "how do we get IBM consulting into the C-suite."[2] While planning the Jam generally takes between twelve and fourteen weeks, the actual Jam lasts from two to three days. During this time employees are invited to spend time away from their daily work to focus on the future of the organization, discussing issues with their colleagues via live chats and message boards. Real-time text mining and analysis is done to help steer the conversations. After the event, IBM analysts spend two to three weeks going through the results, culling trends and conclusions, and then they make recommendations and create action plans.[3] The 2006 Innovation Jam had perhaps the greatest participation, with over four million views of more than 46,000 posts by IBMers, clients, and partners, exploring the theme of "how to combine new technologies and real-world insights to create market opportunities."[4] Several new lines of business emerged from this Jam, including one based on integrated mass transit information and another on digitizing health records. IBM has even turned the Jams themselves into a line of business. It sets up the environment and consults with client organizations to put on their own Jams.[5]

If ideation-type innovation days focus on kicking off the innovation process, celebration-type innovation days are about recognizing achievements. This type of strategic conversation is used by many of the organizations in our study, including Boston Children's Hospital. Innovations have come from employees as diverse as professors, doctors, nurses, and even parking attendants. Some of the ideas celebrated are relatively specific, like the development of heated hats for babies by a nurse who noted that babies who had undergone cardiac surgery had difficulty maintaining their body temperature. Others have much more profound implications for the organization's business model, like introducing technology to allow patients to be treated remotely (telehealth – which we'll discuss further in Chapter 6). No matter the idea's size and implications, making innovation work is almost always arduous. One doctor went through over 300 iterations in the process of developing injectable oxygen for use in patients with acute breathing problems who would otherwise suffer from brain damage.[6] Recognizing these efforts is essential for maintaining energy and commitment.

Both types of innovation days raise the profile of employee-generated innovation, which is always a good thing. But although we believe that it is a good idea to recognize the accomplishments of innovators on a regular basis, ideation-type innovation days can also have a downside. They tend to make innovation a 'special event' instead of the everyday business of every employee. The corporate ethos that institutionalizes strategic conversation treats innovation as an ongoing feature of organizational life, not something that comes solely from an annual event. Again, in today's highly competitive world, innovation must be continuous if the firm is to grab what is often fleeting advantage. We aren't arguing that employees can or should give up their everyday operational responsibilities, but when inspiration strikes it ought not to be delayed until an annual event cycle or formal occasion allows it to be put forward.

Competitions. Like innovation days, internal competitions can provide gateways into rich strategic conversations. Most often, senior management will ask broad questions, like "where can we extend this particular brand," "what are the new opportunities for growth in this specific market?" Participants submit their ideas, often as small teams, hoping to have them recognized and perhaps win a prize. The best competitions involve managers coaching employee teams to hone their ideas and develop the skills to present them. This management involvement and interaction is vital for several reasons:

- It helps transmit management's needs so that the solutions explored are the most relevant to the overall business situation.
- It provides mentoring on how to present ideas to management persuasively.[7]
- It gives management intimate insight into employee thinking.

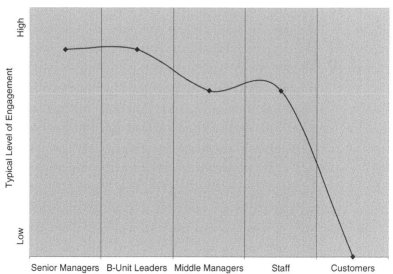

FIGURE 3.2 Shows the typical level of engagement for the different types of participants in "competitions"

All these interactions work to strengthen the strategic conversation.

PricewaterhouseCoopers (PwC) took an innovative approach to competition-driven conversations with its PowerPitch competition. Styled after American Idol competitions, self-selected teams of PwC employees pitch ideas to the company as a whole, and those voted most likely to succeed are given a chance to present to company partners and win a cash prize of $100,000. In this strategic conversation, senior leaders hear ideas for shaping the business – like introducing a data mining service for clients.

Typically, competitions are held episodically and tend to generate fewer ideas than other types of strategic conversations that are more continuous, hence their impact is relatively low even though they are usually open to all employees. Also, an organization's most thoughtful and innovative thinkers may not be extroverts. For every American Idol enthusiast, there may be dozens of shy geniuses cringing in the wings.[8] Nonetheless, competitions can serve as a gateway to deeper strategic conversations. Properly executed, they can generate excitement and an appetite for greater engagement.

Challenges. Challenges are designed to solve very specific problems posed by senior management. Often organizations employ both challenges and competitions, but for different reasons. Competitions like PowerPitch explore broad themes and often explore new territory. Challenges tend to be much more focused.

PwC runs both. Challenges are formalized by using an intranet platform called iChallenge and PwC's mechanism for internal crowdsourcing. Mitra Best, the firm's US Innovation Leader, developed both types of strategic conversations. Mitra sits on the strategy committee and her team acts as interlocutor between executives and employees, soliciting issues from senior management. One business challenge that was revealed in one of her meetings with management related to the acquisition of several assets from BearingPoint. Through this acquisition, PwC ended up owning several offshore software development centers. The problem was that these development centers were serving several of PwC's audit clients, but because of regulations that

Challenges

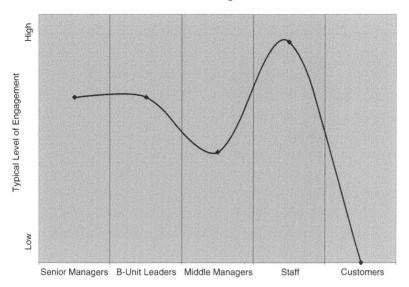

FIGURE 3.3 Shows the typical level of engagement for the different types of participants in "challenges"

don't allow accounting firms to have consulting relationships with their audit clients, PwC suddenly found itself with a great deal of unused capacity. PwC ran an iChallenge to showcase the software development centers and to solicit ideas to put them to work with new clients. Best had originally expected to pick the top 3 ideas, but 120 ideas came in and 50 were chosen for implementation. The top award went to a US employee. No prize money was given, but the winner was given the opportunity to visit one of the software development centers in Mumbai to meet with the people whom his ideas had benefited (layoffs had been a real possibility). According to Best, he came back with tears in his eyes because of the gratitude he received from the development center's employees whose jobs he had protected.

Pitney Bowes, the postage machine company that has since expanded into a wide array of business communications solutions, has issued about sixty challenges over the past four years, ranging from how to better field customer inquiries to various challenges relating to how to grow the business. Challenges were issued and the responses collected and debated in IdeaNet, Pitney Bowes' intranet. Most of the challenges are not issued to the entire company but rather to a selected relevant subset. Nonetheless, the best results arrived when challenges crossed functional lines rather than just pertaining to a single business unit. According to Allison Dahl, former co-lead and manager of communication and engagement for IdeaNet, challenges really took off when senior managers were measured on whether they issued challenges and the quality of the resulting responses.

In general, organizations find challenges are an excellent spur for strategic conversations. They raise issues dear to senior management, are immediate, and they give many employees a chance to better understand and address management's concerns while gaining recognition for their contributions. And, as we'll see later in this chapter, they can lead to even richer strategic conversations if there is follow-on implementation that continues to harness employee energy and creativity.

Sensing and operationalizing platforms. One of the benefits of strategic conversations is that they provide senior management with insight into what's happening at the coal face with customers, partners, and competitors.

Some organizations promote the use of intranets – often the repositories or hosting platforms for competitions, innovation days, and challenges – to have employees and managers post their views of the business and where it should go and then look for which topics are hot. Some, like storage and big data software firm EMC, use sophisticated analytics to mine trends in their intranet. EMC Labs in China experimented with several different analytics packages to better understand the thrust of innovation from their employees' point of view. They used a tool called the Stanford Topic Model Toolbox to textually analyze around 6,000 ideas that had been submitted over five years as part of EMC's annual Innovation Showcase (itself a variety of

Sensing and operationalizing

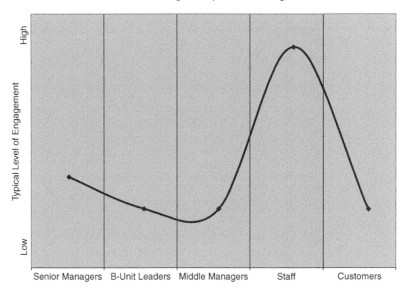

FIGURE 3.4 Shows the typical level of engagement for the different types of participants in "sensing and operationalizing"

the strategic conversation type innovation days). Data Scientist Tao Chen (EMC Labs China) ran a topic-modeling algorithm to create a list of where ideas were clustering. His research revealed that there were twenty-four main topics under discussion.[9] In this study, the hottest topic turned out to be employee engagement and productivity. The analytics package also generated a keyword list for each topic, allowing EMC's management to understand the nature of each topic better. EMC then used this analysis to target future innovation work.

Sensing and operationalizing platforms act as valuable input to other types of strategic conversations by revealing employees' sense of what's important to the organization. Having this 'heat map' of employee attention itself provides senior management with valuable data. It may point them to new and important ideas. It may also indicate that employees are preoccupied with issues that are not driving the organization forward. Either way, they can provide a powerful spur to managerial action.

T-shaped management

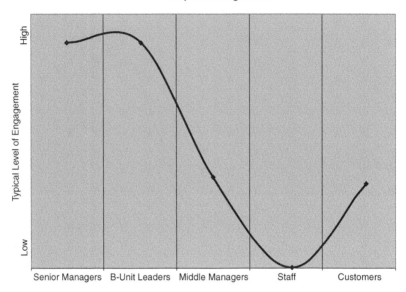

FIGURE 3.5 Shows the typical level of engagement for the different types of participants in "T-shaped management"

T-shaped strategic conversations. We borrow the notion of T-shaped strategic conversations from Morten Hansen's useful book *Collaboration.*[10] His idea is that business unit leaders' focus should be T-shaped: they need to be experts in their business unit but also take responsibility for the overall success of the organization. This type of management is the antidote to the silo thinking that sometimes causes parts of the organization to be optimized to the detriment of the whole.

T-shaped strategic conversations are a way to operationalize T-shaped management. In this type of strategic conversation senior managers gather diverse business unit managers to address the challenges of growth, often off-site or cloistered in headquarters offices disconnected from day-to-day management. Typically, managers gain insight from senior management about broad strategic goals while senior management gains a deeper understanding of the challenges and opportunities faced by their managers. The challenges to be addressed benefit from a diversity of experience being applied. For managers, T-shaped strategic conversations provide a context for the reflection that innovation requires. In a corporate environment, where the focus is on making quarterly targets, they provide an escape from the tyranny of the urgent and a place to create and nurture the future.[11]

While they are a relief from the day-to-day pressures, they certainly aren't an escape from hard work and competition. GE was famous for creating friendly (and sometimes not so friendly) competition among different teams. Ultimately, the teams would report to the CEO Jack Welch (his successor, Jeff Immelt, keeps up the tradition).

ARAMARK also used this technique to good effect. ARAMARK is a provider of food services, facilities management, career apparel, and uniforms. Executive Chairman Joe Neubauer realized that while the company was profitable, its highly disciplined focus on cash flow and quarterly profitability was cutting into its growth opportunities. As one of Neubauer's advisors put it, "the issue was that in the ARAMARK culture there wasn't time to dialogue, to engage people and get them on board with new ways of thinking. They were just so intense, so focused, so transaction-driven, there literally wasn't time for people to put ideas out and discuss and debate them."[12] But it wasn't just a lack of time, there was also a lack of context for proper strategic conversations. Unit managers – who knew the business very well – didn't feel they had permission to question senior management or engage with them on cross-cutting strategic matters. Joe Neubauer, ARAMARK's CEO, recognized that his managers didn't have a forum for imagining where the business should go.[13] They were, to use Larry Prusak's phrase, "too busy to think."

Even though ARAMARK seemed to be in a pedestrian industry, Neubauer's vision was to transform it into a highly profitable hospitality industry-focused professional services firm with a suite of integrated services. It brought in a top-end strategy firm to help it come up with an approach. But instead of letting the twenty-eight-year-old consultants detail specific innovations, Neubauer gave the job to his top 150 people. He created a set of strategy learning teams under the aegis of a new learning organization called the Executive Leadership Institute (ELI). Participating managers were brought to headquarters for two weeks to hear the specifics of the chairman's vision and to bring their perspectives from the field. Instead of using theoretical generalizations to helicopter above the details, they immersed themselves in those details, uncovering the practical constraints to growth and profitability and the immediate possibilities for boosting them. Then they returned to their offices and worked for six months while communicating virtually with their learning team to develop implementation initiatives. One group, for example, focused on ARAMARK's vending machine business. Its complete redesign – including an expansion of the types of customers served and a consolidation of how the machines were stocked and serviced – led to substantial business growth.

The strength of T-shaped strategic conversations is that they are very focused and actionable. Senior managers speak directly with their subordinates about issues they care about. The different views from the varying business units provide a diversity of perspectives on opportunities and challenges and how to capitalize on them. Managers come away more focused and empowered from having been exposed to senior management, and are better able to transmit the organization's strategy to their subordinates. The weakness of T-shaped strategic conversations is that they aren't very inclusive. At best, over the span of five or so years, they will involve a few hundred managers – a small percentage of the total employee population in companies as large as GE and ARAMARK.

Strategy reviews. Too often the strategy process becomes pro forma. Senior management doesn't have the bandwidth to vet plans closely so the business units tend to create what look more like quarterly budgets than forward-looking strategies or novel business model suggestions. Instead of being an exciting moment co-creating the firm's future, the strategy development process decays into a valueless periodic fill-in-the-box exercise.

Employee strategy reviews

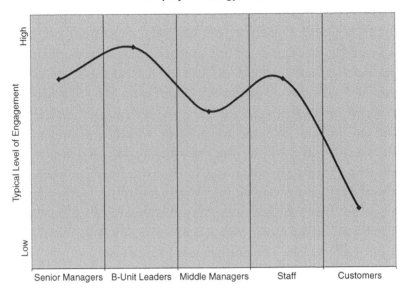

FIGURE 3.6 Shows the typical level of engagement for the different types of participants in "employee strategy reviews"

A few organizations have solved this problem by giving employees a powerful editorial role in the strategy process. One such company is HCL Technologies, a global information technology outsourcing and software development company. HCL Technologies, a spin off from HCL in 1997, has experienced significant growth over the last decade, and today has a market cap of over $10 billion and more than 80,000 employees.

In 2005, in the midst of a down market, HCL's CEO Vineet Nayar realized that he and his small strategy staff had neither the time nor the visibility into the business to critique effectively the hundreds of plans the different businesses were being asked to produce every year. Using the T-shaped management structure described earlier, HCL involved over 100 managers in the strategy development process in an initiative called Blueprint.

Blueprint's greater inclusivity was an improvement, but by 2010 even this solution was no longer sufficient. Nayar realized that he needed to fundamentally change HCL's strategizing process. He needed to create more transparency and opportunity for participation, and HCL needed to completely abandon the hierarchical and often paternalistic model that he had experienced as a young manager and that was still vestigial in HCL. In the old model managers went to 'God's seat' to pitch their annual plan. The CEO, needing to appear intelligent, would opine on the presentation, more often than not without knowing much about what the presenter was describing. Speaking of his own experiences as one of those young presenting managers, Nayar said he would be sure to build his presentation around one of the CEO's favorite hot button issues (e.g., penetrating the Chinese market), then after receiving the CEO's approbation, would more often than not promptly scrap the plan to pursue less grandiose and more grounded objectives.

Now a CEO himself, Nayar wanted to empower employees in what he calls the "value zone" – the interaction between employees and customers, far away from the CEO's seat. So Blueprint was replaced with a review platform and process called My Blueprint, designed to force-multiply the strategy process by giving everyone in the company the opportunity to shape the company's direction.[14]

Having sat in 'God's seat' himself, Nayar admits that its lure is powerful and energizing. But he was willing to surrender that deified position, knowing it was impossible for a single person, or even 100 people, to create strategy effectively in such a large global organization. With My Blueprint, business plans are reviewed not only by top management, but also by the customer-facing employees who will actually implement them. The fiscal year 2010 plans, for example, were reviewed and commented on by 8,000 people throughout the organization. That feedback resulted in significant redesigns of several of those business plans.[15]

Our research reveals that while this type of strategic conversation isn't common, HCL's case is nonetheless not unique. As we'll see, Red Hat, the open source software company, has used this technique to involve its employees in strategy, even to the extent of

Chaordic conversations

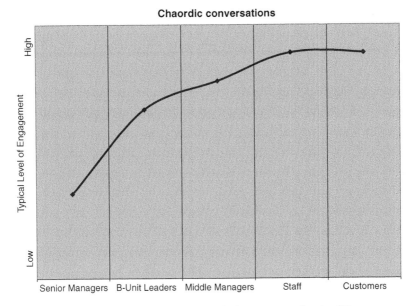

FIGURE 3.7 Shows the typical level of engagement for the different types of participants in "chaordic conversations"

having the company's mission statement edited by employees.[16] And at EMC, Steve Todd, EMC Fellow and Vice President of Strategy and Innovation, estimates that about 20 percent of strategy plans are now being put before employees to engage their insight.[17]

Strategy reviews are an excellent way to engage employees in understanding management's strategy direction and to influence that direction. As discussed earlier, studies have shown that employee familiarity with strategy is strongly correlated with execution and organizational success. The option of getting employees involved in reviewing and editing the strategic initiatives being put forward – when used in isolation and without other supporting options – makes employees more editors than originators of strategy and business model innovation. Nonetheless, this strategic conversation modality can be both inclusive and impactful.

Chaordic conversations. Chaordic strategic conversations celebrate the philosophy that it's better to ask for forgiveness than to ask for permission. In this model, employees, in close collaboration with customers, first take the initiative to make changes to the business model, and *then* communicate what they've done to senior management.

The term 'chaord' was coined by Dee Hock, founder of the financial services corporation Visa, as a combination of the words 'chaos' and 'order' to describe any complex, adaptive, self-organizing system (or organization) that has characteristics of both chaos and order, or in a business sense, both cooperation and competition.[18] His idea was to create a company that was owned by, and existed for, its customers[19] and that eschewed hierarchy so that employees and customer-owners could actively collaborate in setting the organization's direction. His was an early vision of an organization that would be run based on emergent strategy developed at the border of the chaos of the marketplace and the order found in human reason and compassion. Though Visa didn't fully achieve this ideal according to Hock, as it *did* develop its own corporate hierarchy, it was nonetheless a pioneer in implementing this new business model.[20]

Chaordic strategic conversations move organizations towards Hock's ideal. Red Hat certainly exhibits chaordic characteristics, which isn't surprising given its open source roots. Employees collaborate with the external developer community and customers to set direction. The most interesting example of chaordic strategic conversations we've encountered is found in the World Bank. A little background is necessary to be able to fully appreciate the often subversive (in a good way) power of this type of strategic conversation.

The Bank's declared mission is to reduce global poverty. It has traditionally provided technical and financial assistance (often through low-cost loans) to governments, most often at a macro level in the areas of physical infrastructure (e.g., water), health, and education. In this sense it has acted as a commercial, rather than a retail, bank, with a strong consulting arm to help guide investment. Interaction was most often with governments and non-governmental organizations (NGOs), rather than beneficiaries (the people that the Bank was working to help out of poverty).

Not everyone found this model compelling, as the leaders of the Bank's Latin America Region discovered in a meeting with Brazil's president Luiz Inácio Lula da Silva (president from 2003–2010). The team was pitching the Bank's usual portfolio of macroeconomically-oriented products and services, and Lula wasn't buying. He grew up hungry himself, and wanted to know what the Bank would do to feed the hungry in his country. The meeting was going downhill fast and the World Bank team feared that they would be kicked out of the country (not a good career outcome for any of the Bank personnel involved).

The suggestion that saved the day came from a World Bank secretary who was taking notes. She suggested a program she had heard about that was being used by the Mexican government: conditional cash transfers (CCFs). The program was entirely results-based. A family received cash, which they could spend in any way they wanted, as long as their children attended school regularly and received the vaccinations the program required. Lula loved the idea and gave the approach his blessing. The Bolsa Familia program, while not perfect, was a huge development success for a sector where successes tend to be few and far between.[21] It serves 11 million families, who receive small amounts of money – monthly cash transfers to poor families with children average US$35. The program reaches the poorest 40 percent of Brazil's population and 94 percent of funds are spent on recipients.[22] In the first five years of the program, Brazil's absolute poverty rate declined from 39 percent to 25 percent, and extreme poverty dropped from more than 17 percent, to just under 9 percent.[23]

The effect on the World Bank itself has been equally powerful. This work in Brazil is part of a larger chaordic movement transforming the Bank's business model in several dimensions. First, the initial emphasis on transferring western practices to the developing world is being replaced with a multilateral approach that places more value on 'south-south' knowledge transfers (e.g., from Mexico to Brazil). Instead of being the font of development knowledge, the Bank is moving towards adopting a more humble convener role. Second, instead of funding large infrastructure projects, working through large institutions and governments, the Bank is beginning to fund projects that directly affect beneficiaries. This new orientation has had profound effects. The Bank now relies on beneficiaries to provide data on the effectiveness of programs and to alert the Bank to issues of corruption, often through social media accessed by increasingly ubiquitous cell phone use, a truly revolutionary change for the Bank. Finally, this story has begun to erode the strongly hierarchical culture at the Bank. After all, the idea was originally proposed by a secretary working in the Latin American regional office.

Old habits die hard, especially in an institution with as long a history as the World Bank. Nevertheless, in an organization struggling to stay relevant in a world where its traditional lending model is losing its potency (the World Bank lends around $40 billion a year,[24] a number looking increasingly insignificant on a global scale when the average loan size for the China Development Bank is $10 billion per loan)[25] the Bank may be at an inflection point. Jim Yong Kim, the Bank's president as of 2012, has boldly articulated this position – one that would have been seen as wild thinking just five years ago:

> the quality of our knowledge depends on the inclusiveness of the debate. Excluding shareholders from the conversation deprives us of critical data. Thus, if grassroots community voices aren't heard, our understanding of delivery processes will be distorted and incomplete. In our delivery work, the World Bank Group and our country partners will reinforce the participation of beneficiary communities in all facets of program design, implementation, monitoring and evaluation.[26]

With chaordic strategic conversations, the ingenuity and passion of employees working with clients to create successful new models will drive the strategizing process. Good leaders follow. To be institutionalized, chaordic strategic conversations need senior management involvement and need to be transferred to either T-shaped management conversations or to innovation communities, the next and last strategic conversation in our typology.

Innovation communities. The last type of strategic conversation that we've seen in the wild is what we call innovation communities. We define them as:

> A diverse team of employees, empowered by and in constant communication with senior management, who collaborate on specific issues outside of their normal operational duties to promote cross-organizational business model innovations critical to the organization.

Membership in successful innovation communities is determined by whoever is taking the leadership role on the issues, the very people who have the knowledge, energy, and skill to successfully pursue solutions, not by the hierarchy deploying its official power.

This type of strategic conversation is very powerful because the connection between senior management and the innovation

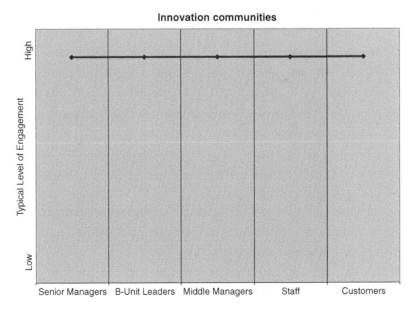

FIGURE 3.8 Shows the typical level of engagement for the different types of participants in "innovation communities"

community team is very close. Oftentimes the output of other strategic conversation types – for instance innovation days or competitions – becomes the input to innovation communities. One can say that innovation communities are where big ideas go to be implemented. A good example of this is Boston Children's Hospital's telehealth group. The idea – to have medical professionals diagnose and treat patients remotely – was the result of an innovation day. Since telehealth is a vast topic, this business model innovation is now being explored in depth by an assigned innovation community.

Because innovation communities are central to the effectiveness of strategic conversations we have dedicated an entire chapter to them later in the book (Chapter 6).

In Table 3.1 we compare and contrast the various types of strategic conversations, and examine where they're most useful, and in what combination. We have rated each conversation type on two attributes, the conversation's impact on helping to grow the business, and its level of inclusivity in terms of involving senior management, business unit leaders, middle managers, employees, and customers. The scales range from '0 = none' to '10 = a great deal.' These ratings, admittedly subjective, are based on the authors' research and experience, both with the organizations profiled in this book, as well as other professional engagements, and are intended to help illustrate the relative strengths and weaknesses of the various techniques, and give insight into when and where to use them.

As we've seen, some strategic conversations are prone to propagate and so engender others. Innovation days, competitions, sensing and operationalizing platforms, and chaordic conversations often lead to T-shaped conversations, challenges, and innovation communities. Many organizations practicing strategic conversations use multiple types of conversations at the same time.

What types of strategic conversation come together into the best combinations? We argue that the primary consideration is always that the strategic conversation modes should be chosen to ensure all stakeholders are highly engaged in one way or another.

Table 3.1 *Comparison of participant engagement levels by strategic conversation types*

Strategic conversation type	Impact	Inclusivity	Comments
Innovation days	4	8	Useful for raising consciousness that all employees are expected to participate in strategy and business model innovation, good for celebrating wins, but can signal that innovation is a 'once-a-year event' rather than a continuous activity.
Competitions	4	8	Another good consciousness-raising device, may exclude shy people from participating, can also signal that innovation is an 'event' rather than a continuous activity.
Sensing and operationalizing platforms	4	10	Properly done, innovation-oriented intranets can foster valuable conversations among employees that can be analyzed and used by managers to set the direction of future innovation.
T-shaped	6	2	Cross-functional management teams working together are often very impactful and benefit the organization by involving managers who are experts in the business in the strategy process, but they don't fully engage employees, and so don't bring the organization's full knowledge to bear.
Strategy reviews	6	8	Strategy reviews are an excellent way to provide employees with insight into management's intent and to solicit their feedback.

Table 3.1 (*cont.*)

Strategic conversation type	Impact	Inclusivity	Comments
			They can reduce the need for change management since employees have a better understanding of strategy *before* decisions are made. Since the strategy is already somewhat 'cooked' before it is presented, employee opportunity to help frame the strategy debate is somewhat limited.
Chaordic	8	6	Chaordic conversations are very powerful because they involve employees and customers at the coal face imagining business models that are optimal from both parties' perspectives. They generally occur in larger, geographically spread organizations. But to make the innovations have an effect organization-wide, senior management needs to be brought into the picture, either through T-shaped or innovation community-type conversations.
Challenges	8	8	Challenges are very effective because they reflect immediate needs from senior management. If employees are properly engaged, they can generate value that's quickly acted upon by management. They can themselves generate T-shaped or innovation community conversations.

Table 3.1 (*cont.*)

Strategic conversation type	Impact	Inclusivity	Comments
Innovation communities	10	7	Perhaps the gold standard of strategic conversations, innovation communities can involve people from all levels of the organization working closely on a cross-functional basis to directly innovate strategy and the business model. They are closely monitored by senior management, giving them the visibility and support necessary for success.

As Figure 3.9 shows, it's not necessary to attempt to implement all types at once to accomplish this. The x-axis shows the potential principal participants to a strategic conversation. The y-axis illustrates the level of engagement typical for the specific strategic conversation mode for a given type of participant.

For instance, chaordic strategic conversations engage customers, staff, and middle managers highly while they tend to involve senior managers less. By way of contrast, innovation communities engage senior managers and business unit leaders strongly. If these two types of strategic conversations were used in combination, an organization could engage most of its participants.

Every organization that decides to use strategic conversations needs to choose the combination of types that best fits its situation and needs. There are no hard and fast rules for doing so, other than the guideline that you should eventually engage all potential participant types in one way or another to reduce knowledge absences to the greatest extent possible. (This is to address the fourth Iron Law of Value Creation, "The better the knowledge

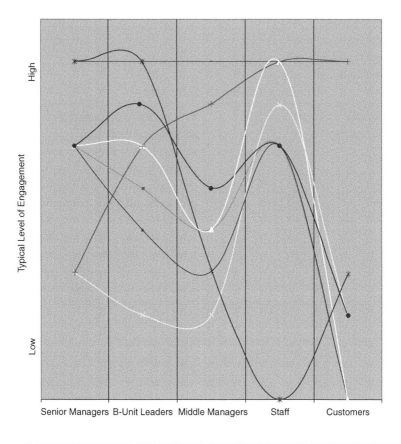

Senior Managers B-Unit Leaders Middle Managers Staff Customers

—♦— Innovation Days	—✳— Sensing & Operationalizing	—+— Chaordic
—■— Competitions	—✳— T-Shaped Management	—— Innovation Communities
—▲— Challenges	—●— Employee Strategy Reviews	

FIGURE 3.9 Graph showing typical levels of engagement of primary
stakeholders for all types of strategic conversations

flows and the more relevant perspectives brought to bear, the more
opportunity there is for innovation.")

This chapter gave an overview of the different types of strategic
conversations. The next two chapters will address the challenges of
how to make them work.

How would you start strategic conversations in your organization?

- How would you determine which strategic conversation types could be best adapted to your organization?
- Which type(s) would be best to introduce first?
- If you're the leader of your organization, who could be your interlocutor (like PwC's Mitra Best) to ensure that the right people are actively engaged and that the topics under discussion provide value?

4 Engaging employees in management's agenda

> Circumstances vary so enormously in war, and are so indefinable, that a vast array of factors has to be appreciated ... The man responsible for evaluating the whole must bring to his task the quality of intuition that perceives truth at every point.
>
> Carl von Clausewitz, *On war*[1]

On the surface, the two companies couldn't be more dissimilar. To get to Rite-Solutions headquarters, you turn off the strip malls of Route 114 in Middletown, Rhode Island onto a nondescript side road named Corporate Place. The building is in a business park like thousands across America, definitely not a candidate for a write-up in *Architectural Digest*. There is even something generic about the company's name. Its CEO and co-founder, Jim Lavoie, dresses business casual. By way of contrast, Kirshenbaum Bond Senecal's (KBS+) headquarters occupies a spacious loft in Manhattan's ultra-hip Tribeca neighborhood. KBS+'s Chairwoman and CEO Lori Senecal is as sophisticated as her surroundings and reputedly dresses in one color, black. Rite-Solutions' 200 employees design mission-critical software for the Department of Defense and gaming industry. KBS+'s 500 employees help market premier brands like BMW and Puma.

Despite their differences, both companies evolved convergently (as biologists would put it) to adopt a common philosophy that allows them to capture lightening in a bottle. They both believe that success depends upon harnessing the genius of their employees to shape their organizations' future. Senecal works to ensure that every employee "at all levels of the company adopts a growth mentality and essentially is a creative entrepreneur."[2] If anything, Lavoie's vision is even more radical. Rite-Solutions is an employee-owned company that eschews the notion of hierarchy entirely; every employee in every function has an equal opportunity to contribute to shaping the business' strategy. (Lavoie is fond of saying that a pyramid, as in the shape found in most org charts, "is a tomb for dead people.") The results transcend stylistic differences: when we spoke to their employees the energy was the same. They were visibly energized to personally and collectively grow the organization. That energy, even to the most hard-bitten cynic, is contagious.

Alas, few organizations achieve what Rite-Solutions, KBS+, and a select few others have accomplished. Tiny Rite-Solutions is a McKinsey/Harvard Business School award winner because its management practices are the exception and not the rule. Too often, employees are disenfranchised from strategy development and business model innovation. Business units are left out of the loop because the strategic planning group or R&D department dominate the agenda. Employees aren't given guidance on what ideas are welcome or how to pursue innovation. Other groups are simply disconnected. Service areas like HR, IT, and legal think of themselves as order takers rather than as agents of change. For instance, we recently attended a meeting of company officers at a company trying to move beyond selling supplies to computer chip manufacturers to providing maintenance services for their customers' fabrication machines. When the agenda turned to innovation, the chief legal officer asked to be excused – even though the conversation dealt with a fundamental change in the business model that could have benefited greatly from creative legal ideas.

The tragedy is that most businesses don't start off this way. Leaders at the entrepreneurial stage of a business often inspire – pulling employee participation – by their presence and energy. Over time, however, the feeling of shared entrepreneurship often fades. As successful organizations grow, the press of formal structures, lines of reporting, and procedural rituals undermine intimacy. Global organizations, with their diversity of cultures, languages and attitudes, face even greater challenges as leadership struggles to maintain connection to the very same employees whose contributions are crucial to generating and implementing business model innovation.

Often leaders try to recapture the entrepreneurialism of their company's youth in ways that actually make the situation worse: they try to exhort or bribe employees to be entrepreneurial. In so doing, they fail to appreciate the essence of entrepreneurialism. Employee entrepreneurial potential is inherent and is there to be released, it doesn't need to be manufactured or forced. Imagination and creative problem solving exist in all employees. It's a source of identity and pride, deeply personal and unique.

We've observed what happens when companies try to spur innovative thinking with financial rewards: it's generally ineffective and often backfires. Research results are clear that incenting employees with financial perks almost always robs potential innovators of their curiosity and passion. Employees don't bother exploring the maze of potential solutions to arrive at novel solutions; they just seek the shortest path to the cheese.[3] Ultimately, the financial incentives are at best ineffective; sometimes they are even viewed as insulting. Why would employees need incentives to express their basic humanity?

What's the antidote to employee engagement dysfunction? How to spur employee entrepreneurialism without either carrot or stick? Ironically, the solution starts with strong leadership. To be useful to an organization, employee imagination doesn't just need to be released, *it also needs to be shaped and harnessed.* For diversity of thought to be effective, there needs to be commonality of purpose. Just like any other kind of energy, unrestrained employee imagination will dissipate if not channeled; if directed at the wrong objective it can actually be destructive.

Employees will not allow their imagination to be shaped by just anyone: the leader, first and foremost, must convince employees of his or her expertise and moral character. The presence of a leader (or leaders) is an absolute necessity for any organization to maintain sustained and fruitful strategic conversations. The leaders of organizations with successful strategic conversations – like Senecal and Lavoie – all exhibit a profound immediacy in their organizations that is felt by all. They actively engage their employees in town hall meetings, through their writings, and in daily interactions. In larger companies, personal interactions between leaders and employees can't always directly involve everyone. Here leaders work to ensure that the personal interactions they do have are well socialized to all. A poignant conversation in the hallway with employees becomes lore through multiple channels, including transmission by subordinates, blogs, and all other manner of electronic water coolers. Joe Tucci, the CEO of EMC, a global company with over 60,000 employees, is able to project his presence effectively through storied interactions that have demonstrated his intelligence, competence, and character. His leadership was palpable even when we spoke with employees as far from EMC's Massachusetts headquarters as St. Petersburg, Russia and Shanghai. We've noticed that employees often refer to these leaders by their first names because they play an active and quotidian role in their lives, even though the conversations they have most often are just in their heads.

Earlier works on employee involvement in strategy development sought to turn employees into internal consultants that would know more about the business than any external consultant could.[4] But strategic conversations go further. Employees aren't working for the leader as 'internal consultants' – they are acting *as if they were the leader* him or herself within their own domain, whether it be as a business unit leader or someone on the front lines with customers. This effect is profound. Think of Steve Jobs, whose presence was legendary. If you were a designer at Apple would you even think about creating a complicated interface for a device? No, Steve Jobs' voice in your mind would direct you, without a word said, to keep it clean.

Leading with personal presence is necessary but not sufficient. Creating employee entrepreneurs also requires appealing to personal pride and community. To a large degree, organizations in our study like the World Bank, YMCA Canada, and Boston Children's Hospital are mission-driven, so this element of leadership's job is made easier. But the leaders of successful commercial organizations in our study also create meaning for their employees. Lori Senecal's motto for her company is "Do things that matter"; her employees are on a journey to remake the advertising industry through their actions. Jim Lavoie is creating a community of employees dedicated to each other's success. Red Hat's employees are dedicated to building a vital open source community through their work. Without creating this context of actionable meaning, employees will neither be fully dedicated to the purpose of the organization, nor will they offer the fruits of their imagination, or allow it to be shaped by organizational imperatives.

Students of rhetoric will recognize the appeals to character and higher interest (ethos) and to personal commitment and passion (pathos) as two of the three key elements for convincing listeners to take action. Rhetoric in many circles has a bad reputation these days as being vacuous and manipulative. But what great organization can you think of today that doesn't employ these two elements of rhetoric, and to great effect? When extrinsic motivation and appeals to self-interest are ineffective (and they usually are), leadership must look to the other arrows that can be pulled from its quiver.

Too many organizations rely solely on the third pillar of rhetoric, logic (logos) to motivate employees. Research clearly shows that extrinsic motivators like higher salary and better benefits are initially appreciated but quickly just become part of the new normal. Intrinsic or social motivators, on the other hand, deeply resonate. Recognition by superiors and peers for achievements hard-won bring deep satisfaction. In organizations where strategic conversations are strong, attaining higher pay or career advancement is a by-product of employee actions, not their object. Ethos and pathos speak to the employee's inner needs for identity, belonging and meaning.[5]

Most MBA curricula tend to stress rationality and logic above everything else. So, if you're a manager squirming a bit at the thought of needing to engage employees at a more emotional and less rational level, you're probably not alone. But business is a place of passion, so this point can't be glossed over if you want to engage employees in strategy and business model innovation. Logic by itself is, at best, a weak instrument for shaping behavior, and it can backfire.

Researchers at Carnegie Mellon University provide a wonderfully poignant example. They wanted to see if people would give more to a charity based upon a rational appeal or an appeal to emotion. Participants were asked to fill out a survey for which they were given $5.00 for completion. (The survey was irrelevant to the experiment, it was just meant to give participants a fixed amount of money.) The researchers then presented two different solicitation letters to participants, both ostensibly from Save the Children, and asked how much of the payment they received for doing the survey they would be willing to contribute to the charity. The first letter objectively described the scale of the hunger challenge in Africa with statistics that clearly showed its magnitude. The second letter painted the picture from the perspective of 'Rokia,' a poor seven-year-old girl from Mali.

The results were striking. Participants were willing to donate twice as much money to the charity if it presented the second letter with the poster child than if they were presented with the 'facts' about famine in Africa, $2.28 versus $1.14. Researchers then gave another cohort of participants both letters. Surely, combining the emotional appeal and the objective 'facts' would result in higher contributions. But no, the emotional appeal alone was far more effective. Those who were given both letters gave only $1.43. The appeal to emotion, unburdened and undistracted by the facts, was a far better impetus for charitable action.[6]

A truly diabolical example of logic backfiring

Big Tobacco understands well the limits of logic and the power of appealing to identity. How else could it be so effective at selling a product that is objectively unpleasant, unhealthy, and expensive? As Tina Rosenberg describes in *Join the Club: How Peer Pressure Can Transform the World*, tobacco companies were brilliant at shaping the anti-smoking movement to their advantage. In 1998 the four largest tobacco companies settled with forty-six states to pay for the health costs associated with smoking and to supply funds for promoting anti-smoking advertising.

The tobacco companies encouraged anti-smoking campaigns that targeted teenagers and pre-teens, and focused on the negative health effects or addictiveness of cigarettes – themes that were proven failures. This type of campaign was beneficial to tobacco companies because their audience already knew about the downsides of smoking. If anything, when surveyed, youth tended to overestimate smoking's dangers. The problem for anti-smoking advocates was that these messages represented authority, the very thing that youth was busy rejecting. In some cases, the appeal to logic actually had the opposite of the desired effect. Anti-smoking tee-shirts became popular with young smokers, who used cigarettes to burn holes in them and then wore them in defiance. Logic was a horrible advertising strategy that Big Tobacco was perfectly happy to support![7]

Some anti-smoking campaigns saw the light and steered away from emphasizing the negatives of smoking and appealed to youth's emotions and identity. Instead of saying "smoke and you'll get cancer," these campaigns used internal tobacco company documents to show how they were consciously manipulating youth to get them to smoke through advertising specially targeted to fourteen to eighteen year olds (like Joe Camel). These campaigns did result in substantial reductions in teen smoking. Instead of rebelling against annoying adults telling them that smoking wasn't cool, they now rebelled against the machinations of tobacco executives. It just goes to show, in trying to get people to change behaviors (e.g., to become more entrepreneurial), logic often doesn't work. Prospective change agents (known to the Greeks as the rhetors) need to be credible and speak to their audience's sense of identity and pride.

Given the limits of logic in stimulating engagement, strategic conversations require that leadership trust its rhetoric and stop relying on hierarchy, position, and title as the source of authority. Leaders, real leaders, need to face their workforce with palms open, carrying neither carrots nor sticks. They need to convince individuals to give up the fruits of their imagination to benefit the organization without these props of authority. If this sounds like a tall order, well, it is! Strategic conversations require that leaders project their presence to individual employees, even (and especially) when they number in the tens of thousands and are distributed across several continents. But as challenging as this may be, it is by no means a fool's errand: strategic conversations scale.

It is probably no coincidence that the first example of a significantly scaled strategic conversation was carried out near where rhetoric was held in high esteem, ancient Athens. It is a testament to the universality of strategic conversations that it could occur in an era without the communication technology enjoyed by today's business leaders. And perhaps unexpectedly, Athens, especially during what has been characterized as its golden age, had many similarities to the situations faced by business leaders today. As classicist, business scholar, and practitioner Brook Manville points out, Athens at this time was around the size of a typical large corporation (about 60,000 citizens) and, as is common in today's global business environment, had far-flung operations and complex relations with its trading partners and competitors. Competition was as fierce as, if not fiercer than, that faced by any contemporary company. In fact, when dealing with the Persians, fellow Greeks, and others, many of Athens' challenges truly were matters of life and death. Yet, against this uncertain and frightening backdrop, Athenian democracy and commercial interests flourished for nearly 200 years. (Perhaps our great, great, great, great grandchildren will be able to witness whether Apple's reign lasts as long.)

Pericles is often mentioned as the greatest of Athenian leaders. Like today's business leaders trying to engage knowledge workers, Pericles couldn't rule by fiat. Athens was a participative democracy of free men who could choose where to direct their energies. He couldn't incentivize them either; even if gold could have bought their allegiance, he didn't have it. The only workable option he had was to convince them with his words. And those words were carefully chosen. An analysis of his speeches reveals that he didn't emphasize rationality (*logos*) above all else. Instead he stressed his own moral authority for speaking, his dedication to Athens above his own interests (*ethos*), and he appealed to citizens' sense of what was right given their identity as free Athenian citizens.[8]

His views were discussed in a series of forums where all citizens were allowed to speak. These conversations allowed them to test their own understanding of the issues in the presence of their leaders and peers, relating the issues to their experiences and to the challenges of their particular situations and towards sharing their insights. In these forums strategic conversations broke down the barriers of structure and formality. Cold, dispassionate communication became personal discourse, with leaders needing to be present and engaging listeners deeply, encouraging their imaginations towards challenges. And while not all citizens attended all conversations, at some point in their lives most citizens did actively participate, creating tens of thousands of people deeply steeped in the decision-making process and outcomes.

Because these conversations engendered a common understanding, trust, and sense of purpose,[9] Athens had the ability to move quickly and decisively under threat. This is a crucial point. One of the arguments against strategic conversations is that they will take too long and delay action on seizing opportunities or reacting to threats. Athenian society generally reacted quickly when necessary. Like any organization, it made mistakes. But because of the structured conversations carried on by its citizens, it had a remarkable ability to learn from errors and often emerged stronger for having made them.

Today's innovative companies do much the same thing. The Japanese call it *nemawashi* – lengthy discussions that precede action but ensure it goes smoothly and swiftly once begun. Soon after Jim

Whitehurst took over the position of CEO for Red Hat he started this very kind of conversation to orient himself and the company. It was a conversation that established him as a present and credible leader while helping him to create focus that would allow Red Hat to develop strategy effectively. It allowed him to gain profound insight into his employees and the market in which they operated. And it changed his own view of the nature and practice of leadership. Having been COO of Delta Airlines in his previous job, he was used to quasi-military command and control. Red Hat employees showed him the power of emergent and participative leadership.

To get a feeling for attitudes and methods used, it is worth quoting him at length:

"During my first few months as CEO, I traveled to Red Hat offices around the world and was often floored by the passion people felt about the company. I began to ask myself, how can we bottle this passion? Can we channel all of this energy and point it in the same direction?

In my experience, one of the most important tools of management is a core company mission that helps the company point all of its resources and energy toward a set of positive outcomes. That mission should answer two questions – what we are trying to do and how we are going to do it – in a simple way that any employee can understand.

When I arrived at Red Hat, there was already a vision for the company ... and it read as follows:

> To be the defining technology company of the 21st century, and through our actions strengthen the social fabric by continually democratizing content and technology.

This was a heady statement ... but, as I began to discuss it with employees around the company, I got the distinct impression many people didn't understand what it meant or what it was telling them to do. Meanwhile, as is often the case in an open source organization like Red Hat, a passionate group of folks had come together and were already thinking about how to solve the problem.

This group was made up of people who'd joined forces to ensure Red Hat's corporate strategy wasn't just words on paper, but instead was deeply embedded within the organization. They had quickly come to the conclusion Red Hat needed something more directional than the 'defining technology company' vision to connect the overall vision to the strategic plan.

By the time they approached me, the team had already crafted some sample 'mission' statements for me to look at. We gathered around and looked at all of the things they had come up with, debating the merits of each. In a few short hours of work, we developed a statement that felt pretty comfortable to all of us. But then we did something most companies wouldn't dream of doing.

Rather than going straight to my senior executive team to get their opinion first, or continuing to muck around with the words for weeks or months to get them just perfect, we employed an open source technique our engineers sometimes refer to as 'release early, release often.'

Rather than continuing to craft the company mission behind closed doors, we showed it to the whole company. In draft form. Before it was perfect.

And we asked everyone what they thought of it. We asked which parts resonated most. We asked them what we should change. We asked for suggestions to make it better. Anyone could give us feedback, and many did. There was thoughtful discussion, some fantastic suggestions for wording changes, even some argument and disagreement about whether this truly reflected what the company was trying to achieve.

I believe this was a conversation the company needed to have.

One benefit was that it engaged many thoughtful employees in a discussion about why they were doing their jobs. It's not often during a hectic day (especially in a growing technology company) that people take the time to think about the forest instead of the trees, and opening up the process of defining the Red Hat mission gave them an excuse to do exactly that.

But perhaps the biggest benefit was that, by asking employees to become a part of the process, and then taking some of their best feedback and using it to improve the mission itself, we gave them ownership of the mission.

How many company missions have you seen where it was clear that it was written by either a) the CEO sitting alone late one evening or b) an executive committee that came to a sterile compromise?

And how do most employees react to those mission statements? Case closed . . . We believe the best ideas should win, no matter where they come from.

In many organizations it is not possible for the best ideas to win because they are hidden in the brains of people who sit many layers of management deep in the organization. The best ideas get lost as they make their way up through the hierarchy. We cut through the hierarchy, and took our draft mission right to the people. We were able to get the best ideas, unfiltered by management, and apply them right away.

Our final Red Hat mission is this:

> To be the catalyst in communities of customers, contributors, and partners creating better technology the open source way."[10]

As is clear from Whitehurst's statement, Red Hat's strategic conversation strove for excellence. In our conversation with Whitehurst and Jackie Yeaney, Red Hat's Executive Vice President for Strategy and Corporate Marketing, they made it clear that while Red Hat is highly participative, it is by no means about majority rule or comfortable consensus decisions. Certain people's opinions carry greater weight than others because of their expertise and prior successes. Yeaney was especially adamant that it was imperative that the best ideas be allowed to shine and not to accept mediocre results dictated by committee.

While some organizational cultures, like Red Hat's, seem naturally open to strategic conversations, other businesses may need to be more judicious in selecting which employees to engage. Especially where bottom-up strategizing hasn't been the norm, some employees will be more open to sharing their ideas than others, who may feel burned or cynical about becoming emotionally involved. By choosing and supporting "positive deviants"[11] – employees who are willing to engage despite the prevailing culture – leadership empowers those already with the program, reduces the antibody-like response to change, and makes it easier to change a passive culture to a participative one.

How can these positive deviants be cultivated? In these cases, some organizations employ T-shaped strategic conversations involving business unit leaders. With fewer people involved, senior management can more easily inculcate a culture of participation under watchful eyes. They know that these conversations are working when people become eager to participate. Managers at GE often have to wait ten years to be selected, and many never get the opportunity. At food giant SUPERVALU, only fifty to sixty managers a year are chosen to lead innovation activities.[12] Competition to head one of Honda's innovation teams is stiff; participation is often the high endnote to a senior manager's career.

In other organizations, such as Pitney Bowes and Pricewater-houseCoopers, senior management starts by using the strategic conversation types of competitions and challenges. In these cases, willing participants self-select to join the conversation. These participants often end up forming teams that draw yet more employees in.

Once you have your employees engaged in the idea of business model innovation, the question becomes "what to innovate?" Without a clear agenda for strategic conversations, the result is apt to be Brownian motion: randomized and vacuous blue-sky ramblings that address key business issues haphazardly or not at all. Without a focus, idea generation seldom creates genuine dialog and learning. Rather, it wastes time and attention, which are always management's scarcest resource. Sometimes the lack of focus can be almost comical. Shortly after taking over as CEO of AOL and meeting with the firm's strategic planners, Tim Armstrong was astounded when they presented him with over 900 potential business deals.[13]

Ask many business people how to generate ideas and they'll suggest a brainstorming session. Brainstorm facilitators emphasize that creativity requires clearing participants' minds of preconceived notions while providing a completely non-judgmental environment for exploring new thinking. The concept of brainstorming originated with the publication of *Your Creative Power* by advertising executive Alex Osborn in 1948. Osborn wrote: "Creativity is so delicate a flower that praise tends to make it bloom while discouragement often nips it in the bud. Forget quality; aim now to get a quantity of answers. When you're through, your sheet of paper may be so full of ridiculous nonsense that you'll be disgusted. Never mind. You're loosening up your unfettered imagination-making your mind deliver."[14]

The problem with brainstorming is that research has pretty much debunked its effectiveness.[15] One early study found that the ideas generated by individuals were generally judged to be more valuable than those resulting from small group brainstorms. And the individuals came up with twice the number of ideas.[16] Talk about a productivity killer!

It turns out that context matters. Thinking informed by, but not bound to, current reality has the potential to be the most fertile. Business and science author Stephen Johnson writes of the "adjacent possible" as the most likely source for innovation. For instance, Gutenberg didn't invent the 'press' of the printing press. He borrowed that idea from the screw-type wine presses of the Rhine Valley.[17] Henry Ford came up with the idea of the moving assembly line from observing meat packers in Chicago, who shunted the carcasses from one area to the next as they were processed. Both of these ideas revolutionized the world; neither was *sui generis*, but was based on already existing concepts from different domains. The power of their imagination lay in their ability to take something familiar to one situation and apply it to another, triggering an innovation with far greater impact.

For these reasons, strategic conversations aren't brainstorms. They are carefully focused conversations between leadership and employees, grounded in current practice and challenges, that seek to address knowledge absences and imagine a better way to fulfil the organization's mission. But if brainstorming isn't the way to go, what technique works for creating an actionable insight, that magic moment when we're able to imagine a way to reinvent a business model that significantly improves the organization's strategic position? Our way of thinking about strategic conversations is, not surprisingly, derived from an adjacent possibility, the development of military strategy for war. Business isn't (contrary to some belief) war. But as we'll see, it is close enough to provide business leaders valuable insight.

Carl von Clausewitz, whose early nineteenth century study *On War* is still taught at West Point, is perhaps the most profound thinker among modern strategists (though he had real battlefield experience too). Strategy is a term relatively new to the English language. The first known use was in 1810,[18] the time of the Napoleonic wars.[19] As a Prussian general, the problem Clausewitz faced was how to understand, and ultimately counter, the strategic genius of Napoleon Bonaparte. Napoleon had redefined war in Europe and beyond, and at one time or another had defeated all of Europe's major armies, including Prussia. Clausewitz puzzled about how Napoleon was able to act decisively within the "fog of war" and consistently take advantage of situations others did not seem to see.

Clausewitz concluded, and the authors agree wholeheartedly, that leaders have a profound responsibility to contribute to strategic insight in the face of the irreducible uncertainty found in both war and business. They must shape the strategic conversation into something useful by grounding it in their experience. Clausewitz believed those aspiring to be great military leaders should be dedicated students of military history, stocking their minds with knowledge of past wars, down to the sort of minute details on which battles often turned. But while great leaders had one foot in the past, they kept the other firmly in the present, establishing a 'presence' that saw the situation as unique and open to yet-undiscovered possibilities. Only when these two conditions existed, a mind well stocked with past situations and an imagination open to seeing the new, would the flash of strategic insight become possible. Clausewitz called this flash the *coup d'oeil*: "the rapid discovery of a truth which to the ordinary mind is either not visible at all or only becomes so after long examination and reflection."[20]

Lest this seem like German romantic mumbo jumbo, business scholar William Duggan points out, in a work written for the United States Army, that neuroscience confirms Clausewitz's model of the flash of insight.[21] Firefighters, emergency room doctors, and soldiers in battle rely heavily on their experience to make snap judgments. This 'muscle memory' is the result of years of deep and profound reflection. MRIs reveal that the entire left/right brain dichotomy between rationality and creativity is misunderstood – during decision-making both hemispheres fire at the same time. And when one side cannot function, for instance in individuals with lesions in their right hemispheres (the side associated with creativity and intuition), we are rendered incapable of making even simple decisions.[22]

But for Clausewitz, experience and presence were only two pieces of the leadership puzzle for addressing uncertainty: leaders also required resolution. In a state of uncertainty, there would be doubt and doubters. The leader should stay true to his or her initial insight ('maxim') that resulted from the *coup d'oeil*. As Clausewitz wrote in *On War*:

> We must firmly believe in the superior authority of well-tried maxims, and under the dazzling influence of momentary events not forget that their value is of an inferior stamp. By this preference which in doubtful cases we give to first convictions, by adherence to the same our actions acquire that stability and consistency which make up what is called character.[23]

A leader without 'resolution' would constantly change tack, confusing the organization and wasting valuable energy by going to and fro. (Of course, Clausewitz didn't argue that in the face of new facts that invalidated a maxim, the leader should obstinately hold to outdated positions. The best generals also knew how to pivot gracefully in the light of new facts on the ground.)

Tim Armstrong's strategic intuition, based upon his own previous experience as a marketing executive at Google and his overview of AOL's prospects, was to play to the strength of AOL's web presence and to focus on digital journalism tailored to small communities that often didn't have their own local papers. With the new strategic agenda defined, the 900 business ideas were quickly winnowed to just 5 strategically significant deals. Crucially, the conversation was two-sided: even though he had his own favorite in the race, Armstrong gave it up at the urging of his managers. Whether or not AOL's new business model ultimately results in profitability, Armstrong has brought direction to a firm that has lacked it for years.[24]

The leaders in our study who successfully practice strategic conversations all have the Clausewitzian qualities of *experience* and *presence* from which they achieve *coup d'oeil*. They also possess *resolution*, through which they pursue the 'maxims' derived from their *coup d'oeil* even in the face of uncertainty and doubt. And while they are strong leaders who actively shape the imagination of their employees, they are also skillful listeners. They make sure that they too are open to being shaped by the conversation, and thus able to work effectively to eliminate key knowledge absences in their own strategic thinking.

Following are examples from three of our case studies: Rite-Solutions, KBS+, and YMCA Canada.

Rite-Solutions. CEO Jim Lavoie likens his job to that of a mechanic aligning the magnets in an electric motor to optimize its performance. The dynamics of the engine require balancing between aggressively pursuing new opportunities and exploiting the organization's current expertise. Too much chaos and the engine spins out of control, resulting in problems with cash flow and potential cata-strophic failure. Too much order and the organization fails to adapt to changing circumstances while making the organization an undesir-able place for entrepreneurial employees. Lavoie is the first to admit he doesn't know where the motor will take Rite-Solutions; his function is to ensure that it's running smoothly wherever the journey takes it. Lavoie's *coup d'oeil* has given Rite-Solutions significant latitude: from its Department of Defense roots, employee innovation has enabled it to branch out into gaming (like the DOD, Las Vegas also needs high availability software), and from gaming to educational toys for Hasbro (the idea for moving into the toy industry came from a secretary).

KBS+. If anything, KBS+'s CEO Lori Senecal has given her colleagues even more latitude while running the firm's employee-fueled innovation engine very hard since taking it over for its original partners in 2009. She introduced the mission statement "Do things that matter," which made clear that her focus was on remaking the advertising world, and that she was interested in impact and not clutter. Her *coup d'oeil* revelation is that the energy and network power of social media is creating massive and diverse unrealized opportunities in the advertising world. Where they may be, she can't know for sure, but she knows that they're out there and will keep her army of experienced executives, finance experts, technology geeks, and young creative talent moving to find them. She made it clear that any idea has to be both good for the client and the company. Within those parameters, KBS+ generated an incredible blossoming of new initiatives in less than three years, including: KBS+ Ventures, an investment arm that backs entrepreneurs focusing on advertising and marketing technology; KBS+ Spies and Assassins, a creative tech-nology boutique; KBS+ Action Sports and Lifestyle Brands, which caters to sports like skateboarding and surfing, as well as lifestyle brands and independent culture; and the Hyde Experiment, a large physical space in KBS+'s office where artists from within and outside of the agency can come together and create projects that reveal new creative possibilities (we'll expand on the Hyde Space in Chapter 6).

As in the case of Rite-Solutions, hierarchy is not a factor. Some of the ideas for these innovations have come from senior members of her staff, like KBS+ Ventures; others, like the Hyde Experiment, were conceived by the youngest people in the firm. Despite the lack of hierarchy, Senecal's leadership is very present. She wields the 'soft power' implicit in her encyclopedic knowledge of the advertising world (and beyond), and her presence and resolution to see ideas implemented have cemented her leadership and put her stamp on the firm. Senecal admits that she hasn't slept much in three years – it's the price she has paid for ensuring that the massive amount of business model innovation that has occurred under her watch has been well executed, and results in a coherent overall strategy. She'll concede that KBS+ has had the pedal to the metal of its innovation engine in a way that isn't permanently sustainable, and that it is probably time to milk the rewards of innovation a little before venturing out further into chaos. (She's also the first to admit that a little sleep in the coming years wouldn't be a bad thing either.)

YMCA Canada. If you're a CEO and think achieving alignment in your company is difficult, consider Scott Haldane's situation. As CEO of YMCA Canada, Haldane is responsible for the overall strategy for a federation of fifty-one local chapters across the country. Over its 150-year history, YMCA Canada's chapters have traditionally been very independent, and there had never been a federation-wide strategy. The situation for each chapter is quite different: some cater to French-speaking populations, others to First Nations peoples, and others to Canada's many large immigrant populations. Some chapters are tiny, like the one in Moncton, New Brunswick, which served 1,500 individuals and families in 2011.[25] At the other extreme is the Greater Toronto Area chapter, the largest YMCA chapter in the world. Haldane has a mandate to optimize the Y's efforts in Canada, but like a latter-day Pericles of the great white north, has no authority to force solutions on the chapters, and so must engage them in collaboration around a strategic vision.

Like Pericles, Haldane has gained the respect of his audience: his thirty-three-year YMCA career has taken him from the West Island of Montréal, where he began as a lifeguard, youth worker and branch executive, to a position in the national office, to chapter CEO (including seven years as CEO of the YMCA of Greater Toronto). He is known to be a good listener, humble but effective. So, as a leader he has *ethos* covered – a leader well worth listening to. What about pathos, the ability to stir his listeners' emotions? Haldane played on the sentiment most shared by chapter CEOs – one that he himself had as a chapter CEO – that YMCA Canada was missing opportunities to serve its community by not having a clear focus. Because of this, YMCA Canada wasn't able to create the impact it might if it succeeded in speaking with one voice. The facts on the ground also confirmed Haldane's intuition: Canada's federal government, especially the office of the Minister of Health in Ottawa, was interested in deepening its relationship with YMCA Canada, but it didn't have the time, organization, or resources to deal with fifty-one separate chapters. Haldane saw there was a great strategic opportunity open if YMCA Canada's Federation could only be brought together. But what should the unifying theme be and how would the services that support it be determined?

Haldane initiated a strategic conversation among all of YMCA Canada's CEOs and their chapter boards to develop the theme and decide on common services. Over a series of meetings – many of which were face-to-face in order to create trust and build common understanding – a central theme emerged. It was based on adjacent possibilities – literally and figuratively. Chapters in Ontario had become aware of the Strong Kids program from interacting with US chapters in neighboring states. The Ontario chapters gravitated towards it as a theme. It played to the Y's strengths – providing recreation options for communities through its gyms and sports programs. And of course the 'Y' in YMCA stands for 'Young.' This was Haldane's *coup d'oeil* for creating focus: healthier children, teens and young adults (under the age of twenty-eight) would lead to safer, more wholesome communities and fulfill the YMCA's broad mission.

To solidify this concept, he convinced chapter heads that the first common service the federation should supply, a service that would be funded out of chapter monies, was marketing their Strong Kids program. This was widely considered to be a smart move. It would allow YMCA Canada to speak with one voice in regard to Strong Kids. And since marketing had never been a strong point for YMCA Canada, or any of its chapters, marketing services would be an easy sell. It was needed and would not interfere with any chapter initiatives already in place.

For all these reasons, Haldane's intuition made practical sense, and was greeted with enthusiasm. That didn't mean that implementation would be easy, or that Clausewitzian resolution wouldn't be needed. For some chapters, especially those located in cities like Vancouver or Toronto that had large young immigrant populations, the theme was an easy fit. But for chapters like Moncton that served an aging population, the Strong Kids concept was more difficult to sell.

When the authors discussed this dilemma with Haldane, we hit upon the notion of fractals to describe how YMCA Canada would deal with this diversity of situations. Fractals are patterns that repeat at different scales. Fractals are phenomena of practical mathematics – especially the mathematical properties of shapes in nature. While nature is well stocked with smooth shapes – an egg or pebbles on the beach – many of its shapes are rough. Coastlines are a common instance: headlands jut out, bays are broken by river estuaries and so on. Fractal mathematics explores an unexpected discovery, that this kind of roughness exists at every level of scale. You can see the coastline's roughness from a circling space capsule; you see it as you walk along the beach, and still see it as you crouch with a magnifying glass and look at the sea's edge. There is no scale at which roughness is replaced by smoothness – the patterns of roughness are repeated at endlessly greater or smaller levels. So too with Strong Kids. Through the strength of the strategic conversations, every chapter clearly understood the intent of the program and could apply it in a way that, at their level, made sense. The national Strong Kids pattern would repeat, but would vary to account for local differences. So, in the Greater Toronto Area implementation of Strong Kids, CEO Medhat Mahdy might emphasize providing athletic outlets to kids who otherwise could be attracted to gangs. Moncton's CEO Zane Korytko, who doesn't face a gang problem, might focus on mentoring programs for young adults that leverage its adult population. Different, but recognizable, implementations of the same strategy.

This is a key point, and one of the most powerful advantages of strategic conversations. When leadership establishes that everyone should participate in the development of strategy and then provides a clear but flexible agenda, employees at all levels of the organization act as if they are part of leadership, but at their own zoom level of the fractal. Leadership hasn't just communicated its intent, it has also fully engaged employee agency. In the heat of battle, subordinate officers in the Prussian army were empowered to act without the need for direct orders because they had discussed the general's strategic intent and understood it. They knew what the battle was about. Command and control style management was no longer necessary. As Mahdy and Korytko plan their implementations, they assimilate Haldane's intent in their actions, they're transformed. But the effect is not merely top-down – as in any productive conversation, all parties are open to change. Haldane also has Mahdy, Korytko, and the other chapter CEOs in his mind, guiding him as he learns from conversations about their experiences and issues. The conversation is focused, engaging, and transformative for all participants.

Some have described strategy as a science. But from our discussion above, we see that it isn't. Both in war and business, there are no repeatable experiments, there is no one solution set. Yet, as military scholar Christopher Bassford notes, Clausewitz didn't consider strategy to be art either. Bassford writes:

> In both art and science, the actor is working on inanimate matter
> (and, in art, the passive and yielding emotions of the audience),

whereas in business, politics, and war the actor's will is directed at an animate object that not only *reacts* but takes independent actions of its own. War is thus permeated by "intelligent forces." ... It is a wrestling match – a contest between independent wills, in which skill and creativity are no more important than personality, chance, emotion, and the various dynamics that characterize any human interaction, including raw strength and power. When Clausewitz wrote that war may have a grammar of its own, but not its own logic, he meant that the logic of war, like politics, is the logic of social intercourse, not that of art or science.[26]

Thus, strategy is a form of social intercourse. Strategic conversations are inherently social. As such, they take upfront time to initiate, all participants must invest themselves, commit to the process. But once trust is built and a common vocabulary emerges, strategic conversations allow organizations to address challenges and shape their future with the advantage of superior knowledge, clarity, and the capability to quickly seize advantage.

Are employees engaged in leadership's agenda? A simple test:

Visit ten employees from across the organization and do the following:

- Ask them to describe the firm's strategic vision. Are you satisfied with their answers? (By the way, the compensation of Red Hat's CEO as well as that of his direct reports is partially dependent on how well employees understand the company's strategy.)
- Ask them why they come to work. Do they respond with explanations of pride and a deep sense of meaning? How do you react to their explanations? Do you feel more or less energized by them?
- Pose a strategic problem with which you're currently wrestling. Listen to their response. Do they enthusiastically rise to the challenge? Do they frame the problem in accordance with your strategic intuition or are their suggestions off-the-wall?

5 Strategizing and the leaders' role

Entrepreneurial versatility is a somewhat different quality
from managerial or technical versatility. The latter two
qualities are primarily questions of administrative and technical
competence; the former quality is a question of imagination
and vision.

Edith Penrose, *The theory of the growth of the firm*[1]

By now you should have a good appreciation for the need for strategic
conversations, and an understanding of how organizations employ
them to gain a leg up. This chapter's focus is on you, the leader, and
what you need to do to deliver on the promise of strategic conversations: strengthening decision-making under uncertainty, promoting
an entrepreneurial workforce, and accelerating growth. It will provide
guidance – a recipe – for developing business models in the strategic
conversations way. But before we delve into the process, we'll address
how leadership is different under strategic conversations and how you
need to comport yourself to be successful.

These lessons apply whether you have a position on the org
chart that bestows authority, or whether you find yourself somewhere
at the bottom of the pyramid. Neither of these circumstances deter-
mines your ability to lead. As we saw at the World Bank, a secretary
far from its Washington DC headquarters was able to provide the
catalyst for a change that radically altered the business model of a
hidebound institution. The opposite is also true: just because you
have a leadership title doesn't make you a leader. We've all seen
high-ranking people abdicate their leadership potential by playing it
safe and doing what is politically expedient.

Leadership is a choice, and it's available to us all.

If strategy development is no longer a solitary or small-group effort, if it is to engage the energy and imagination of employees, then the context in which it is developed is crucial. Leaders have the ability to spark and enhance strategic conversations; they also have the power to snuff them out before they even start. (Conversational health is vital too. Chapter 7 will discuss the new norms for dialog that promote strategic conversations.)

Scholars have identified three different leadership styles in practice today: we call them coercive, transactional, and conversational.[2] Most organizations exhibit aspects of all three of these styles, but in any institution one is generally much more dominant.

Predominantly coercive organizations are relatively rare today, but they are not unheard of. Recently, outsourced manufacturing has been associated with this kind of leadership practice, where workers are subjected to threats and humiliation to maintain management control.[3] It goes without saying that this style of leadership alienates employees and is wholly inappropriate for organizations looking to improve their performance by engaging employees in the strategy development process.[4]

Transactional leadership is probably the dominant style today. In the transactional model, the predominant one taught at most economics departments and business schools, employees are viewed as free agents who act in their own self-defined best interests. Employment is simply an exchange of value between two parties – employees agree to do a unit of work for a measure of compensation. In the past, employees could count on long careers at an institution as long as they stayed out of trouble, which created a certain loyalty to the firm. But for most employees, those days are behind them (or for younger employees, never existed) because almost everyone is now considered contingent labor. While leaders in transactional organizations may spend some effort to create employee loyalty to the organization and its purpose, more often than not what fealty there exists is directed to individual managers rather than to the institution. Neither side expects to be transformed by the interaction, any more than you would expect to be transformed by a trip to the store to buy milk. As we've seen, this style is also inimical to generating employee involvement in the strategy development process. This is reflected in a long and downward trend of employee engagement: globally the percentage of employees who are willing to put in high levels of discretionary effort is thought to be lower than 20 percent.[5]

Our research confirms that organizations are increasingly moving towards the conversational style of leadership. Conversational leadership uses neither sticks nor carrots. Rather, these leaders use rhetorical techniques to engage employees by tying the employees' understanding of the firm's goals to their own. In high-performing conversational organizations, employees act as if they were leadership, their decisions and actions guided by their interpretations of management's values and objectives. This leadership style is not mere smoke and mirrors, fancy words laid onto the same old practices – it gains commitment by giving employees a stake in defining their work goals and purpose. As Chris Argyris has shown, the more power people have to shape their lives, the more commitment they have.[6]

Conversational leadership may demand a different leadership posture from the one you're used to, one in which you don't need to have all the right answers, but rather are armed with an inquisitive mind. Business author and philosopher Fred Kofman names the old style of manager "controllers." These managers believe they know how things are and what needs to be done to get them to where they should be. They enjoy "being in charge" and giving orders, no questions asked. The new type of leader he calls "learners." They are curious about the world and believe that everyone has the potential to help inform decision-making. They ask lots of questions and are open to considering the perspectives of others rather than just imposing their own.[7] Leaders who are learners are exactly what strategic conversations need.

The transition from knower to learner management doesn't necessarily require an injection of new blood; such transitions can occur within every individual. Before becoming Red Hat's CEO, Jim

Whitehurst was COO at Delta Airlines, an organization famous for its command and control style of leadership. To his credit, Whitehurst was open to changing his own style, and when he moved to Red Hat he allowed himself to be transformed to embrace its radically different conversational style of leadership. He quickly learned the new leadership style from his employees. As we've seen, it was employees who initiated the effort to redefine Red Hat's mission. As he has shaped the organization, Whitehurst has allowed himself to be shaped.

At this point you may be thinking this all sounds well and good, but aren't some of the most successful companies in the world run by CEOs with a tyrannical bent that makes them more controller than learner? Our observations suggest that the age of the controller CEO may have crested, with learner CEOs on the ascendency. Captains of industry like Jack Welch (GE), Andy Grove (Intel) and Steve Jobs (Apple) have much more collaborative successors, Jeffrey Immelt, Paul Otellini, and Tim Cook respectively. Heroic leadership is certainly powerful, and can create ardent followers. But those shoes are hard to fill when the hero leaves, and in today's economy you need leaders at all levels of the organization working to create its future, not just at the top. Heroic leadership can condition employees to 'look up' passively to the boss instead of 'looking forward' actively to address and conquer the challenges they find within their own sphere of influence, non-adaptive behavior for today's business climate.[8]

What does a conversational style of leadership mean for the org chart? How does it affect span of control and delegation of responsibilities? As we'll argue later, conversation trumps structure. Rearranging the hierarchy won't save a company in poor conversational health. Nonetheless, flatter organizations are typically less rigidly formal and less siloed, which helps to promote strategic conversations. And the data show that this is the direction in which organizations are going, especially those in fast-moving, highly competitive industries, where decisions can't wait to go up and down the hierarchy.[9]

What do flatter hierarchies mean for CEOs? According to a recent study by Harvard researcher Julie Wulf, several things. First, data shows that CEOs in flat organizations tend to have a greater span of control and are more involved in the details of the business. The percentage of organizations with COO positions is falling – business areas as well as service functions like CIO are now more likely to report directly to the CEO than they were just a few years ago. CEOs are also spending more time in meetings and less time by themselves. As a result they are closer to their organizations than at any time in recent history. By the same token, when CEOs spend more time in meetings interacting with and influencing subordinates, they have less time for the contemplation required to reinvent their organization's business model (as our third Iron Law of Value Creation requires). Thus flattening is not the same as decentralization – to the contrary, the CEO and his or her directs have their fingers in more aspects of the business. And this is precisely as strategic conversations would have it – the presence of the leader is amplified across the organization. Nevertheless, something needs to give if CEOs are to avoid being overwhelmed. This is where the fourth Iron Law – "the better the knowledge flows and the more relevant perspectives brought to bear, the more opportunity there is for innovation" – comes to the rescue. In a flattened but centralized organization, it is incumbent upon leadership to engage employees in helping to innovate the business model. The CEO may not have the time or knowledge to reinvent the business model constantly, but an engaged workforce is more than happy to help.

Before he joined the World Bank as its President, Jim Yong Kim was President of Dartmouth University, and a physician and anthropologist. In a 2012 speech to the World Knowledge Forum, Kim talks about creating labs for what he calls "the science" of delivery. His thinking is profound, and it starts at the level of the individual employee. His notion is to create and nurture an organization that can effectively institutionalize practitioner learning:

> The foundation of success in delivery is the knowledge that is present in the heads of implementers. In the habits of effective

action that have become second nature to them, what we might call their "muscle memory," like the unhesitating movements of a musician executing a piece learned through tireless practice.

Development implementers working on the front lines acquire this "muscle memory" over the course of a career. They test solutions, observe the results, make corrections, test again. As they go through many of these learning cycles, their accumulated experience becomes practical know-how. ...

The challenge is to move from excellence in individual performance to broad improvements in the quality of delivery across ... [the organization].

For that ... we must create effective mechanisms to share delivery knowledge, so that implementers can continuously learn from each other. And we must set up "virtuous cycles" of learning, in which practitioners continuously test innovations, capture results, and use these results to design new experiments.[10]

The Bank is currently working on building the methods for implementing Kim's vision, to develop the types of strategic conversations that can capture the practical knowledge gained by the organization's field staff and to embed it into the strategy and operations of the organization.

Key to the thinking of leaders in organizations that use strategic conversations is that while many are consulted in strategic conversations, the strategic development process is not based on consensus. Kim, Whitehurst, and the other leaders we have observed aren't interested in voting on which ideas are acted upon. The best ideas win, not necessarily the most popular. "Diversity in counsel, unity in command," is the byword of the conversational leader's philosophy. Like the Athenians in Periclean times, conversational leaders and their organizations must move quickly to address challenges and take advantage of opportunities.

We've discussed the context required for developing strategy the strategic conversations way. We now turn our attention to how leaders should develop strategy. What are the tools that can be used? What's the process? And what are the outputs? And for that matter, *what is strategy*? In order to answer these questions, it's helpful to overview how business strategy has historically been viewed and practiced.

If you've ever had niggling uncertainty about the definition of business strategy, you're in good company. Neither consultants nor business schools have made a clear or practical distinction between strategic and other types of managerial decisions. Strategy has become an activity that is often defined as 'you know it when you see it' – often synonymous with 'long-term' or 'big' thinking that addresses a well-defined market space and business environment. The problem is that it is nearly impossible to be sure what part of the environment is 'not relevant,' and significant business model innovations can arise from actions that initially seem insignificant.

Take Wrigley's chewing gum. In 1892, William Wrigley Jr., the company's founder, began packaging chewing gum with its cans of baking powder as an advertising give-away. The chewing gum eventually became more popular than the baking powder itself, and Wrigley's completely reoriented the company to take advantage of the opportunity.[11] Post-it® Notes are another example of a small, seemingly insignificant development that took on 'strategic' dimensions. Ideas like 'long-term' and 'big' miss the happenstances and opportunism of business life. Freddie Laker's involvement in the Berlin airlift foreshadowed his creation of Laker Airways in 1966, the first to disrupt the traditional stodgy airlines with no-frills services, and the conceptual parent of companies like Southwest Airlines, Ryanair, and AirAsia. Steve Jobs' visit to Xerox PARC's facilities led to the popularization of such mainstays as the graphical user interface and devices like the mouse. It's pretty much impossible to know in advance which actions are tactical versus strategic.

To lift the veil on the purpose and methods of business strategy it will be useful to go on a brief "strategy safari."[12] This background will sharpen our arguments, and as an added bonus will give you ammunition if you ever run into a business strategy professor.[13] (If you don't have the time or the inclination to explore the history of business strategy with us, no worries. Skip the next several pages and rejoin us at the next section of this chapter: "So what is the goal of strategy?".)

As strategy textbook authors are quick to point out, strategizing is an ancient topic. Prior to the Second World War the business strategy field was dominated by references to historic war campaigns and to senior managers' own 'war stories.' After the Second World War and the successful application of rational planning methods to the use of logistics, especially by the Americans, to coordinate the massive effort of fielding a huge army, 'strategic planning' spread through business, often led by consultant firms though increasingly supported and theorized in business schools.

The beginnings of a more formal theoretical approach came with Alfred Chandler's analysis of the relationship between 'strategy' as the firm's chosen market engagements and 'structure' as its chosen administrative organization.[14] He presumed a functionally efficient 'fit' between environment and firm, between strategy and structure. This External-Internal-Fit paradigm dominates the strategy textbooks to this day. And it also dominates the way managers 'strategize,' for instance in the commonly used SWOT assessment, where an organization's internal Strengths and Weaknesses are considered matched against its externally based Opportunities and Threats. The External-Internal-Fit paradigm was considerably elaborated as post-Second World War firms became larger and more complex, often by acquiring dissimilar operations and effecting vertical and horizontal integration. These conglomerates' portfolio of separable operations – a new phenomenon – begged additional strategic questions about their governance, and managing the funds flow and risk allocations among them. Consultants responded by developing strategic tools like the Boston Consulting Group's Growth-Share Matrix (remember those cows, stars, dogs and question marks?), and the GE/McKinsey and Ansoff matrices.

In the 1980s and beyond, the External-Internal-Fit paradigm was severely jolted by Michael Porter's Competitive Strategy and its "five forces" analysis. Porter's thinking derived from monopoly theory and industrial organization economics and paid little attention to fit or efficiency. Rather, it focused on protecting the firm's profits from those economic actors able to disturb or appropriate them, specifically competitors, suppliers, buyers, potential substitutes, and potential new entrants. The underlying presence of market power ('force' in Porter's terminology) showed that firms are not the passive adapters implied in the External-Internal-Fit analysis but can push back aggressively against those actually eroding their monopoly profits, or threatening to – with re-pricing, R&D, new products, negotiating, and signaling, for example. The shift from efficiency to rents was also in tune with that time's changing politics, when Reagan's and Thatcher's attitudes towards antitrust legislation resulted in changes that gave monopolists freer rein.

As fond as big firms were of the idea of being able to capture monopoly profits, the center could not hold. Innovations in information technology, logistics, and other domains increased competition dramatically and the idea of being able to 'control' a market became, for many industries, a fond pipe dream. By the end of the 1980s many strategy researchers were abandoning the "five forces" model and looking for ways to explain how firms might acquire and protect their rent-streams in dynamically competitive situations.[15] One of the principal conjectures was that a firm's profitability was a function of its ownership of valuable, rare, and inimitable resources and its ability to integrate them into the firm's operations. This approach was labeled the Resource-Based View. Examples of these resources could include the Coca-Cola recipe, Toyota's car manufacturing process (the Toyota Production System), or Apple's design skill and know-how.

Missing, though, was any explanation of how firms might (a) acquire these resources without their rent-potential eventually being stripped by market forces or (b) transform these resources into economic value. Some began to suspect that the Resource-Based View was based on a tautology. How do we know which resources are valuable, rare, and inimitable? Valuable resources stand out and beget value because they are valuable. Nonetheless, this strategy theory became wildly popular among strategy academics, in spite of being little supported by empirical research or evident practical managerial application. Its enduring appeal provoked a second conjecture, sometimes dubbed the Knowledge-Based View or KBV.[16] The primary intuition of the Knowledge-Based View was that the firm's learning can produce new rent-yielding resources internally, where they will be shielded from market forces and cannot easily be copied by competitors.

The popularity of these two conjectures ensured that strategy researchers converged on 'organizational learning,' which is where the knowledge that created value would be created. There was greater attention to the dynamics of learning with notions like 'dynamic capabilities,' resources that would enable firms to generate new rents when changing circumstances eroded their existing rent-streams. Missing was a theory of what was being learned and by whom, or how it translated into competitive advantage or value. Does the organization learn by building a more effective inventory of 'organizational routines,' or is it only people who learn?

The struggle to define strategy and its practice continues. But the sheer number of strategy authors and the variety of their initiatives has led to deepening confusion about business strategy's nature and the problems it addresses. Strategy guru Henry Mintzberg has listed ten distinct schools, each with its own sub-groups.[17] At the same time the consultant's inventory of strategic tools has expanded, especially after the introduction of the Balanced Scorecard in the 1990s. But no tool has met all needs. Researchers complain the field is fragmented and look urgently for its defining characteristics and overarching concepts. All to little avail, the confusion grows apace.

While the External-Internal-Fit paradigm remains dominant in strategy teaching, researchers have left its simplicities far behind. Today strategy academics discuss; (a) economic, international, political, psychological, and institutional theories, underpinned by models of human decision-making, and (b) a range of models based on mathematics such as game theory, small world phenomena, and agent-based models, or on biology and neuro-science. *Strategic Management Journal* alone, where academics publish their latest thinking on these matters, puts out thirteen issues a year, and the list of business strategy journals, both academic and professional, expands relentlessly.

So if you're confused, join the crowd. Given this profusion of thinking, some have called for the 'theory police.' But most corporate leaders are more interested in clarity than police action. So many of the practitioners we know eschew theory altogether and fall into one of two camps: strategic planning aficionados or strategy nihilists.

For those in the strategic planning camp, the purpose of strategy is to reach the firm's goal as efficiently as possible. So data or evidence-based planning should shape activity. The method is computational: first perform data collection and analysis, then solve the problem and draft a plan. Strategy becomes something akin to project planning. In the background is a single over-arching methodological metaphor – the image of the strategist viewing the firm's situation objectively, gathering definitive information and processing it rationally to a rigorous and actionable conclusion.

But strategy development is not project planning, and there are plenty of reasons to doubt that metaphor's usefulness. The track record of those – from Herbert Simon to Nassim Taleb – who view the business landscape as a highly complex system riddled with uncertainty is considerably better than those who claim to have a crystal ball into the future. Nuclear power was the wave of the future. Sugar or corn-based ethanol was a sure bet until it wasn't. Coal was going to be the cheapest fuel possible for the next 25 years until the discovery of vast new sources of natural gas. The remarkable inability of energy 'experts' to predict the supply and demand *of a commodity* has been stunning.[18] For products that involve quickly shifting consumer tastes, global labor markets, global suppliers, and complicated logistics, prediction is, if anything, even more fraught.

What computer program could have told William Wrigley, Jr. to put sticks of gum in his baking powder, a strategic move that turned out to be his company's most important? What spreadsheet told Apple, at the time a computer manufacturer, to invest in becoming a music distributor through its combination of the iTunes store and its iPod device? In busy New York City, with an abundance of delis serving coffee in a Greek-themed paper cup for a dollar, could an algorithm have predicted that a company like Starbucks would be successful at luring customers to drop $5 for coffee while relaxing in a cafe? Would those same strategic moves have been successful a year or two earlier or later? All that seems obvious to us now, was in actuality unknowable beforehand.

For the 'strategy nihilists,' the comments above clearly illustrate that strategic plans are nothing but an apparatchik's dream: a "thick binder, gathering dust on a shelf next to other thick binders from five and ten years past."[19] The nihilists tend to work in fast-moving industries like technology. They claim that planning is a fool's errand because their markets are so fluid and chaotic. In this environment you 'make your moves' and 'react' in real time. Taking time to decide on a strategy is just a waste because it will be out of date before the ink dries.

The problem with the nihilists' view is that it makes a chaotic situation even messier. As Roger Martin, Dean of the Rotman School of Management in Toronto, puts it, "Without making an effort to 'do strategy' though, a company runs the risk of its numerous daily choices having no coherence to them, of being contradictory across divisions and levels, and of amounting to very little of meaning."[20] As we've learned from Clausewitz, even in the chaos and fog of war, strategy is vital to success.

It's time to end our strategy safari and delve into strategy's purposes and processes under strategic conversations. We'll do our best to answer the question of "what is strategy?" We'll describe the following: its goal, the nature of strategic leadership, and its processes.

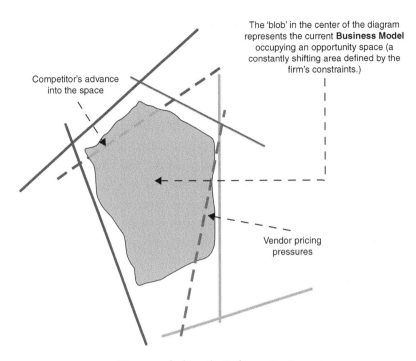

The 'blob' in the center of the diagram represents the current **Business Model** occupying an opportunity space (a constantly shifting area defined by the firm's constraints.)

Competitor's advance into the space

Vendor pricing pressures

FIGURE 5.1 Diagram of a hypothetical opportunity space

Our exploration of these issues will be heavily informed by the Five Iron Laws of Value Creation discussed in Chapter 2.

So what is the goal of strategy? In a constantly shifting business environment, we assert that the job of the strategist is to expand the organization's opportunity space. If you recall from Chapter 2, the opportunity space is defined by the organization's ability to create new opportunities or push back or elide the constraints to growth: things like competition, legal and regulatory pressures, costs, resource availability, customer perceptions, etc. The sum of these actions is what defines the organization's business model, which from the first Iron Law, we argue is the primary driver of growth and profit. Since as we've already seen, every organization's opportunity space is unique, every organization's business model is likewise distinct. Strategy is the process of conceptualizing the business model as uniquely situated and adapted to the firm's goals and the empirical situation's constraints and possibilities.

Of course, building effective business models is easier said than done, especially given the fact that it is impossible to know all of the relevant factors, and that these factors are, especially in our sped up world, constantly changing. Strategic conversations address these challenges by taking a different approach and focusing on how strategists respond imaginatively to knowledge absences. *Strategizing is redefined as the application of entrepreneurial judgment to knowledge absences, complementing the gathering and rigorous analysis of available data.* It is an imaginative form of organizational improvisation that is continuous rather than discrete. The product of strategic conversations isn't a 'strategy' that is updated after a year or two; it is a carefully managed process of constant re-evaluation and adaptation.

Within the process of strategizing, there is a fundamental connection between uncertainty and profit, and so between strategizing – the process of selecting and engaging uncertainties – and corporate performance. As mentioned earlier, we take this principle from the work of the economist Frank Knight, who argued that real profit (rather than accounting profit) can only be generated by engaging uncertainty, by acting intentionally or purposefully through the application of judgment in uncertain circumstances. Because perfect markets are perfectly competitive and perfectly informed, by definition, they have no space or need for entrepreneurial judgment, nor is profit available in them. But under uncertainty, the situation cannot be forecast or anticipated fully or objectively. Consequently the focus of strategy shifts from the situation and towards the leader – and towards her/his entrepreneurial and imaginative responses to what isn't known – to the situation's knowledge absences. In other words, drawing reasoned conclusions under bounded rationality means introducing something else, beyond the situation's incomplete data. This something else is the strategists' judgment.

Key here, and this may pain some business academics who believe in prioritizing rationality, are the leader's values. Values are beliefs and ideals, guidelines to behavior, and their key characteristic is that they are freely chosen by the actor in a situation that is otherwise underdetermined. When there is no single 'right,' calculable answer as to how to shape the organization's business model, then strategizing hinges on the values the strategist chooses to impose on the uncertain situation. Consequently strategy is both personal and entrepreneurial. Under certainty the data alone drive the action and the strategic task is independent of the strategist's values. But under uncertainty, rather than the numbers determining the practice, it is the values and meanings that the strategist attaches to the numbers that matter. If values applied generally they would be just another kind of data driving the conclusion. Profit results from judgment.

Strategizing is at its most powerful when the bland generalities of theory are replaced with the unique and passion-filled particularity of practice under uncertainty. Thus strategizing is bounded first by those aspects of the situation that are determined (constrained) and are not open to being freely chosen, and then by the strategist's judgment and values, and the strategist's intention, as manifested in the firm's chosen strategic objective.

Don't wait for big data to come to the rescue

As of late, a great deal of attention has been placed on big data and analytics. With the astonishing quantity of data being generated by commerce, science, and social media, and through the use of powerful new computer programs to analyze it, some managers now have at their disposal more knowledge about their customers and the world than ever before. Can we expect these tools to rid us of Knightian uncertainty and Herbert Simon's bounded rationality? Probably not.

In a recent New York Times article, writer Steve Lohr recalls an MIT conference where a panel was asked to cite examples of big failures in big data. Silence. Roberto Rigobon, a professor at MIT's Sloan School of Management, was all too happy to come up with an example: the massive failure of hedge funds such as Long Term Capital.[21] There are those flash-crashes too.

(*cont.*)

David Brooks, also in the New York Times, lists several issues with computer-driven analysis, including its poor record at understanding emotional states, creating context, dealing with big problems (like the economy or markets – e.g., the kind of thing that hedge funds need to know), plus noting that the more data you have, the more statistically significant correlations you have, even when none exist. And, as we've already noted, Brooks remarks that what data you collect and how you analyze it is value-driven. In other words, judgment is inescapable in all but the most simple of situations.[22]

Neither Lohr nor Brooks deny the value of data and rigorous analysis. Strategizing doesn't either. On the contrary, it celebrates the need to understand the particulars of any business situation as well and as thoroughly as possible. But ultimately any real-world business system is too complex to be understood by a machine. Insight and judgment, informed by values, are crucial to strategizing, and remain the sole province of humans.

THE STRATEGIZING PROCESS

Armed with as much data as can be reasonably obtained (but never enough to act upon with certainty), and informed by his or her values, what does the strategist do? How can the strategist arrive at a justifiable strategic decision when that choice will necessarily be uncertain, selective, subjective, and personal? Despair not. While there is no formula, there *is* an approach. We would argue that something like the following approach is in fact used by all strategists, whether they know it or not. Because as much as strategists might wish to do strategizing as rigorous computation, we have seen that it is impossible.

The approach involves five strategizing modes: (1) Discovery, (2) Judgment, (3) Persuasion, (4) Practice, and (5) Learning. Since strategizing in a fast-changing world is best when it is a continuous process (this is why we use the verb 'strategizing'), in practice these modes will overlap, often running simultaneously. As we'll see, Discovery is informed by Learning, Learning is an outgrowth of Practice, and Persuasion draws from all four of the other modes. And while we believe that all strategists perform all of these types of conversations, they do so with varying levels of skill. Good conversations lead to better strategies. Poor conversational health degrades strategizing. (This is, of course, the principal thesis of this book. We'll discuss conversational health further in Chapter 7.)

Strategizing mode 1: Discovery. In Discovery mode the strategist must discover the degree or manner in which the situation is unconstrained and open to judgment. This is depicted in the opportunity space we described in Chapter 2. Real-world choice is always constrained by some facts, but never to the point of being fully determined. Conversely, we always have choices, even under the most constraining of circumstances. It follows that the facts to be taken into account must be selected; they are never self-evident and beyond doubt. Which facts and constraints are most relevant to the business' situation will depend on your choice of objective – what is germane to one objective may be irrelevant to another.

As mentioned earlier, strategizing is bounded by the strategist's values and intention, and the organization's fixed constraints. Each firm – or rather, its business model – is unique, and no two firms can occupy the same socio-economic space. Each organization will be shaped by a different set of constraints. In the private sector, some of the matters over which the business strategist has little choice may be government regulations affecting the firm's goods and services, patents and other forms of intellectual property to which the firm has no access, labor contracts made on an industry-wide basis, constraints to the supply of the relevant factors of production, certain costs such as transportation costs and taxes, and so on.

How many constraints should be taken into account? Herbert Simon argued that managerial attention was the organizational resource in shortest supply, so the nub of strategic choice lies in knowing what to pay attention to and what to ignore, on the presumption that much of what we know is irrelevant to any particular action. Yet there is good reason to doubt the wisdom of oversimplifying, for salient details may get squeezed out. If, as we noted earlier in this chapter, you can't know in advance which actions will prove tactical and which strategic, then how can you know whether details lost in simplification may later prove strategically crucial? Perhaps you can't (after all, we are dealing with uncertainty), but the continuous and inclusive nature of strategic conversations should both provide as comprehensive a view of the business' environment as possible, and enable the organization to be agile and adaptable, so that it can quickly detect changes or problems in its situation and make adjustments to its strategy and business model.

Every analysis begins by making simplifications. Here the strategist has some help. The strength of popular strategic consulting tools lies in their confidence that the strategic problem can be boiled down to a few essentials. Thus tools like the SWOT analysis (the analysis of the business' strengths, weaknesses, opportunities, and threats) and the Balanced Scorecard (with its focus on financial, marketing, internal processes, and organizational learning) can help elicit new growth areas or challenges and turn long lists into manageable categories. And so in Discovery mode, the strategist must simplify the number of constraints to be actively considered. Empirical research by one of the authors suggested most business models address around a dozen strategic issues, a rough guideline we endorse.[23] Ultimately, determining the 'right' number of constraints to consider for your organization will be a practical matter of sensing when you have the makings of a reasonable case to support that focus, and when the more urgent need is to advance the strategizing process.

With an inventory of constraints in place (perhaps categorized using a tool like a SWOT analysis), the strategist needs to explore the nature of the opportunities to push back against or modify those constraints, and thus expand the firm's opportunity space. In practice, the constraints to a firm's strategic maneuvering are seldom immutable facts, but rather are open to interpretation and manipulation.

Constraints of ignorance can be shifted to the firm's strategic advantage by applying its research powers. If the constraint is insufficient knowledge to enter a new market, then R&D might have an impact, or data mining, or business intelligence. Thus the strategist's job becomes to engage with, and to the extent possible, reduce knowledge absences. Sometimes external forces, such as regulatory bodies, have established certain constraints. These may be moved to strategic advantage by exercising the firm's social powers, and negotiating either directly or indirectly with the regulators, such as through lobbying or well-connected intermediaries. Other constraints may seem powerful, for instance Microsoft's dominance of much of the computer software industry seemed unstoppable not long ago. Web-based or 'cloud' computing and a shift away from the dominance of PCs has seriously relaxed that constraint for Microsoft's competitors. Some constraints may be a matter of physics, such as gravity or space-time. But even these types of constraints, seemingly unconquerable, may be overcome or turned to advantage. Anti-gravity may not have been perfected yet, but airplanes allow millions to fly.

Discovery is where entrepreneurship begins. It's about looking at the current situation and seeing where reducing knowledge absences and fostering creative ideas could crack open new opportunities. Once the organization's constraints have been discovered and selected, and their nature and causes examined, the strategist and the firm have various powers to respond to those constraints, and expand into or refashion their strategic opportunity space.

Strategizing mode 2: Judgment. In Discovery mode, data was collected and rigorously analyzed and steps taken to reduce knowledge absences. In Judgment mode, the strategist must determine what direction should be taken based on the resulting understanding of the organization's situation and its constraints. There is no one right answer. The strategist must make the call, and there's nowhere to hide.

Here the second Iron Law comes into play – all business models require a leap of faith. Because it is not possible to know all variables or predict all outcomes, the exercise of strategic judgment requires trust. Trust that you've chosen the most relevant constraints to consider, that you have involved employees and other stakeholders in filling in knowledge absences, and that you have simplified your choices as much as reasonably possible. With the bounds of Simon's bounded rationality in place, and the nature of Knightian uncertainty inescapable, you are poised to take that leap.

Here we return to Clausewitz and his notion of *coup d'oeil* from Chapter 4. This is where you, the strategist, armed with the data, analysis, and a profound understanding of the field from having been its student, can clear your mind and pause to reflect, allowing that flash of strategic insight to arrive. Rational left-brain thinking colludes with right-brain creativity to imagine a new future. With this strategic Judgment comes the potential for true innovation, actively changing the business situation to secure new value and competitive advantage, rather than simply adapting or responding to it.

Strategizing mode 3: Persuasion. After the strategist's exercise of strategic Judgment, the business model begins to come together. It is a firm-specific language, and it becomes the means to justify the choice of constraints and how they are interpreted. But how to communicate the strategist's judgment? Much of the literature on organizational communication presumes the firm is like an electrical network, with instructional signals passed without loss through the administrative apparatus to individual work roles that are thereby fully controlled – while accountability and performance signals flow back to the strategic nerve center. The firm is envisaged as the rigorous solution to a communication system design problem.

Real-world strategizing bears little relationship to this metaphor. We have already seen how strategists are always working with imperfect information. Strategizing works by capturing the vitality of the firm's participants, a group of creative people brought together by the firm-specific language of the business model. These individuals collaborate and apply their judgment to engage the firm's chosen uncertainties and constraints. The key to managing the distribution of uncertainties is not to pass them willy-nilly to others to deal with as they wish. On the contrary, employee judgment has to be directed, harnessed, and channeled towards the objectives the strategist has chosen.

Therefore, strategic decisions involve both the situation's data and the strategist's values. Two people with the same data could arrive at different, yet equally justifiable, decisions. But an organization pursues multiple strategies simultaneously at its peril. Inevitably, such strategies will contradict one another in some ways, reducing or even destroying their respective effectiveness. (For instance, high-end retailer Tiffany's would probably be ill-advised to pursue a low-cost branded strategy in partnership with WalMart.) The data, and the strategic direction, must be given meaning.

As we have already seen, rhetoric manages meanings, for they cannot be communicated as data. Meanings are what humans attach to data in order to make sense of it. The logos, ethos, and pathos modes of human communication reflect the different ways in which human beings know, understand, and debate meaning. Logos concerns communication that appeals to the audience's rationality and objectivity and is the mode of communicating that works well with data. When meanings are not problematic data appears as 'fact' and taken for granted – time of day, number of units sold or customers served. Ethos is the appeal to the social relationship between the audience and the leader/strategist, and draws people towards letting their meanings be changed by others they respect. When an admired person speaks, we listen; we may be persuaded to think in a new way simply because we respect the speaker, and focus less on what he or she said. Pathos appeals to the audience's emotions. Emotion is the driver to human action.

When strategists are armed with the persuasive powers of rhetoric, employees are drawn into contributing imaginatively and become immersed in the organization's value-adding practices. They become aware of the nature of the uncertainties being engaged and of the subtlety of their relationship with the leadership. That said, their commitment is vulnerable to doubts. They look to the strategist to reassure them that the firm (a) has a viable business model able to survive because it adds real value, (b) has a means of estimating the viability of its strategy ahead of implementing it, (c) appreciates the principal threats to its viability, (d) has a sense of how to change the firm's business model as the need arises, and (e) has a sense of how long it will remain viable before it must be reinvented. The strategist has to use all three rhetorical modes – logos, ethos and pathos – to be effective. Without persuasion, both strategy development and execution will suffer from a lack of engagement and confusion of purpose.

Strategizing mode 4: Practice. The ultimate test of strategizing is "does it work?" The essence of Practice is strategic conversation with those others whose judgment might bear usefully on the situation, increasing the strategist's confidence without, of course, ever entirely eliminating uncertainty. Our fifth Iron Law states that an organization can only benefit from organic, internal business model innovation. This is true both from the standpoint of employee engagement and buy-in to the execution of the model, and also from the perspective of the business model as the language and culture of the organization. Would Red Hat still be Red Hat without the open source mindset that pervades the organization? Red Hat's business model is so thoroughly perfused throughout the company that it amounts to an attitude. You could say that the employees have internalized the 'commander's intent,' but that falls short of the reality. To a very real degree, the employees have each become the commander, executing on what's best for the company.

When the rhetoric of Persuasion has been effective, employees' values and judgment will have been influenced and aligned with the strategy of the organization, and they can be relied on to implement the business model consistently and creatively. A strategy or business model innovation imposed externally will necessarily lack the employees' intrinsic motivation and engagement, won't be aligned in values and meanings, and thus is far less likely to succeed or realize its full potential.

Practice is the ongoing conversation that implements the business model and thus creates value for the firm. Strategic conversation types like sensing and operationalizing can be particularly valuable to this mode of strategizing, continually transferring information between employees and management, and enabling ongoing Discovery and Learning.

No preparation can secure the actors against being surprised. The doing is always different from the thinking about it. But like reaching closure and selecting the constraints to attend to, there comes that crucial point when the actor must 'jump in with both feet' and expose her/himself to the unconsidered, to the unknown-unknowns. In business situations the loneliness of this act is ameliorated because most business activity is collaborative. Others can help. So the essence of step 4 is strategic conversation with those others whose judgment might bear usefully on the situation, increasing the strategist's confidence without, of course, ever entirely eliminating the risk. The strategist remains responsible.

Strategizing mode 5: Learning. Strategizing modes 1–4 imagine an organization's business model and help put it into practice. During this entire cycle, the business model is both a bridge out from thinking to practice, and a bridge back from practice to better thinking.[24] Thus step 5 of the strategizing process measures the firm's performance against its strategic intentions. But it doesn't stop there – it also embraces managing what those involved have learned throughout the previous steps. The business model provides a language and a frame for not just looking backwards at past performance, but also for once again thinking about and reimagining its future. Step 5 completes the cycle of strategizing and closes the loop of the business model as a dynamic pattern of managed responses in an ongoing and incompletely predictable context.

We argue, perhaps audaciously, that *all* strategists use something like the strategizing cycle we've just described whether they realize it or not. It doesn't matter what strategy framework you subscribe to, under the uncertainty faced by every strategist you must

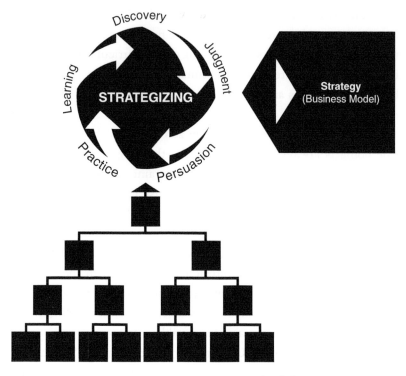

FIGURE 5.2 Strategizing in an organization that fails to engage employees in its strategizing process

do your best to discover the constraints to success, make a judgment as to the direction in which to go, persuade others to go along with you, put the strategy into practice, and then learn from the results. (Even organizations that seemingly never learn, at some point do so when they have to close their doors.) The problem, as we have argued throughout, is that most organizations don't engage enough of their employees in the process.

Their strategizing process tends to spin in isolation at the top of the hierarchy. We know hierarchies aren't amenable to absorbing new information and promoting change, the very purpose of strategizing in a competitive and dynamic environment. First, a hierarchy's strategizing suffers because new information must go up and down, suffering harmful bottlenecks at the senior level. Discovery, Learning, and ultimately Judgment are impaired because the interactions with customers, competitors, and suppliers, which should provide invaluable grist for the strategizing mill, are watered down, aggregated, or blocked. Persuasion is likewise adversely affected because the leaders' strategic intent is diluted, or sometimes never communicated. Second, hierarchies themselves are allergic to change because they articulate power structures and for those in power, especially in the middle of hierarchy, change is threatening.[25]

Strategic conversations are a way of turbo-charging the strategizing process with more and better knowledge, energy, and buy-in. Instead of one narrow bureaucratic pipe with low bandwidth informing the strategizing process, strategic conversations provide multiple channels that bypass the hierarchy's choke-points. Strategizing can then become more of a continuous rather than an intermittent discrete process and the C-suite is no longer a bottleneck. This doesn't mean the formal processes of management are abandoned, for most firms require accountability and periodic performance measurement against goals to manage their budgets, finances, overall strategic balance and so on.

Keeping the strategizing wheel turning using strategic conversations implies a different type of leadership. That this chapter, the one on leadership, is this book's longest may be surprising given its focus on augmenting employee involvement in strategy-setting and business model innovation. But leadership under strategic conversations is essential and transformed; it needs to be more nuanced, skillful, and rich than under a command and control regime. There is nowhere to hide: the leader's identity, intentions, and imagination are all exposed to all those engaged in or affected by the strategizing. The leader can't duck behind a cloak of rationality to justify decisions.

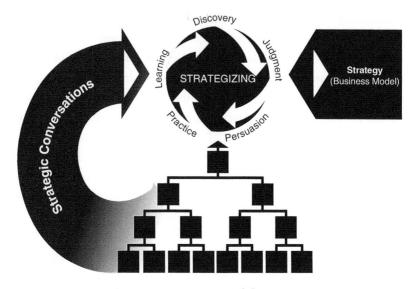

FIGURE 5.3 Strategic conversations and the strategizing process

Given that any strategic decision has to cope with uncertainty, strategy can't be separated from the strategist's human judgment. Strategy is necessarily value-laden.

But this is not all. Under strategic conversations strategizing is also *ethically burdened*. A leader's power lies in the capacity to persuade (through the rhetorical techniques we've described). When the intent is to engage employee imagination and energy in strategizing, the motivation must be intrinsic: the employee must internalize the mission, values, and goals of the organization as his or her own. The leader's intent isn't just to engage in a transaction with the employee. Strategic conversations eventually reinvent and transform employees as they make the purpose of the organization their own. They are ethically burdened because the purposes and practices of the organization can be either beneficial or exploitative. Strategic conversations thus take strategizing far away from the rationality-based strategic models: external-internal-fit, five forces, resource-based, and all of their permutations. Until computers develop a sense of human values, until they can imagine, and until they can emotionally persuade others, they will not be able to do strategy, nor grasp the need for it. Strategizing is a uniquely human endeavor, a reflection of who we are and how we operate.

Strategizing is about change, and change creates anxiety. What questions does the leader need to address?

Here are some of the questions that need to be answered by leaders to allay employee (and shareholder) anxiety, and thus for successful strategizing:

1. Do we have a business model with value-adding potential in today's situation? This is the fundamental starting point for any business model. (Salespeople know they have to believe in what they are selling).

2. Do we have a means of measuring the business model's viability – other than trying it out? This seems to be a technical issue but is related to the ethos dimension of the conversation. The employees will only listen to the leader's ideas when the case for them feels compelling. To declare a mission statement such as "We shall be number one in this industry" is counter-productive if there is no way of establishing that as a realistic possibility rather than a punt in the dark.

3. The third question is wonderfully illustrated in Porter's five-forces model: "Who and what threatens our business model's viability – competition, technological change, labor legislation, etc.?"

4. The fourth question reflects the point that strategizing turns on the constraints discovered, but that these in turn are seldom fixed and can be moved and replaced. "What about our business model is malleable and how can it be changed?"

5. A fifth question is the inverse to question 4: "How robust is the business model against unexpected shocks – the stuff we do not know we do not know about the firm's situation?"

6. A sixth question places the business model into real time: "How long do we expect our business model to remain viable?"

7. Finally, a seventh question brings us back to the firm's specific people: "How exposed is the business model to our losing the particular people whose activities comprise the firm?" We might call this the Jobs question, given it will be a while before we, or Apple Inc., can see the real strategic significance of Jobs' death.

6 Putting strategic conversations into practice – innovation communities

Do not wait to strike till the iron is hot; but make it hot by striking.

Anonymous (eighteenth or early nineteenth century)

In Chapter 3, Strategic conversations in the wild, we documented seven different types of strategic conversation as they are currently practiced. But we've waited to fully describe the last one: innovation communities. Of all of the different types of strategic conversations – innovation days, competitions, challenges, sensing and operationalizing platforms, T-shaped, strategy reviews, chaordic – innovation communities may be the most potent at both engaging employees in strategy and business model innovation and in creating connections with senior management so that the ideas are implemented.

Recall that we defined innovation communities as:

A diverse team of employee leaders, empowered by and in constant communication with senior management, who collaborate on specific issues outside of their normal operational duties to promote cross-organizational business model innovation critical to the organization.

Innovation team members can be from anywhere in the organization – participation in the most successful teams tends to span the hierarchy. Whatever their source, membership in successful innovation communities is determined by who is taking a leadership role on the issues, people who have the knowledge, energy, and skill to successfully pursue solutions, not by the hierarchy.

This type of strategic conversation is so powerful precisely because the connection between senior management and the team is so close. As we'll see from the cases presented in this chapter, innovation communities can be an outgrowth from other types of strategic conversations – such as innovation days or competitions. One can say that innovation communities are where big ideas go to become deeply embedded in the business model.

Before delving into the 'hows' of innovation communities, it is probably worth spending time exploring the 'whys.' We've already explained why the structure of hierarchies is poorly suited to promoting business model innovation: ideas take too long to go up and down the chain of command and hierarchies tend, by their very nature, to be hostile to changes to the status quo (Figure 5.2). In organizations with distinct profit centers (or in non-profits, distinct program areas), business model innovation is also difficult to pursue for three additional reasons. First, because of financial analysts, the rhythm of the business requires results often measured on a quarterly basis. But business model innovation isn't amenable to being rushed. Second, business units are most often tightly delineated (e.g., the jet engine division) whereas business model innovation often spans domains (the iPod was both a technological advance and a play to become a music distributor). Finally, business unit budgets are generally closely controlled – with precious little in the way of discretionary funds. But exploring business model innovations, like the iPod, is often expensive.[1]

For these reasons organizations with strong profit centers often have difficulty innovating their business model. They aren't provided an incentive for exploring the white space between or outside of their own business units. For example, a major financial institution we know is having trouble implementing a plan to address an entirely new customer segment – the middle market – because it requires coordinating services across several of its asset classes, each run by different managers. The units can't make the margins they have come to expect from their larger clients, and so they are resisting innovation that would benefit the entire corporation. It is outside their scope – no single unit is in charge of making this happen. The change would be too costly, and the benefits would take too long to realize for any one unit to justify the investment – they are focused on their own quarterly profits. The strategy is effectively stymied.

So, leading companies have begun to explore ways of systematically fostering business model innovation. The origins of the innovation community concept aren't clear; they are most likely an extension of the entrepreneurial role played by product leaders. Tracy Kidder's *The Soul of a New Machine* describes a skunk works operation set up by product champion Tom West back in the late 1970s at Data General Corporation. Fuelled by an internal rivalry, and the desire to beat competitor Digital Equipment Corporation to building the first 32-bit microcomputer, the team worked day and night under West's inspired leadership. West exemplifies the type of leadership we've spoken of and fully employed the rhetorical techniques of ethos (he demonstrated a passionate understanding of the computer market and what was needed to be a leader in it) and pathos (he created strong bonds as his group raced against internal and external rivals, and made everyone on his team know that success would guarantee that they would be the Jedi warriors chosen to develop the next generation of computers.)

Unfortunately for Data General this type of innovative practice remained in the shadows of a disapproving hierarchy, and eventually the company lost steam and was acquired.[2] But some innovative product companies have institutionalized the capture of this energy and imagination. At 3M, every major new product development program is led by a champion who writes the initial product concept, gathers management support for the program and recruits most of the team. A champion, essentially an internal entrepreneur, is expected to keep working on a good idea even if the program is killed by management.[3] A similar role is played by the Chief Engineer at Toyota, who spends time studying the target market, writes the vehicle concept document, establishes the overall design, and is responsible, in the end, for the economic performance of the vehicle.[4] These champions aren't just managers, looking to manage to schedule and cost, they are true leaders with a profound sense of ownership.

Product champions can be game changers. But they don't often work across the organization to help reimagine it. Innovation communities do. We've observed innovation communities created top-down – commissioned by senior management to address white spaces in the business model – as well as bottom-up communities proposed by staff and then supported institutionally because they conform to senior management's vision and goals.

The rest of the chapter presents several cases that demonstrate the power of strategic conversation to innovate organizational business models.

BOSTON CHILDREN'S HOSPITAL TELEHEALTH INNOVATION COMMUNITY (COMMISSIONED BY SENIOR MANAGEMENT)

Boston's Children's Hospital's telehealth innovation community is an example of the top-down type. Boston Children's Hospital (BCH) is one of the largest pediatric hospitals in the United States and is the primary pediatric teaching hospital of Harvard Medical School. Founded in 1869 as a twenty-bed hospital for children, it is now a comprehensive medical center for pediatric and adolescent health care, providing patient care while seeking new approaches to the prevention, diagnosis and treatment of childhood diseases, as well as educating the next generation of leaders in child health. The hospital houses two multidisciplinary intensive care units, a neonatal intensive care unit, a cardiac intensive care unit, a bone marrow transplantation unit, and a clinical research center. There are more than 100 outpatient programs ranging from primary care to a wide variety of specialty programs. The hospital's clinical staff includes approximately 1,000 active medical staff and 900 residents and fellows.

The Children's Hospital has one of the largest research infrastructures for pediatrics in the world. Its research facilities are situated in the center of the Longwood Medical Area where Harvard

Medical School and three other major teaching hospitals are located – including Brigham and Women's, Beth Israel Deaconess Medical Center, and Dana Farber Cancer Institute. The Hospital is within a block of the Joslin Diabetes Center, the Massachusetts College of Pharmacy, the Harvard School of Public Health, the Harvard Dental School, the Harvard Institutes of Medicine, the Channing Laboratory, and the Center for Blood Research Institute of Biomedical Research.

In 2010, the Children's Hospital's CEO started the "Innovation Acceleration Program" (IAP). According to its program head, Chief Innovation Officer Naomi Fried, PhD, employee surveys indicated it was difficult to initiate innovation at the hospital. Nonetheless, there was significant untapped staff energy; what was needed was some seed money and guidance. The IAP is focused on enhancing the innovation culture and community within Boston Children's Hospital. The program supports grassroots innovation by providing employees with a variety of formal and informal resources. The program's goal is to turn BCH's employees' innovative ideas into products, technologies or clinical improvements to make health care safer, better, and less expensive. IAP offers innovation boot camps to would-be entrepreneurs, innovation forums where those interested in innovation can support one another and learn together, information technology awards to support software development for innovations, innovation days to celebrate successes, and an investment grant program to test new clinical innovations.

Like many innovation programs, the hospital's IAPs began with a focus on discovering and promoting innovative point-solutions. Participation has been broad-based. A neonatal nurse with twenty-three years tenure at the hospital noticed that infants who had just undergone cardiac surgery had a hard time maintaining their body temperature. With IAP's support, she developed, tested, and helped spread the use of a warming cap that significantly improved patient outcomes and is soon expected to become part of the standard care protocol. Even parking attendants have contributed innovative ideas that have been incorporated to improve the BCH parking service.

As important as these efforts have been at improving hospital service and patient care, and for engaging the staff, the IAP's charter also includes identifying strategic institutional innovation initiatives and unmet business model innovation opportunities. It then catalyzes solutions in those areas. Senior management realized that as a leading research hospital BCH had the opportunity to transform how health care is delivered, financed, and even the very economics of health care.

One area that senior managers decided deserved special attention was telehealth, a process and system that delivers specialized care beyond hospital walls by using communication, information and biometric technologies to extend, and even enhance, clinician, caregiver and patient relationships. Dr. Fried, acting as an interlocutor between senior managers and staff, performed her own strategic discovery process. The statistics[5] convinced her telehealth was an area that merited special attention:

- 74% of teleconsults led to a change in diagnosis or treatment (and improved outcomes)[6]
- 60% of telehealth cases solved without a face-to-face visit (cost reduction)[7]
- $30 for a telehealth consult vs. $75 for an office consult (yet more cost reduction)[8]
- 75% of US consumers say they would use telehealth (clearly there's demand)[9]
- The market for telehealth is projected to be $6.28 billion by 2020;[10] 80,000 homes had already been wired for remote health care monitoring (market validity had already been established).[11]

Dr. Fried established a telehealth working group to begin the process of developing a strategy. Over time, staff were hired and Dr. Fried and her team laid the groundwork for an institutional telehealth strategy and program. Goals for telehealth included:

- make BCH's cutting-edge resources and skills available to more patients (especially those for whom traveling to Boston was a burden);

- reduce overall cost by delivering care in lower cost settings, including patient homes, community hospitals, or primary care doctor's offices or clinics;
- increase clinician efficiency; and
- enhance the patient experience.

From the start Dr. Fried knew telehealth was much more than just getting the communications technology right. Solving the legal, financial, risk, and organizational challenges was likely to be at least as complex. These issues weren't going to be addressed by helicoptering above the details but only by digging into the complexities on the ground. Senior management knew a lot, but they couldn't possibly know everything about the challenges. If the telehealth nut was to be cracked, she needed to recruit practitioners.

Based on her fast-growing network within the hospital, Dr. Fried discovered Dr. David G. Hunter, Children's Hospital's Ophthalmologist-in-Chief, Professor and Vice Chair of Ophthalmology at Harvard Medical School. It was quickly apparent that he was exactly the kind of partner she needed. Dr. Hunter is a well-regarded, affable clinician and teacher with an entrepreneurial bent. And he came ready with a telehealth application that clearly demonstrated the power and benefit of telehealth in the community hospital setting. Better still, this wasn't some sort of wild-eyed idea and passing fancy; Dr. Hunter had been working on his concept for over eight years. The possibility of using Dr. Hunter's mature idea for a quick win in the telehealth arena was very attractive. Fried gave Hunter her full support.

As it turned out, he'd need it.

Retinopathy of prematurity (ROP) is a disease that affects some infants with low birth weights or with less than eight months gestation. Untreated, it can lead to total blindness. It is a result of poorly regulated vascular development in the retina. As a fetus develops, blood vessels grow from the central part of the retina outwards. This process is completed a few weeks before the normal time of delivery.

However, in premature babies the vessels don't yet reach the peripheries of the retina. In some premature infants, their eyes overcompensate for this lack of development by producing too much of a blood vessel growth hormone resulting in vasculature that is outsized, jagged, and prone to bleeding. The result is often band-like membranes that can cause retinal detachment and, eventually, blindness.

If detected early, treatment is possible and usually involves burning the periphery of the retina with a laser. This effectively turns off the over-stimulation of blood vessel growth and saves the retina. While an invasive and somewhat brutal procedure, the results are generally just minor visual impairment.

The problem was, the entire in-person diagnostic routine was quickly breaking down, medically, legally, and financially. Medically, diagnosing ROP was difficult and literally involved as much art as science. Specially trained physicians would look into premature babies' eyes with a light and then record retinal vasculature, using pen or pencil, on a paper form like the one shown below. Getting the diagnosis wrong could be catastrophic. A false negative and the child would probably go blind. A false positive and the child would be unnecessarily subjected to a procedure that would burn its retina with a laser.

The stakes were high and this was reflected in court. The parents of babies who went blind because they weren't properly diagnosed often received multi-million-dollar court judgments. This led to physicians refusing to examine babies because their insurance wouldn't cover them. Especially in smaller hospitals, the shortage of local doctors willing to diagnose ROP became acute. So, in the Boston area, they began asking specialists from Children's Hospital to visit them. This wasn't a good solution either: having specialists travel for hours wasn't a good use of their time, and often the babies would be napping when the doctor arrived. And all this led to even higher costs.

Dr. Hunter thought he had the solution. New technology allowed patients to be screened by nurses, not physicians, using a specially devised camera that could be operated locally. Baby sleeping patterns needn't be disturbed by traveling physicians; nurses could take the

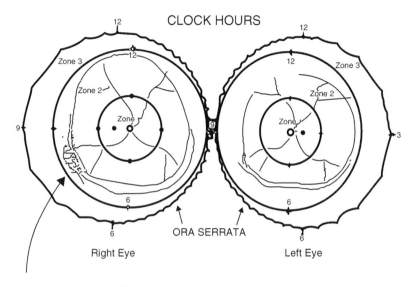

FIGURE 6.1 Physician drawing documenting extent of retinopathy in one examination of a premature infant. Lines are drawn freehand on a preprinted template, provided courtesy of Boston Children's Hospital

images when the baby was awake. And instead of a hand-drawn image, physicians could now consult on the diagnosis using photographic images, and they could do so remotely. A telehealth solution!

As always, the devil was in the details. Could the equipment and nurses effectively capture enough of the vasculature at the required resolution? Would local hospitals spend the money to train their nurses? How would payments – which were often triggered by hospital visits – be handled when the diagnosis was being done remotely? What would be the workflow from image acquisition, to diagnosis, to reporting, to following up on treatments with the patient's parents?

Fried's innovation team provided Dr. Hunter with access to senior hospital leaders, some funding, and mentorship on how to address all these cross-functional areas. With this help, and a lot of hard work, an idea that had been germinating for eight years finally took root. As is the case with all innovation communities, the effort was cross-functional. Children's hospital's legal team, IT group, medical records group, credentialing function, billing, privacy, and ambulatory services participated. Local hospitals were also part of the team, as were vendors of the imaging equipment.

And as is often the case for successful innovation communities, the result was profound business model innovation. The new process took diagnostic and financial risk away from a large, distributed group of physicians and concentrated it at Children's Hospital where it could be more effectively managed. Instead of hundreds of physicians only doing a few examinations, now tens of physicians did many, allowing them to gain world-class experience. They could also share their experiences much more readily, and cross-check their diagnoses when useful, because there were now photographic images as opposed to hand sketches. The result would be better care, resulting in more manageable malpractice insurance costs. And the new model was more efficient. The examination and diagnosis process was uncoupled: nurses could do the examination at the local hospital when it was most convenient for them and the infant's sleep schedule. Similarly, diagnosis could be done in batches at Boston Children's Hospital at a time that fit the specialist's schedule.

The full impact of this project, and the others being promoted in the telehealth innovation community, on Children's Hospital's business model isn't yet fully knowable. What is certain is that as long as Boston Children's Hospital continues to cultivate the garden of innovation, innovators like Dr. Hunter will be more than happy to help the hospital reap telehealth's benefits.

How innovation communities are different from communities of practice

Many companies have been using what are called communities of practice (CoPs) for decades. CoPs are self-organizing entities – sometimes supported by management, but generally without much management participation – that serve as knowledge-sharing vehicles. Innovation communities are a distinct concept. As this table indicates, their purpose, membership, and practices are quite different from CoPs.

Innovation communities	Communities of practice
Crucible to create solutions to key business problems	Space to spread best practice
Problem-based	Interest-based
Cross-functional	Birds of a feather
Strategic	Tactical
Limited duration	Endure as long as participant interest exists
Purpose defined by senior management	Purpose defined by group
Action-oriented	Clubby
Continuously rechartered by senior management	Created by participants

KBS+'S "HYDE" INNOVATION COMMUNITY (PROPOSED BY STAFF)

Our focus now shifts to another doctor altogether, Dr. Jekyll and, more to the point, to his alter ego, Mr. Hyde. As we've said earlier, innovation communities can result from other types of strategic conversations. So it was with the Hyde Experiment at advertising agency KBS+. Lori Senecal, KBS+'s hard-charging CEO, introduced in Chapter 4, held a competition in July of 2012 to crowdsource ideas from employees to improve company operations and morale. Out of thirty entries her senior managers chose the Hyde Experiment.

The competition itself was part of Senecal's plan to engage employees from every level to help set the direction of the firm. The winners of the competition, Mark Jensen and Nick Vodovich, were twenty-two and twenty-three years old. Their idea was to create a place where artists, both within and outside of the agency, could come together to create, display, and discuss their art. Their insight was that there was a great deal of artistic surplus (perhaps a close relative to Clay Shirky's notion of cognitive surplus) that went unexpressed by all the Dr. Jekylls in the office – Mr. Hyde's responsible side – whose day job was to satisfy clients. They proposed creating a 4,500-square-foot space on the sixth floor of KBS+'s headquarters in Manhattan where this work would be done. Employees who chose to do this would be given up to 15 percent time off to pursue these projects.

To say that they were shocked to have their project chosen would be an understatement. As they put it, "we didn't think we had a bat's shot in hell." They were asking to literally and figuratively reshape the firm. Physically they were proposing to radically reconfigure KBS+'s office space to make room for the studio. The space was obscenely large for downtown New York, some of the most expensive real estate in North America. Asking management to allow employees to take time off work in the fantastically frantic world of advertising was a long shot, at best. Oh, and this request was coming from two junior employees.

But the Hyde Experiment was neither proposed nor accepted in a vacuum. Through this competition and other strategic conversations, Senecal had already carefully crafted the matrix in which ideas like Jensen and Vidovich's emerged and grew. Senecal knew she needed to attract, grow, and retain the best talent for KBS+ to thrive, and the Hyde Experiment could be an ideal structure for doing just that. "Keeping our talent excited is also important in terms of moving client work forward by encouraging new approaches and thinking outside norms."[12] And as a leader she had the intuition that giving the inherent talent in her office, and the adjacent community, another channel for expression could both indirectly and directly benefit her clients.

The competition itself was a pitch to twenty-five of KBS+'s managers; as Jensen and Vidovich put it, "anybody with their name on an office was a judge." The competition was filmed, "which was terrifying." Feedback was given in real time. "It was like American Idol, but not so mean." Two senior KBS+ employees, Jonah Bloom the Chief Content Officer and Darren Herman, the Founder and Managing Director of KBS+ venture capital group provided significant help while the contestants were preparing their entry's content and presentation.

The entire competition was designed to reinforce and generate excitement for Senecal's vision at every level of the organization while having the organization take that vision in unexpected and useful directions.

We were able to interview Jensen and Vidovich before the Hyde Experiment launched. They were clearly very enthusiastic about the project and knew what they wanted to do. But when we pressed, they weren't entirely clear about the benefits to KBS+. But their doubts evaporated as they saw how the Hyde Experiment became the Hyde innovation community. Making sure that the investment paid off and worked well with KBS+'s numerous other initiatives became the responsibility of Ed Brojerdi, President and Co-Chief Creative Officer, and Izzy DeBellis, the other Co-Chief Creative Officer.

Brojerdi and DeBellis, according to Jensen and Vidovich, were instrumental in organizing Hyde into an "executable format." The centerpiece, the work they hoped would start the flywheel of creativity spinning, was a film Jensen and Vidovich were writing and animating simply called "Hyde." Some joined to help with the film, which incorporated wood models and detailed shadow puppets to recreate a twenty-first-century New York scene with a nineteenth-century feel. Others joined to help with different aspects of the film. DeBellis himself worked on the film's pace and detail. The wood buildings were designed by members of the KBS+ team and the laser cutting was outsourced to Fabrication Guide in Brooklyn.

The grand opening of Hyde was set for March of 2013. As the date approached, more and more KBS+ staff came to help, to install their own work, and to just hang out and eat their lunch and drink coffee. Fifteen staffers put in significant time.

The opening itself was a big hit. Virtually everyone in the office attended and there were numerous guests. There was a palpable sense of surprise with a variety of work shown; staff revealed talents and artistic directions that had up till then been mostly hidden. The opening did, as hoped, give the Hyde Space's creativity flywheel a strong spin.

FIGURE 6.2 Screen capture from "Hyde," provided by and used with permission of KBS+

Since then, the Hyde Space has become something like KBS+'s "Building 20," the famous hub at MIT where physicists, musicians, designers, and others co-mingled to create a dynamic, innovative stew that spawned dozens of successful companies and thousands of successful academic lines of inquiry.[13] The Hyde space allows for multiple uses simultaneously, such as running a photo shoot, filming interviews, and product demonstrations. The space also plays host to all agency-wide events, from karaoke, to big client presentations, to live performances. And besides spreading goodwill and providing staff with a meaningful alternative area for expression, Hyde is already paying off dividends for clients. The Action Sports Team within KBS+ ran a focus group for Nike's skateboarding division, bringing in local skaters to discuss the brand.

Of course serendipity favors the prepared, and the Hyde Space so far has generated several interesting opportunities. The father of a KBS+ staffer is a 3D sound engineer (3D sound is a spooky new technology that can make a listener hear sounds with eerie precision – imagine a bee buzzing around your head). She asked if her father could install some equipment to test it in Hyde's large space and to demonstrate it to anyone who wanted to hear. They got the green light and soon thereafter a client walking through the space was intrigued by the possibilities. KBS+ and the client are now working on concepts based on this chance experience.

Where will the Hyde Experiment go from here? The future is still unfolding. What is clear is that the original idea of a place to create art for art's sake has evolved. It is now a space where KBS+'s broad range of talents, and connections to the talent of others, is exposed, mixed up, and reconstituted in ways that hadn't happened before, and could neither have been planned, nor anticipated. A younger, more experimental approach to advertising is emerging that is allowing KBS+ to pitch to clients with non-traditional ideas in non-traditional media. This is exactly as CEO Senecal wanted. Before the Hyde Experiment was launched, nobody could have known the path taken or the exact results. Senecal is fond of saying "action creates opportunity." This is a close paraphrase of the Clauswitzian notion of "armies in motion" by which military forces don't focus on a particular objective like a hill or a bridge but rather through constant motion explore the most fruitful opportunities to impose their will. KBS+ president Brojerdi told us that the benefits of the Hyde Space go beyond the ability to profoundly engage clients. The Hyde Space has become the literal and figurative heart of the organization, whose beating is felt at all levels. He spoke with a sense of amazement of how it has created a self-organizing, siloless "harmony." Around a table a group shares snacks while exploring ideas before a meeting. In another area someone is tinkering with a model for a client. In the back others attend a course on a new technology that can be used for marketing displays. Brojerdi calls it a "palette" for the firm's creativity: a living, breathing space where artistic installations appear, decay, and are replaced by new works.

The Hyde Space, itself a product of strategic conversation, has now become a place which engenders yet more employee-initiated business model innovation. It's an investment unquestioned by Senecal and her team.

RITE-SOLUTIONS' "RITE TRACK" INNOVATION COMMUNITY (PROPOSED BY STAFF)

Rite-Solutions, the Rhode-Island-based software development company introduced in Chapter 4, has routinized and further democratized the creation of innovation communities. It developed a game called "Mutual Fun." (CEO Jim Lavoie is a unrepentant punster, as will become clear.) All employees are given $10,000 in Mutual Fun money to place bets on innovation ideas generated by other employees. As Lavoie explains:

> Any player [employee] can propose an idea – from a cost saving or efficiency measure (which gets listed on "Savings Bonds") to an extension of the company's current capabilities ("Bow Jones"[14]) to a truly disruptive venture into a new business or technology ("SPAZDAQ"). The creator fleshes out his or her proposal in an "Expect-Us" (rather than a "prospectus"), assigns it a ticker symbol, and follows a detailed template to describe the value-creating potential of the idea. Ideas are advertised on the Ticker Tape as initial public offerings (IPOs) with a starting price of $10. Colleagues can make dollar investments in stocks, volunteer time (via "assists" – discrete activities to help move the idea forward), or express interest (in the threaded comments attached to every idea). An algorithm dynamically derives individual stock values (from the collective activity and investment around an idea), portfolio values (from an individual's activity), and a player's place on the leader board (from an individual's own idea stock values and activity in assisting, investing, and discussing their co-workers ideas).[15]

Lavoie says that the game relieves him and his senior managers of the burden of being the sole arbiters of what is the "next big thing" for the company. With a bit of encouragement, Mutual Fun acts as the company's idea generator. One of the key features of the game is that it isn't the extroverts that end up deciding the company's future. Lavoie firmly believes that companies routinely waste their best talent by not promoting the ideas of the shy. Mutual Fun allows introverts to promote their ideas without going in front of what Lavoie calls "murder boards" – senior manager committees used in other companies where ideas are publicly given thumbs up or down.

Some ideas submitted to Mutual Fun are responses to challenges issued by senior managers. These are called "Penny Stocks," where players are asked to provide their "2 cents via a simple template." As Lavoie puts it, "The 'Challenge' template is a way to get a thinking blitz going around a focused topic – and to allow the people doing the thinking to weigh in on the other inputs provided." In 2012, for example, management sent the following Mutual Fun challenge: "What commercial product could we make with our knowledge of real-time asset tracking, optimization, and visualization for the military?" Note in Lavoie's description of the response, each participant brought their own expertise, experience, and passions to their actions to create unique value. As Lavoie describes it:

> Chuck Angell, a systems engineer and a father, won the challenge with his idea to apply the company's expertise to make transportation of children to and from school safer. His idea received Mutual Fun "assists" (volunteered time and effort) from three other employees: software engineers John Hubbell and Al Gains and installer Mike Augustus, who has a degree in Criminal Justice with an emphasis on juvenile justice and thus has special interest in the issue of child safety. The system they developed is called Rite-Track, which provides en-route alerts with voice over IP, route monitoring, individual child tracking at stops, and video for school buses. It's helping schools save money, reduce the carbon footprint of their buses, anonymously identify peculiar driving habits, and solve behavioral issues. We know of one child in particular who had been the victim of bullying on his way to and from school who is no longer targeted.[16]

When we spoke with Lavoie about Rite-Track, he was honest about the program. As of the end of 2012 it had been installed in a little over 300 school buses in Connecticut and Rhode Island. He told us that

Rite-Track may not have been a big part of revenue in 2012 "but it is helping us to penetrate a new market with technology we already were using elsewhere in our business."[17]

That said, most ideas are generated without management's prompting. But even here, this doesn't mean that blue-sky brainstorming is encouraged – the point is to go after the "adjacent possibilities" like Rite-Track. As Lavoie points out,

> The point of Mutual Fun isn't unstructured free play. If you offer up a truly irrelevant idea, 175 people will not budge it forward. We're after constructive disruption. We're not trying to predict the future. We're trying to provoke it to arrive. Most companies say, "this is what we do." We say, "what can we do with what we know or what we've done before that will be of value?" This ethos helps to continually open up the field of play at Rite-Solutions to new products, technologies, and directions. The innovation engine is about more than pure idea generation, it's about decision making. Your portfolio is your belief about where the future is.[18]

Whether the strategic conversation starts as a challenge or competition (Mutual Fun is essentially a competition), at some point the best ideas coalesce into an innovation community. People join because of their interest and ability to contribute. They are never "volunteered." Originally ideas were assigned to "prophets" – more experienced people who could help mentor the team to success. The culture has matured so that this is no longer necessary. There are enough people skilled in innovation that the mentoring happens without mediation.

One of the most impactful ideas was suggested by an administrator with no engineering experience. As CEO Lavoie describes it:

> In the process of planning the company's annual holiday party and helping her daughter with a school project, she came up with an idea for using a bingo algorithm we created for our casino clients to create a web-based educational tool. That idea, "Win/Play/Learn" (symbol: WPL), immediately caught the attention of some

engineers, who developed her idea into a [game architecture] ultimately [used] by toy-maker Hasbro."[19]

Rite-Solutions continues to work with Hasbro on other projects – an entirely new market segment for it.

BEST BUY "WOLF PACK" INNOVATION COMMUNITIES (PROPOSED BY SENIOR STAFFER)

Best Buy has been in the news quite a bit of late, generally for the wrong reasons. The big box electronics retailer has suffered declining revenues, a stock price tumble relative to the S&P 500, and its former CEO Brian Dunn resigned recently under a cloud of personal scandal. All while facing ever stiffer competition from purely online competitors, especially its arch-nemesis Amazon.

But it wasn't always so. During Brad Anderson's tenure as CEO, Dunn's predecessor, Best Buy thrived in a highly competitive market. During the Anderson era, from 2002 to 2009, Best Buy consistently beat the S&P 500. It grew even as competitors like Circuit City and CompUSA closed their doors. And during this time, it supported, and benefited from, the largest innovation community that the authors have ever encountered. It's a story that illustrates the power of innovation communities, the type of groundwork that needs to be done for them to flourish and, unfortunately, their fragility when they're not properly nurtured by senior management.

Anderson joined Best Buy in 1973 when it was a regional chain called Sound of Music. As the company grew, and then became Best Buy, Anderson moved up the ranks and became known as a self-deprecating but unrelenting innovator. By 1981 he was made a vice president and was widely considered to be founder Dick Schulze's right-hand man. During the go-go 1980s Schulze and Anderson began to open the giant "blue box" superstores that turned Best Buy into the dominant electronics retailer in the Midwest. Never satisfied with the status quo, this duo was able to vanquish rivals like Crazy Eddie with new thinking. In perhaps its most daring move during this period, Best

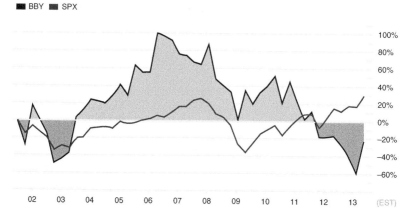

FIGURE 6.3 Best Buy stock returns charted against the Standard & Poor's Index, 2002–2013

Buy converted its salesforce from a commission-based compensation plan to salary. The plan had many detractors; one Best Buy executive reported that for brands that relied on salespeople to push their most expensive products, the move went over poorly, to say the least.[20] Nonetheless, consumers were happy to be rid of high-pressure pitches and revenue grew by 25 percent a year.

When Anderson took over as CEO in 2002, Best Buy faced new challenges. The bursting of the internet boom had depressed demand. And new competitors like direct marketer Dell, plus other big box stores like Walmart and Costco were entering its market. Anderson initiated two major business model innovations. The first was around service – he surmised that as the electronics market grew, more and more technophobes would be buyers, and that they would need help beyond the point of sale to manage their purchases. So he acquired the Geek Squad, a company that at the time had only fifty employees and revenue of $3 million, and rapidly grew this business – the Geek Squad as of 2013 has over 24,000 employees.

The second initiative was an effort to attract and retain Best Buy's most profitable types of customers. Called "centricity," it focused on configuring stores to serve the archetype customers found in that store's market. Stores would choose to cater to one or more of the following categories: affluent technology enthusiasts, young early adopters, busy suburban moms, or small business owners. Products and displays were optimized for these groups; employees were extensively trained to best serve them to ensure that they would be repeat customers.

Market watchers and a number of internal senior managers viewed this strategy with considerable doubt. Anderson fully realized that his strategizing carried risks. He once remarked that "Whether we're doing it in the right way is a highly challengeable premise."[21] But true to the Clausewitzian notion of "resolution," Anderson stayed true to his initial insights resulting from his *coup d'oeil*.

While sticking to his guns, Anderson also opened up Best Buy in a way it never had been before to bottom-up innovation. He believed that employees' proximity to customers gave them particularly valuable insights.[22] In 2003 he hired Kal Patel, previously a senior partner at Strategos, a leading strategy and innovation consulting firm in North America and Europe, to be Best Buy's vice president of strategy,[23] and to become a strategic conversation interlocutor. Patel immediately set up sensing and operationalizing (one of our strategic conversation types) with a special focus on insights that Geek Squad members gained from their customer interactions. As an example, Geek Squad team members in Silicon Valley worked with the founders of SlingBox – a device that allows consumers to view and control their home's cable, satellite, or personal video recorder remotely over the internet – to help it better meet their understanding of consumer needs. The interaction secured Best Buy a special relationship with the company. In a similar vein, Patel supported a grassroots effort by store managers to discuss store strategy. These General Manager Forums both helped Anderson to communicate his "centricity" strategy and helped refine it through interaction with those who worked with customers every day.

In 2004 Anderson was approached by Julie Gilbert, who was leading the effort to attract the affluent technology enthusiast segment. At the time, she had already made considerable headway configuring and promoting Best Buy's Magnolia Home Theatre stores, the segment's centerpiece. She had been hired in 2000, coming from Deloitte and Touche's Minneapolis office. On joining Best Buy, she was struck by the degree to which the headquarters executives were inwardly focused. When she mentioned to them that she felt it was her job to visit stores and talk with customers, she was met with indifference and incredulity. At one point, she even received a call from Best Buy's ethics department worried that she might be too aggressive in her outreach efforts.

Nonetheless, that outreach was producing valuable insights. As a former CPA, she was well versed in the transactional data on shopping behaviors; she didn't go into these interviews cold. But she also considered herself to be a cultural anthropologist. When she visited consumers at their homes, it was generally to speak with husbands who were putatively the affluent technology enthusiasts. She was often greeted by their wives, who almost universally told her how much they disliked the store. There was clearly a gender gap. Gilbert saw this as a huge opportunity. The women's market for electronics was about $90 billion, of which Best Buy had $10 billion. There was clearly room for growth. But Gilbert's tenure at Best Buy made it clear that to bridge that gap, Best Buy itself would have to fundamentally change. Women were poorly represented in management and it felt like a good old boy network. "How can any corporate strategy to serve women consumers ever work when the voices you need in the corporate strategic discussions don't exist?"[24]

Her insights coalesced as the result of two incidents. The first was when an employee confided in her that the reason Gilbert often received hugs from the female employees on her trips was that she was viewed as a role model in an industry in which females were undervalued. The second experience, later that same day, occurred when a senior male executive told her that even though she was respected, there were people who "hated her." What was most depressing was that these haters were fellow executive women, some of whom had never actually met her.

According to Gilbert, who had grown up in a tiny rural town in South Dakota, that night she had a dream. It harkened back to when she would climb the giant silver maple in the family's front yard and listen to the howling of coyotes.

> When I had the dream I felt a paradox surfacing. Wolves, like women, are being misperceived or misunderstood. Wolves are loyal to others, unlike what I have experienced with women in corporate business. Without women supporting women, businesses in all industries will not be successful because the top levels of all corporations have so few women's voices...
>
> To overcome this paradox, I knew I needed a completely new way to reinvent the company that did not look anything like a traditional "top-down" approach. I woke up and immediately mapped out how I would attempt to reinvent Best Buy by bringing the women's voices from inside the company together on teams and then bring the female consumer voices together – giving them every facet of the company to reinvent through a female lens. I built the business plan the next day, focusing on building this innovation movement and targeting three business metrics that would remain valid: 1) female revenue, 2) internal female retention, and 3) internal female recruitment. I knew that there was something there. I called on some women I knew in California and said, let's meet next week. When they asked why, I only responded that they would see. As any entrepreneur would, I just went ahead and started talking about my vision of a new day – inside the company – and the architecture I was building to make it happen for women.[25]

The meeting took place in the Miramar Hotel in Santa Monica. The hotel was a famous hangout for Hollywood stars, especially during the roaring twenties, and Gilbert told her entourage that they were stars too that would change the business landscape. She laid out her plan to create WOLF Packs: she had to rebook her plane reservations back three times because no one wanted to end the conversation.

For all the energy and excitement, Gilbert knew that making WOLF successful wouldn't be easy. Best Buy had been built largely by men to serve male customers. It was, at that point, arguably the most successful electronics retailer in the world. Change would not be easy. To address these challenges, Gilbert architected the richest and most robust innovation community the authors have ever seen.

She knew that to have a chance at success, she would need to recruit the support of key Best Buy male managers – she called them the alpha wolves. Without this support, many female employees would find it too risky to join. She started at the top: both Brad Anderson and Brian Dunn (who was then COO) readily gave her their support. Armed with their agreement, she then approached other senior male managers she knew. She asked them (around sixty at the beginning of the program) three things:

1. to use their network inside the company to communicate to their friends in California where she was launching WOLF Packs, what WOLF was, and to allow women in their stores to go to the WOLF meetings;
2. to deliberately greet women in the stores first when they entered the stores; and
3. to attend, and be visible at, WOLF events.[26]

Once the program was up and running, there were approximately thirty-five WOLF Packs in existence at any one time. They quickly started generating ideas and spurring actions, many small-bore, but in aggregate they fundamentally changed Best Buy.

To appeal to female consumers, the packs suggested training greeters to make eye contact with women coming into the stores, improving lighting in stores, and adding more women-oriented displays. Another idea put into practice was a pamphlet for parents about internet safety for children. One WOLF Pack came up with the idea for a line of Liz Claiborne bags and accessories for laptops, phones,

MP3s and cameras. Recognizing that highly organized women often get holiday shopping done early, Best Buy extended its normal thirty-day return policy to run through January 25 for purchases made after November 1.

To provide more opportunities for women employees, the packs suggested and helped implement job-sharing, so that women who wanted to spend time at home with young children could still pursue their careers. And of course, the WOLF Packs themselves greatly increased mentorship and exposure to senior management.

Gilbert had anticipated these changes would be difficult, but she didn't expect the level of animosity that she received. Men she didn't know would derisively make wolf calls. Her car was even keyed. "Merely walking down the halls was a typically painful experience. People who didn't know what WOLF was about thought I would paint the stores pink with WOLF and alienate male customers."[27]

Fortunately for Gilbert, and for Best Buy, the results were strong:[28]

- revenue generated by females increased by more than $4.4 billion in less than the five years of WOLF@Best Buy;
- female market share increased from 14.7% in Q1 2006 to 17.1% in Q1 2008;
- female turnover was reduced company-wide by over 5% each year;
- female recruits increased by more than 37% in areas where WOLF Packs existed;
- female district managers increased by 300% and where no female executives existed in retail prior to WOLF, as of 2009 there were an unprecedented two out of the eight Best Buy territories in the US led by women executives;
- brand perception of Best Buy increased by four points from the baseline;
- to top it off, it turns out that women customers' business was more profitable than the men's; women's return rate was 60% lower than the men's.[29]

With these impressive dividends, one would think that WOLF would continue to be supported within Best Buy. But Brian Dunn, Brad Anderson's successor as CEO, didn't have Anderson's faith in bottom-up strategizing and, while not shutting WOLF down, he de-emphasized it. With the connection to senior management largely broken, the strategic conversation faded. Is this the reason for Best Buy's declining prospects, or part of it? It's impossible to say, but at a time when Best Buy needed all hands on deck, it reverted to more of a command and control mentality and lost the edge gained from har-nessing employee imagination. Best Buy demonstrates the power of strategic conversations, and in particular, innovation communities. But it also demonstrates their fragility. Even when they have great success, if senior management isn't a willing participant, strategic conversations simply can't exist.

How innovation communities are different from 'Tiger Teams'

WOLF Packs, the drivers of Gilbert's vision, had all the hallmarks of successful innovation communities, and in this way are very much related to the innovation communities we've just seen from Boston Children's Hospital, KBS+, and Rite-Solutions. Because they operated through newly created and missioned communications between charged-up imaginative employees and senior management:

- *They were closely tied to the leader's vision as they explored business model innovation.* Because of Gilbert's close connection with Brad Anderson, and because of her own work in developing the affluent technology enthusiast segment, she had a deep understanding of Best Buy's strategic intent. In perfect congruence with that strategy, she had the WOLF Packs focus on: (1) growth of female market share, (2) recruiting more women to the company, and (3) retention of women.
- *They were cognitively diverse.* They represented both retail and corporate players (who otherwise rarely interacted.) Through energetic employees reaching out they had strong input from

(cont.)

customers. They included people from different levels of the
hierarchy. And, by design each WOLF Pack had to include at least
two men.

- *They were of limited duration, demanded significant commitment,
  and were viewed as prestigious.* WOLF Packs' primary reason for
  existence was to change Best Buy's business model in the service of
  the three WOLF goals. They weren't meant to be debating societies
  or networking clubs (though of course issues were discussed and
  networking occurred). Their limited duration helped to maintain
  focus. And they were limited in size to twenty-five members to put
  a spotlight on individual contributors and to create accountability.

- *Their linkages to senior management stimulated conversations
  with high strategic content.* WOLF Pack members were given
  collective access to senior managers to review their ideas and, when
  appropriate, fund and execute them. WOLF Packs allowed members
  and senior management to bypass Best Buy's hierarchy and directly
  converse in a meaningful way about the business.

- *They prepared members for strategic conversations.* Members were
  coached on how to think and present strategically so that their
  conversations with senior management would be valuable to all
  parties. Members were given stretch assignments to help them
  grow. Line people were taught how to read a profit and loss
  statement. As Gilbert put it: "Every single meeting had a recipe, a
  flow and exercises to ensure they led the meetings, thereby building
  leadership skills into the essence of the meeting. In the first six
  months of WOLF, I would put out an exercise to the pack and then
  watch how they react and build more, or less, content into the
  meeting plan."[30]

7 Conversation trumps structure – new norms for dialog

> Argument based on knowledge implies instruction, and there are people
> whom one cannot instruct. Here, then, we must use, as our modes of
> persuasion and argument, notions possessed by everybody.
>
> Aristotle, *Rhetoric*

When managers are looking to reinvigorate a company, often their
first thought is to reshuffle the organizational structure. But this puts
the cart before the horse. Conversation trumps structure. A company
having meaningful strategic conversations can thrive even when the
org chart isn't quite right; the best organigram won't save a company
with poor conversational health. Conversation may be a soft topic
but it is about hard truths. At the end of the day, not having
honest dialog is as serious as running out of cash.[1] All the elements
essential for good strategizing – from understanding customers to
engaging employees to developing leaders to sparking innovation –
depend on it.[2]

At the most basic level, leadership needs to convince employees
to participate, to join the energized circle of innovators from which
many feel excluded as they talk about the leadership as 'them.' At a
large financial firm for which we've done work, information technology employees we surveyed didn't believe it was their job to innovate
the business model and couldn't name any innovations that had come
from their group. But in fact the group *was* actively involved
in profoundly changing the organization's business model. By using
advanced algorithms, they were automating trading in several asset
classes, radically reducing transaction costs and creating new hedging
opportunities for customers. By explaining what innovation was,
and by illustrating areas in which the group had already made a

contribution, we helped convince these employees to be more engaged in the strategizing process.

Good strategic conversations aren't necessarily polite, but they do need to be managed. They are absolutely not free-form brainstorming. Management must, like a good host, draw all guests into the conversation while guiding it in ways that enrich all participants.

When the dinner discussion turns to politics, sex, or religion, a good host knows how to manage the conversation so that it remains provocative without becoming mired in awkwardness and acrimony. Business model innovation is likewise a delicate subject that needs to be managed. It's all too easy to crush the young shoots of an idea. Research has shown that in many organizations, employees who propose new ideas are viewed as less intelligent than those who criticize them.[3] If you want to impress your colleagues and peers, why not take a few pot shots at someone else's not fully-formed ideas. In the knowledge economy, such attitudes are beyond bad manners; organizations that don't promote new ideas are not long for this world. Leadership must willingly embrace the occasional *faux pas* and eccentricities. Statements that may seem unwelcome may nonetheless – like the mold in Alexander Fleming's cultures that ruined his experiment but led to the discovery of penicillin – take the conversation in unexpected and worthwhile directions.

Sometimes an attentive host will notice that guests are talking past one another. This often happens when innovative ideas meet overly rationalistic left-brain thinking. In general, business culture has great difficulty being fact-driven while simultaneously having to deal with a messy world that can only be vaguely grasped.[4] Managers need to help employees bridge this gap. Strategic conversations help establish a *corpus callosum* connecting the creative and analytical right and left sides of the organization's business brain.

For instance, organizations that stress programs like Six Sigma are especially likely to need such interventions. While disruptions and variations are the enemies of efficiency and quality, they're precisely what facilitate innovation. The innovator seeks to introduce something

FIGURE 7.1 Strategizing wheel

new even if the quality is inferior (think of iPhone or Skype in their early days). Starwood Hotels has successfully bridged this gap. To increase their share of their clients' wallet they embraced a staff innovation to introduce massage services for guests. To prevent worker injuries and reduce workers' compensation claims from slips and falls, employees introduced stretching routines for hotel staff. The ideas were allowed to see the light of day in their rough form and *then* were burnished by Six Sigma black and green belts to enhance their efficiency and quality.[5]

How does the strategist use conversation to promote useful business model innovation? How does conversation help to expand the firm's opportunity space? This chapter will reiterate the intimate connection between strategy and conversation. It will show how to foster healthy conversations that create a fertile context for conceiving, building, and executing innovative and resilient business models.

Conversation has four major roles in supporting the strategizing process:

1. **Fostering knowledge exchanges to reduce knowledge absences**. While reducing knowledge absences is important throughout the strategizing process, it is especially important at the beginning of the process, in Discovery. Management should always be scanning the world for trends that could help it improve the business

model. Employees, given half a chance, also try to push the boundaries in their own work. So it was at Boston Children's Hospital (BCH). Dr. David Hunter spent eight years working on the implementation of a telehealth solution to diagnose premature babies for eye disease (see Chapter 6 for the longer story). As he struggled with implementing his solution, Dr. Hunter achieved a detailed understanding of the implications and challenges of telehealth. This knowledge proved invaluable to management. But management was also able to help solve institutional problems that Dr. Hunter encountered around the legal and financial implications of what he was doing. Through a strategic conversation, mediated by BCH's Chief Innovation Officer Naomi Fried, both parties reduced each other's knowledge absences and together expanded BCH's opportunity space. (This type of knowledge exchange is important for all eight types of strategic conversation we identified in Chapter 3.)

2. **Shaping conversations to make them productive**. As we've stressed throughout, unstructured conversations and open brainstorms can be fun, but their outcomes are rarely productive. Unless the participants have a focus shaped by a point of view that reflects management's strategic concerns, the results are generally incoherent and inconsequential.

For this reason, effective leaders actively shape strategic conversations, and they do this through conversation. We earlier mentioned how Steve Jobs, even after his passing, deeply influences Apple employees' thinking through his insistence on the simple, clean design aesthetic that pervades the thinking of Apple software and industrial engineers. When considering a design, they still ask themselves "would Steve do it like this?" Likewise, KBS+ CEO Lori Senecal is careful to shape the conversations that take place in her company. In her conversations with her subordinates she insists that everyone in her advertising firm should "Do things that matter." She's not interested in "me too" advertising or working on low-profile accounts. Senecal's thinking is deeply embedded in her employees' psyches because of her active presence in meetings, hallway interactions, and active blogging. She is consistent and relentless, talking with employees about her expansive view of the company. All of the employees we spoke with at KBS+ have internalized Senecal's vision.

Science is just now starting to give us insight into what this process looks like at the neurological level. In one study subjects were placed in an MRI machine that measured their brain waves. One subject was "the speaker" while the others took on the role of "listeners." The experimenters found that the more actively the listeners listened, and the greater their comprehension of the speaker's story, the more the brain waves of the listeners actually synchronized with those of the speaker. Much like the spooky coupling of particles found in quantum physics, the speaker's and the listeners' brains coupled. Remarkably the brain wave patterns of listeners with the highest comprehension actually began to antici-pate those of the speaker, as if finishing the speaker's thoughts before they were uttered.[6]

Of course what this book has suggested throughout is not some kind of mind control over employees. What we have said is that the language developed by leaders should be used to convince employees to support the strategist by pointing out (a) what to pay attention to, and (b) how to interpret and act on what they discover. The strategist harnesses employee skills and knowledge to his or her insight so that they can help inform and then successfully implement the strategy.

When thinking about shaping conversations, it is important to consider the distinction between data and meaning. Machine communication depends on the presence or absence of a signal, of data. The meaning of that data is not considered. But human conversation always contains elements of subjectivity; it concerns both data and meaning. Meanings are what we attach to data, and as anybody who has ever tried to convince someone else knows, managing meanings is often more challenging than securing data. The first step of strategizing, Discovery, involves coming to grips with an uncertain situation, finding and selecting the facts that seem most relevant. Judgment involves imbuing those facts with meaning and, through language, constructing a business model that engages uncertainty as a matter of practice and is likely to create value.[7] The importance of language to strategy becomes immediately apparent when thinking about strategizing in this way. For instance, companies that embrace a total quality management philosophy would probably view an industry with traditionally high defect rates as an opportunity to compete because they would know how to drive both quality up and costs down. A firm not dedicated to quality would be more likely to adopt a discounting strategy. Same data, different meanings, leading to completely different strategies.

How far should leaders go in shaping the conversation? This is a delicate matter and requires managerial judgment. Given their primary function is to lead the firm towards greater value creation and profit, engaging others to help the strategists deal with the discovered knowledge absences and uncertainties leverages their own capacities in ways that result in further added value. So strategic communication needs to be two-way. Effective strategizing has little to do with broadcasting conclusions or giving directions. When leaders take all the uncertainty upon themselves, the result suffers because it is seldom possible for them to resolve all relevant knowledge absences by themselves. The leader's principal contribution should be to shape the workplace through conversation so that additional uncertainties can be engaged and resolved by those working throughout the organization.

However, leaders need to be judicious in how they burden employees to support strategy. Employee judgment and sensemaking must be engaged in ways that reflect the employee's capabilities. On the one hand, employee work is enriched when uncertainties remain unresolved and when their judgment is called on to supplement their day-to-day operational and instruction-following work. Most employees know well the difference between empowering work and mindless labor. But if they are exposed to too many of the uncertainties unresolved by senior management or are provided too little support, their work situation becomes overly stressful, discouraging, and maybe un-doable. Employees want challenges, not crushing chaos.[8]

3. **Persuading employees to pursue a specific strategy.** The third role for conversation in strategizing is persuasion. As has already been discussed extensively in Chapter 5, this is because under uncertainty, any strategic insight can be questioned by others advocating equally valid alternatives. Strategic conversations are implicitly 'critical' in that all participants are open to critique others' ideas. Through active criticism comes growth. So it's up to leaders to convince employees that their strategic insight, their *coup d'oeil*, as Clausewitz called it, is both valid and worth pursuing. This is done through the rhetorical techniques of ethos (highlighting the leader's ability, experience, insight, and commitment to others and the employee's sense of what is right) and pathos (appealing to the employee's desire to act). The CEOs in our study – Senecal of KBS+, Haldane of YMCA Canada, Lavoie of Rite-Solutions, Tucci of EMC, Whitehurst of Red Hat – are indisputably experts at what they do. They care about employees, and are passionate and resolute about their vision for the organization. The notions of ethos and pathos are inescapably embedded in most if not all of leadership's conversations with employees. This has given them the ability to persuade their employees to adopt and act on the management's strategy as if it is their own, and to move from Judgment to implementing the strategy in Practice largely without doubt or hesitation.

4. **Creating a learning 'social apparatus' that constantly creates new knowledge and value.** When strategic conversations flourish, strategizing goes way beyond developing a plan of action to address a chosen objective. In highly effective organizations, these conversations become a way of doing business. This is the fourth role for conversation in strategy. The conversations become systematized into a value-generating social apparatus in which the strategist and employees work together to resolve selected

knowledge absences to expand the firm's opportunity space. Some call this 'culture,' but it is specifically a culture of critique and positive action rather than a culture of passive acceptance. As we've seen in our cases, the very practice of strategic conversations becomes the vitalizing core of a dynamic firm. The product of these conversations is a constantly evolving and adapting business model – the firm's specific language about how it generates value and why.

But even with the business model established, the conversation doesn't stop. The firm isn't a command and control machine. Organizations are problematic and constantly shifting, dynamic and tentative nests of collaborative practices, never entirely tidy, with elements of insight and error intermingled throughout. The business model is a conversation the firm's actors inhabit as they apply their skills and generate value in a constantly changing world. The business model meets the world full on in Practice, and from that collision the conversation turns to Learning. During this aspect of strategizing the measure of the business model is taken. Based on these assessments, changes inevitably will need to be made and the strategizing wheel is given yet another turn.

This revisiting of the strategizing model and its different modes – Discovery, Judgment, Persuasion, Practice, and Learning – in relationship to conversation further illuminates the vital connection of conversation to strategy, and makes clear why conversational health is required for effective strategizing. If conversations are core to all aspects of the strategizing process, what makes them effective in real life? The topic of human conversation is vast and rich. The rest of this chapter is only an introduction; it offers some practical advice and gives suggestions for further reading.

A first step to conversational health is, as a leader, to be very mindful of the language you use to address the organization. Language management profoundly affects a conversation. In a now famous experiment, subjects were shown a video of two three-person teams, each of which was passing a basketball. One team was wearing white shirts, and the other was wearing black shirts. The subjects' task was to count the number of times the white-shirted team passed the ball, and they were specifically directed to ignore the number of passes made by the black-shirted team. During the video a person in a black gorilla suit appears, thumps their chest at the camera, and then walks off-screen. The gorilla is in the frame for approximately nine seconds, yet only about half of the subjects noticed.[9] This experiment is a classic illustration of selective attention. The lesson for strategic conversations comes from what the subjects were told to pay attention to – how their task was framed. Rather than being asked to watch the whole scene, they were given a very specific task and directed to ignore other inputs, and many of them completely overlooked something entirely remarkable.

The type of framing encountered by employees at the workplace may be more subtle, but the effects are no less striking. In Chapter 5 we argued there are two leadership styles most often used by businesses today: transactional, and conversational (the third style, coercive, is thankfully relatively uncommon). The transactional model represents the old norms for dialog, though it's still the predominant model taught at most economics departments and business schools. In it, employees are viewed as free agents who act in their own self-defined best interests. The model asserts that cooperation between employees and the organization is possible, but only when employees are carefully managed and monitored.

There is growing evidence that transactional cultures actually reinforce selfish behavior. If employees behave in their own self-interest, as transaction economics says they are supposed to, and are then rewarded for this behavior (with money or promotions), and if the organization's leaders also assume that employees will always act this way, then employees will become accustomed to using cunning and deceit to gain personal advantage, whether or not they would have behaved that way in another setting.[10] In other words, the transactional theory of management becomes self-fulfilling. In such an environment, cooperation becomes invisible, ignored or just viewed as foolish naivete.

Obviously, transactional framing has dire consequences for strategic conversations. Employee imagination can only be mobilized effectively towards the organization's objectives where straight talk is the norm. Without candid, respectful dialog, strategic conversations can't even get started. The dialogs that undergird strategic conversations require all to follow clear rules. These include: don't lie; pay attention and listen to others; don't sneer; do cooperate; don't shout; let others talk; be open-minded; be prepared to learn and change; explain yourself when asked; don't resort to trickery or conspiracy to push your ideas; do your homework and get the facts right; be prepared to have others check your facts; control your emotions; keep the organization's goals in mind; don't let yourself be dragged down barren alleys.

When strategic conversations are shut down they are often done so almost unconsciously, as a result of the invasion of the transactional mentality that rewards guile. But sometimes they're shut down willfully because they contradict management's interpretation of reality. The results are often calamitous. Kirsten Grind documents such a disconnect between management and employees in her book *The Lost Bank*, a history of the failure of Washington Mutual (WaMu).[11] In 2006, at the very beginning of the sub-prime mortgage crisis, the bank's stated values set the tone: "dynamic and driven." (They had been "fair, caring, and human" before WaMu began its aggressive expansion.) Employees began to notice, and have conversations about, a growing set of disturbing signs. The median price of existing homes declined. The percentage of loans made without documentation of income or assets increased. First payment default (failing to make even the first payment on a mortgage) rates increased. Employees knew that the bank was heading into trouble. But instead of opening up the strategic conversation and reorienting the bank, senior management doubled-down on sub-prime loans. Conversations that contradicted or critiqued CEO Kerry Killinger's narrative were actively suppressed. The bank's Risk Officer, Ron Cathcart (who had just taken over after his predecessor resigned in disgust), at one point notified Killinger that the Federal Office of Thrift Supervision was threatening to downgrade the bank's rating. Stubbornly refusing to hear bad news, Killinger left the room before Cathcart could finish. In September of 2008 the bank was seized by the Office of Thrift Supervision and became the largest bank failure in American financial history. WaMu had all the proper structures for the Bank, including risk officers. All to no avail.

Conversations trump structure.

The sad tale of WaMu is an extreme example of an all-too-common problem that profoundly undermines strategic conversations: managers may say one thing but do another. Chris Argyris and Donald Schon named this phenomenon "espoused theory versus theory-in-use."[12] Employees may find themselves in an untenable position when they are expected to keep others informed, but hide any mistakes; to be honest, but not deliver bad news; be creative, but follow the rules; don't over-promise, but never say no to the boss' demands; be a risk-taker, as long as you don't fail. Argyris and Schon note that, insidiously, employees are being forced to live these lies. Managers insist on not talking about the specific contradictions. They also forbid subordinates from talking about the fact that it is forbidden to talk about the contradictions. Such suppression of reality unsurprisingly leads to stress and lack of engagement for employees.[13]

Today's employees are less tolerant of obfuscation and are certainly less trusting of corporate-speak than the generations who came before, especially after the experiences of the Great Recession. But that doesn't mean that they are naturally cynical. They are attracted to the conversational model of management because they are deeply interested in how their participation gives them a sense of meaning and how it helps them grow and learn. (As we noted earlier, the effects of social rewards are often stronger and longer lasting than financial rewards.) When we spoke to Mark Jensen and Nick Vidovich of KBS+ about the prize money they won when their Hyde Experiment was selected as the winner of KBS+'s 2012 innovation contest, they were adamant that the prize money had nothing to do with them proposing their idea or with the countless hours they put in to make it a reality. Rather, they had taken to heart CEO Lori Senecal's mantra "Do things that matter."

Of course, doing things that matter involves risking failure. Many organizations these days speak of "smart failure" and the importance of taking risks to explore new opportunities. But when push comes to shove, too often a manager's plea for employees to "take risks and be creative" translates to "do crazy things and then I'll fire you."[14] This becomes a fundamental contradiction. According to our second Iron Law of Value Creation, "All business models require a leap of faith," because in competitive markets economic rents only exist if there is uncertainty. If all the relevant facts are known, then there is no room for competitive advantage and above-average profitability. Thus to be successful, organizations can't be ambivalent about embracing smart failure, they need to manage it.[15]

Interestingly, one of the most innovative organizations in managing failure intelligently has traditionally been one of the most hidebound, the United States Army. Modern warfare produces a massive amount of information that is highly time-sensitive. General Gordon R. Sullivan, the Army's recently retired chief of staff, described Information Age war as a paradox of managing huge amounts of information without trying to over-control that information. The value of real-time information – such as enemy location, and the nature and targeting of their weapons – is on the ground. That value is lost if the information has to be run up and down the chain of command first. So long as the commander's intent is clear to the frontline soldiers, the decisions for how to use the information and exploit opportunities should rest at the lowest possible level in the hierarchy.[16]

Failure is endemic in war, which is unpredictable, fast, and where mistakes can cost lives. The Army uses after-action reviews

(AARs) for leaders to become familiar with what's happening in the field by hearing directly from the participants themselves. During these reviews participants discuss what went right and wrong in an action in a very frank way. The object is to learn; properly used they are never the basis for disciplinary action. The format is simple and consistent. Four questions are discussed:

1. What did we set out to do?
2. What actually happened?
3. Why did it happen?
4. What are we going to do next time?

The sessions are forward-looking. According to Army guidelines 25 percent of discussion time should be on the first two questions, 25 percent on the third, and 50 percent on the fourth.[17]

Critically, the Army hasn't fallen into the trap of expecting the AAR process itself to change its culture. It knew that for AARs to be effective, both officers and enlisted personnel would have to fundamentally change their behaviors. Issues couldn't be saluted away: truth would have to be able to speak to rank. The Army has famously used the concept of boot camp to break down recruits so that they could then be reconstituted into a coherent fighting force. The Army is now using extremely demanding war games and AARs to actually *cause* failure and force participants to deal with the consequences. Over the course of these exercises, in which over half a million soldiers have participated multiple times, participants are placed in stressful and sleep-deprived situations and are taught to transform failure into learning by changing the language that they use and their behaviors. Brigadier General William S. Wallace, the former commander in charge of these trainings, wrote that these after-action reviews had democratized the Army, and developed a discipline of constantly examining and critiquing the actions taken. In the process, the leadership style of generations of officers has shifted from command and control to a style more able to capitalize on the distributed intelligence of troops.[18]

An after-action review

After five days of desert combat training exercises, the exhausted tank, HMMWV and armored personnel carrier crews from a team of two platoons converge in a shaded location to perform the review. The observer/controller leads things off by creating a miniature in the sand of the terrain of that day's battle. A gunnery sergeant is asked to come forward and explain the mission.

The sergeant's broad response, to destroy the enemy at a particular location, is met with more searching questions from the observer/ controller, inquiring about the importance of that mission, and what specific role the sergeant's tank was to play in that objective.

The sergeant is unsure of the tank's role. The observer/controller asks the rest of the group for input. Slow at first, the responses grow into a full discussion. It becomes apparent that no one but the lieutenant in charge truly understood the mission, which was to drive the enemy away from an area of weak defenses and towards friendly tanks and artillery. Individual vehicles weren't coordinated, and no one was told where to concentrate their fire.

By eliciting the perspectives of all the soldiers involved in the engagement, and supplementing with video and other data provided by the observer/controller, a comprehensive picture of the battle, and the soldiers' roles in it, is revealed. An ordinary flip chart is used to take note of the day's important lessons, and with repeated such exercises, certain themes appear regularly – everyone in the unit needs to understand the big picture and think for themselves; the mission is more important than the hierarchy; they must be so well prepared that the unexpected doesn't catch them off guard; and they must be able to critically examine their own role as individuals, and within the team.[19]

Other organizations are also beginning to change the conversation around failure as well. When Jim Yong Kim became World Bank President, he introduced the idea of "the science of delivery," an approach that seeks to systematically improve poverty-fighting prac- tices. Kim wants to apply the same rigor to poverty alleviation that doctors do to epidemiology. The laboratory is the field – the regions and countries where the Bank does work. Every action taken becomes an opportunity for the entire system to learn – and in order to learn, smart failures must be embraced.

In a 2012 speech, Kim discussed one of the ways the World Bank Group embraced smart failures. He expanded and systematized existing "Failfair" events, including personally chairing some of the workshops. Similar to the Army's after-action reviews, Failfairs do not place blame, but explore what factors led certain projects to be less than successful. Kim also articulated a desire to further open up participation in the future to include critics and communities affected by the projects, and to publish the conclusions and results of the discussions.[20] Kim's chairing of the workshops has significant consequences and is once again a type of sensing and operationalizing strategic conversation. Kim will increase his presence as a leader. He will learn a great deal about the reality of development work directly from those who do the work, and hence have much greater insight for strategizing. And participants will learn, in a direct and intimate way, much more about Kim's strategic intent.

Sometimes failure is just what an organization needs.

If good strategy is a function of good conversation, then given the poor state of conversation in many organizations, it's not surprising that the results of strategizing are often disappointing. Strategizing in an environment in constant flux is an exercise in reacting to, and initiating, change. As we asserted with our third Iron Law of Value Creation, companies must continually update their business models, since even innovative business models are vulnerable to attack and obsolescence. But most would rate the success of corporate change efforts as grim. Not long ago McKinsey & Company surveyed 1,546 business executives from around the world, asking them if they consider their change programs "completely/mostly" successful. Only 30 percent agreed.[21]

Good conversational health helps in both the formulation and implementation of strategy. Yet conversational skills are generally undervalued. Studies over the last thirty years have consistently shown that managers who are good communicators aren't rewarded, and may even be penalized, in the review process.[22] The focus on individual performance and quarterly numbers undermines systems approaches and the creation of the social networks which over time support effective and sustainable strategizing.

Leading organizations are starting to pay attention to this conversation gap. Google, ever the stickler for data, coded and analyzed thousands of pieces of information about managers – from feedback surveys, performance reviews and other reports – as part of what it called Project Oxygen, and followed that textual analysis with interviews with managers. This research was aimed at determining what characteristics or practices were shared by superior managers, and how Google could help its managers improve.[23] The results were clear, and to the technically-minded researchers, startling. Eight rules for good management were distilled from the findings:

1. Be a good coach.
2. Empower your team and don't micromanage.
3. Express interest in team members' success and personal well-being.
4. Don't be a "sissy": Be productive and results-oriented.
5. Be a good communicator and listen to your team.
6. Help your employees with career development.
7. Have a clear vision and strategy for the team.
8. Have key technical skills so you can help advise the team.

Of the eight, five (1, 2, 3, 5, 6) directly relate to conversational skills, including the top three. So, even at one of the most geeky organizations on the planet, conversational skills are paramount. Having key technical skills was important, but last on the list.

Given the importance of conversation, it is probably bad practice to just hope managers and employees improve their skills one interaction at a time. Organizations need to address the conversation gap systematically. For managers, there are both positive and negative behaviors that will help or hinder strategic conversations. On the positive side is the notion of what business writer and philosopher

Fred Kofman calls "productive inquiry." It requires active and attentive listening, and an attitude of openness and receptivity. Your desire to really understand the other person, to appreciate and respect their viewpoint, must be stronger than your need to show you are right. If your focus is proving that you're right, you're unlikely to show genuine interest in and truly hear what the other person is saying. And if the other person doesn't feel heard or appreciated, they will be less willing to genuinely listen to you, and the potential for a productive conversation is short-circuited.[24] Productive inquiry is foundational to strategic conversations.

Knowledge absences can only be addressed and filled by an inquiring mind. Productive inquiry greatly reduces the transaction costs in filling knowledge absences, the primary goal of strategic conversations and the *sine qua non* of effective strategizing and value creation.

One technique for implementing productive inquiry is "fishbowl discussions," a method used to address potentially contentious issues that could easily become a victim of theory-as-practiced double-speak. It is especially useful when a group is dealing with an issue that has the potential to threaten the status quo and managerial turf. For instance, a T-shaped group we observed came to the conclusion that the company should exit a particular business line. This clearly didn't play well with the managers of that business!

The team members were placed around a table to openly discuss the issue. Their managers sat outside of this circle and were instructed to listen to the discussion without interrupting or challenging the team. They could only ask clarifying questions when the theme of the discussion changed. The group itself just discussed the issues. It did not make recommendations.

A facilitator helped enforce the rules. This technique allowed the task force members to speak the truth with a high degree of freedom and openness. They were able to function much like a team of professional consultants, but with the advantage of being part of the organization, with the richness of their inside knowledge.[25] As it turned out, the group's suggestion wasn't acted upon. But there was no retaliation against those who suggested pulling the plug. The facilitated fishbowl thus helped promote an honest conversation.

Several leaders we've spoken to mention the importance of ensuring that all voices, and not just the loudest, are heard. For instance, at Red Hat, the problem wasn't that conversations were overly constrained by corporate politeness, but that they could become unfettered and distracting. Red Hat's corporate intranet, memo-list,[26] was a vital platform for strategic conversations (as we noted in Chapter 4, it was even used to collectively update Red Hat's mission statement). The problem was that, from time to time, this communications channel was overused by the more aggressive within the company. Some complained that the amount of non-business-related conversation was excessive, while others were offended by the often direct and frank nature of the passionate discussions. As DeLisa Alexander, Red Hat's Chief People Officer, put it:

> On the positive side, memo-list was a vehicle that connected employees to each other around the world and created a shared understanding of our business, values, and culture. It gave every employee a channel from which to provide feedback and was a powerful meritocratic force that could (and often did) facilitate change and increase accountability.
>
> On the other hand, it was also a venue where personal attacks could get out of hand, where conversations could quickly become demoralizing, where misstatements helped to proliferate inaccurate information, and it could be deeply polarizing. Some viewed it as a symbol of Red Hat culture, while others perceived it as a waste of valuable time.[27]

For Red Hat, memo-list acted as a sensing and operationalizing platform that was too valuable to be abandoned. It needed to be revitalized. Management assembled an innovation community to tackle the problem. The core team, fifteen members out of the company of

3,000, was chosen for its diversity but also all shared a common passion for tackling the problem.

> We looked for people from different functional backgrounds and geographic locations. We tried to recruit representatives who worked remotely and some who worked in offices. We looked for old-timers and newer hires. We also specifically included associates who were strong advocates to discontinue memo-list. Our goal was to assemble a team small enough to work quickly and diverse enough to be representative of the Red Hat population.[28]

In order to incorporate the voices of the shy and disaffected the team performed a survey. The results reinforced the urgency of their task: over 42 percent of the respondents indicated that they wanted to unsubscribe from memo-list completely. The team developed etiquette for posting on memo-list that discouraged personal attacks and 'flamewars.' The guidelines also focused the conversation on business and business-related topics. Because the new guidelines were developed by representatives of the community – two of the top posters to memo-list were part of the team – they were widely accepted. Enforcement of the guidelines was handled by members of the team, not management. But the way in which the guidelines were developed created the environment where individuals for the most part self-policed. After the guidelines were announced, 89 percent of survey respondents now said they wanted to participate on memo-list. It had become a safe place for all, including the shy.

Jim Lavoie, CEO of Rite-Solutions, is a tireless advocate for introverts. His hypothesis is that in most organizations the shy are a vast, underutilized innovation resource. He is not a fan of innovation competitions where contestants have to go in front of panels to present (he calls these panels "murder boards.") His experience is that introverts will just keep their ideas to themselves rather than be subjected to the agony of exposing their ideas, and themselves, to the bright light of scrutiny.

That is one of the reasons he developed Mutual Fun, the game described in the previous chapter that allows employees to suggest innovations and buy stock of promising ideas using "Rite-Solutions cash." It's a social game that provides safety for introverts to sell their ideas and to give feedback. Lavoie describes it as the "anti-challenge challenge."

> Most people make innovation a contact sport, which automatically leaves out the introverts. The smarter your organization is, odds are the more introverts you have in it. In a knowledge economy, harvesting the introverts is the new secret sauce. As an extrovert myself; I never had an idea I didn't like. The higher I was in the old organization, the more dangerous I became.
>
> Mutual Fun gives embryonic ideas – wherever they come from – room to breathe and take shape before "the managerial disapproval loop" shunts the discussion to ground. The best thing for an idea is air, and the more air you give it and the more people that breathe that idea, the better it will become. It can also take the sting out of rejection when it's the crowd that doesn't see the wisdom of your idea.[29]

A balance must be struck. In all of the organizations that we've studied that have successful strategic conversations, introverts may be shielded from the aggressiveness of their more extroverted colleagues, but they aren't allowed to be anonymous. Even at Rite-Solutions, probably the organization most assertive in protecting introverts that we've observed, all actions (creating new funds or supporting existing ones) are attributable to the employee.

The reason for resisting anonymity is that it degrades the strategic conversations. Beer and Eisenstat describe one of the failings of two standard methods of collecting information about organizational problems. Surveys of large numbers of employees, or interviews by outsiders (such as consultants or HR specialists), assume that the anonymity of these processes is necessary to elicit objective and truthful responses. But this also creates a distance between the senior executives and the people who have actually seen and experienced the problems. That distance enables the leaders to misjudge the severity of problems, or to ignore them or delay taking action.[30]

Chuck Hollis, Global Marketing CTO at EMC puts it even more starkly: "Anonymity is the plague." People need to own up to their opinions and be visible in the .conversation.

Conversational health is essential for successful strategic conversations. This chapter has just scratched the surface in identifying the issues that can affect conversational health and describing and enumerating the techniques for taking corrective action. Human conversation is a rich and complex phenomenon, and as we've argued, central to the strategizing process. If an organization's leadership isn't paying close attention to the conversational health of the organization, then it isn't performing one of its most important functions.

PUTTING INTO PLACE HEALTHY SPEECH PATTERNS

Do the conversational norms at your company promote strategic conversations, where employees are encouraged to share the fruits of their knowledge and imagination with management?

Are you often surprised by new, employee-generated ideas that challenge your view of the business?

Suggestion: if the answers to the questions above are 'no,' it is urgent to tailor a set of conversational norms that work in your company to promote truly strategic conversations. Test them with the management team and any existing innovation communities. Adjust as necessary. When you have a set that work, make sure that they are part of the conversation with prospective employees and are part of the on-boarding and evaluation processes, especially for managers.

SUGGESTIONS FOR FURTHER READING

There is a great deal to be read on this and our hope is that alerting the reader to the central place of conversation will encourage further interest in the ancient art of rhetoric and its pervasive application in our lives, most especially in politics and management. We believe an excellent place to start is with a couple of books that adroitly examine rhetoric in both historical and contemporary contexts: Jay Heinrichs' *Thank You for Arguing*,[31] and Sam Leith's *You Talkin' to Me?*[32]

8 Strategic conversations across geographies, generations, and the multitude

It is difficult or even impossible to name an individual that acts as "the entrepreneur" in a concern.

Joseph Schumpeter[1]

Perhaps you work for a huge company with hundreds of thousands of employees spread all over the world, and with significant cultural and generational differences. Then you may be saying, strategic conversations are all well and good for smaller organizations, but how can they help me? The answer is, actually, quite nicely.

It's not by chance that Apple, one of the largest companies in the world by market capitalization, is superb at managing its language space. Management's agenda embodies the thinking of Steve Jobs – still vastly influential after his passing – and it informs every conversation. What would Steve say about this design idea, about this packaging, this part of the Web site? With Steve's sensibilities in everyone's mind, the designs that don't fit Apple's aesthetic are self-censored before ever seeing the light of day. Borderline cases are discussed and the conversation goes on. Thousands of employees across the world self-manage as they implement Apple's business model, speeding up work and reducing management costs.

As Apple illustrates, strategic conversations don't require technology to be effective, even in very large organizations. Perhaps an even more striking case of technology-free strategic conversations is Periclean Athens. As we noted in Chapter 4, their democratically run society, with strong leaders who used rhetorical techniques to align and engage citizens, created very effective, robust, and geographically dispersed mercantile and military operations using strategic conversations.

While strategic conversations can be successful without relying on technology, many organizations are taking advantage of technology combined with social media principles to enrich interactions between management and employees. In this chapter, we'll see how enterprise social networking offers new and useful ways of strengthening strategic conversations and how it can provide an especially effective medium for engaging younger generations of employees.

Best Buy provides an amusing example. Management decided that Geek Squad engineers should electronically share solutions to commonly found hardware and software problems. So it created a wiki, a modern-day way for users to add and update content in a non-hierarchical way. But it was not modern enough for Geek Squad employees and usage of the wiki was scattered. Confused, Best Buy management spent time with Geek Squad members observing how they solved problems. They discovered that the wiki had been bypassed. Instead of using the wiki, Geek Squaders traded technical tips while playing video games with each other. A warrior located in Minneapolis, after decapitating a victim in Juneau, would be observed providing pointers on router configurations. Thereby a very useful and effective tool was created bottom up. The moral of the story: strategic conversations worked, employees solved a problem identified by management. But they did it their own way. Management shouldn't be surprised when a solution to a problem they raise looks different from the one they originally envisioned.[2]

Along these lines, let's say you are a global accounting firm like PricewaterhouseCoopers (PwC). How about using American Idol or the Apprentice as a model to generate new ideas? This was the idea of Mitra Best, a former engineer who is now US Innovation Leader at PwC. She borrowed ideas from these shows, including live chats and an online platform for discussion and voting. "We tried to create a collaborative and competitive environment. This was not like inspiring fifty people, or thirty people, where you can periodically take them on a field trip," she says. "The question is, how do you connect 30,000 people? We figured if gaming can connect millions, let's try it." But the idea wasn't just to bridge a huge company spread all over the world, it was also to bridge generations. "We have an average age of 27, but we have roots in tax and assurance," says US Chairman Bob Moritz. "So how do you make this place feel like a Google or a Facebook? A place that feels leading-edge?"[3]

The result was PowerPitch, events where self-generated teams of PwC employees pitch ideas to the company as a whole and those voted most likely for success are given a chance to present to company partners and win a cash prize of $100,000. In this strategic conversation, senior leaders hear of ideas to shape the business, like introducing a data mining service for clients. Participants achieve a deeper understanding of PwC management's strategic intent. The finalists are coached by partners for even more in-depth socialization. The results have been encouraging – strong participation and the implementation of innovative ideas.

We've observed that the notion of involving younger generations in strategizing is a recurring one in organizations using strategic conversations. This reflects management's realization that the best generation X and Y employees demand to have more say in shaping the organization, it's their *quid pro quo* for engagement and loyalty. And smart management also realizes that today's younger employees embody a different way of thinking about work and life – more collaborative, more social, more networked and less accepting of hierarchy – and that is already affecting the products and services that companies produce. By involving younger employees in strategizing, companies can anticipate these trends better.

KBS+'s embracing of the Hyde Space, a major business model innovation and significant investment, proposed by two of its youngest employees, is the embodiment of this type of thinking. This in no way means that the young employees were left to their own devices. In strategic conversation fashion, senior management was involved throughout, making sure that it fully understood what was being done and to offer encouragement and advice to ensure that the implementation was relevant to KBS+'s business.[4]

It is no surprise that in countries where the proportion of youth is the highest, progressive companies are especially assiduous in involving younger employees in strategizing. India-based global IT services giant Infosys created what it calls its Voices of Youth, panels of high-potential young employees that participate in strategy development activities. Infosys Chairman N. R. Narayana Murthy instituted what he calls the "30/30" rule, which stated that for strategizing meetings at least 30 percent of participants should be under thirty years of age. Infosys also worked to involve yet more young employees in the strategizing process – thousands by their count – through electronic tools like "strategy graffiti walls." It developed software to sift through responses to detect patterns in the massive quantity of submissions. Murthy points to these activities as being responsible for spurring strategic initiatives in the areas of health care, education, and others.[5]

As these examples show, strategic conversations can scale and help to bridge generational gaps. With care and skill, they can also help to bridge cultures in a way that can contribute mightily to firm success. Herminia Ibarra and Morten Hansen note that:

> [M]any companies spend inordinate amounts of time, money, and energy attracting talented employees only to subject them to homogenizing processes that kill creativity. In a lot of multinational companies, for example, non-native English speakers are at a disadvantage. To senior management, they don't sound as 'leader-like' as the Anglophones, and they end up getting passed over for promotions. At a time when innovations are increasingly originating in emerging markets, companies that allow this to happen lose out.[6]

They write about how French food company Danone works to remedy this situation at their annual review sessions. They quote CEO Franck

Riboud: "We spend a fortune on interpreters so that being less articulate in English is not a barrier. Some of our executives have even presented their business case in native dress. This helps us steal away talent from competitors where those who don't speak perfect English get stuck."[7]

EMC is similarly committed to involving all their employees in strategic conversations regardless of geography. Like many large, global companies, it started developing overseas research centers as a cost-saving device. But by the mid-2000s, EMC executives realized that the real advantage of their offshore presence was that it gave them access to people in the middle of dynamic markets in places like India, China, Israel, and Russia.[8] These markets exposed the company to a rich set of new opportunities and ideas, innovations that often had applicability in other EMC markets.

To take advantage of this potential, EMC needed to attract and retain the best talent in countries were employee loyalty was often fleeting. EMC began to offer something that the companies in their native counties rarely did: senior management support for local initiatives and ideas. This was highly attractive to employees who were more used to the traditional command and control management styles in their home countries. EMC created local Centers of Excellence (COEs) that established clear channels of communication between headquarters and the overseas offices for senior management to make their strategic intent clear and for locals to promote their ideas across the organization. According to some of the people to whom we spoke at EMC, if anything, these offshore offices were more innovative than the ones in EMC's headquarters in Hopkinton. Peter Madany, a manager within EMC's Unified Storage Division and one of EMC's Distinguished Engineers, described the COEs as "hothouses of innovation." He explained that, whereas in Hopkinton each company division tends to be in another building and interaction is rare, offshore you often have all ten company divisions in one building, leading to more cross-functional idea generation. The diversity of experience combined with commonality of purpose is powerful.

This is a key point. The purpose of strategic conversations is *not* to homogenize the discussion, to gloss over differences or deny how employees experience their work. Just the opposite: these differences are celebrated as providing solutions to the business model puzzle, offering novel and unexpected ideas for expanding the business' opportunity space and for parrying threats to existing lines of business.

This celebration of diversity has contributed to an attitude of "coopetition" according to Madany. The different COEs compete to have the most ideas adopted company-wide while at the same time sharing ideas through a collaboration wiki developed by someone from the Shanghai office. Like painters in the Renaissance that competed with each other not by denigrating each other, but rather by trying their best to top the other's latest masterpiece, EMC has created a powerful innovation dynamic.[9]

How do organizations successfully create effective strategic conversations that span geographies, generations, and cultures? From our observations, there are several commonalities.

- The environment for strategic conversations is architected and driven by an "intrapreneur" dedicated to creating an organization in which they, and all entrepreneurial employees like them, can thrive;
- the strategic conversation is informed by an enterprise-wide, social networking mindset;
- there are clear rules for discourse, and enforcement of these rules relies mostly on social pressure (soft governance) rather than top-down enforcement;
- electronic interaction is supplemented by periodic face-to-face meetings;
- special attention is paid to ensuring that middle management is supportive;
- intranets are conversation-rather than document-centric.

The first thing that can be said about starting strategic conversations that connect geographies, generations, and cultures is that it's not a task for the faint of heart or for those who can't dedicate significant time to the effort. The organizations we've observed that have had success have all had an intrapreneur champion who drove the program relentlessly. This person is generally high enough in the organization to be able to communicate directly with senior management, but not so high up in the organization as to have senior management responsibilities that would distract them from the effort. As such, they (and their staff) act as interlocutors between senior management and employees, helping both to sharpen their communication skills.

For instance Mitra Best sits on PricewaterhouseCoopers' Strategy Team while being point person for several different types of strategic conversation initiatives. She, and her staff of ten, provide the glue to make the following firm-wide programs work:

- PowerPitch – the American-Idol-like competition described earlier. Focused on involving younger employees in developing new business ideas, Best guides partner mentors to prepare contestants to hone and deliver their presentations and to navigate the organization.
- iChallenge – an internal crowdsourcing platform that presents challenges raised by senior management. Best and her team work with senior management to formulate the challenges to improve the number and quality of responses, while working with employees to create awareness and provide feedback on submitted ideas.
- iPlace – an idea management platform that's available 24/7. Everyone can see and vote on ideas. It is a managed space – Best's team reviews the ideas offered every 30 days and makes sure the most promising ones get management attention.
- DoItYourselfIdeas – a part of PwC's intranet dedicated to addressing everyday challenges for ideas that don't require investment (e.g., how can we better reach clients in a particular geography or industry with PwC thought leadership material). Best and her group curate these ideas as well.

When we asked Best why she became involved in fostering strategic conversations in the firm, she gave an answer that was typically personal for these intrapreneurs:

> I'm an entrepreneur and software engineer and when I initially took a job with PwC I was looking to experience what it was like to work for a very large company. After two or three years I expected to leave PwC and start a company, perhaps using the insight at the firm to prepare me to serve large clients. Instead I have been here for 13 years now. Why? We have a great flexibility program for family work-life balance, a strong brand, what tipped it was that I was able to continue to be heard and to make a difference.[10]

Her goal is to make the opportunities she found at PwC pervasive. She remarked, "Hero maker is my job! I want talent to rise to the top; to ensure that their efforts are recognized and communicated. I want to reduce the barriers to innovation so that our intrapreneurs can be as successful as I've been."[11]

Julie Gilbert at Best Buy, the force behind the WOLF Packs innovation communities described in Chapter 6, similarly wanted to enable employees, with a focus on women, to be able to benefit from the same opportunities to be entrepreneurial as she had enjoyed (she had been leading Best Buy's marketing effort targeting the affluent technology enthusiast segment). Her passion was derived from the realization that the talents of Best Buy women weren't being tapped effectively. Women didn't enjoy support in the male-dominant culture, and perhaps worst of all, it was women managers who were often the worst offenders at preventing promising female employees from advancing. She surmised that this unrealized potential could be a huge boon to Best Buy with the right encouragement.

She knew from the start it would require full-time effort to make the necessary changes. She was able to convince then-CEO Brad Anderson to make WOLF her sole focus. In her new capacity as Senior Vice President: Wolf; Enterprise Innovation & Learning she could effectively act as a bridge between senior management and employees. Gilbert mobilized employees (male and female, WOLF Packs were required to have male members to ensure that their work would be relevant to all) in a series of emotionally charged and lively meetings that eventually involved thousands of employees. From the first WOLF event in 2005 and throughout the program, Gilbert brought Best Buy executives to these meetings so that they could hear what participants were saying and to give participants exposure to senior management's thinking and encouragement. CEO Anderson attended the first event, and feeling the energy in the room reportedly told Gilbert "You have started a fire that no one will ever put out!"[12]

Chuck Hollis came to his role in a different way. Rather than seeking to create something new like Best and Gilbert, he became a strategic conversation evangelist to preserve something he felt was being lost. In the mid-2000s, Hollis' intrapreneurial instincts were troubled by the direction he, and others, saw EMC going. What had been a hard-driven but very entrepreneurial company was, as it grew, becoming increasingly bureaucratic and political. Hollis related that many employees by the mid-2000s had begun saying, sardonically, that EMC2 really meant "Email, Meetings, and Conference calls squared." Employees were looking up (for direction from their superiors) rather than forward to pursue business opportunity. Employee satisfaction was dropping and the organization wasn't scaling effectively. And while he didn't give up his role as the Chief Technology Officer for Global Marketing, he modified it so that he could dedicate significant effort to what became EMC's social networking proficiency initiative. Hollis' mission became recapturing EMC's storied past when it was small and hungry and every employee was expected to contribute to innovation and take responsibility for solving the problems at hand.

Hollis, of course, realized that what had worked when EMC was a smaller and younger company wasn't going to succeed now that it was a global behemoth. The "just get it done" ethos of the early days would create chaos in a company which today has over 60,000 employees. And in any case, those days were far behind the company. "Many aspects of our traditional corporate culture can be described as 'command and control.' And certain audiences within EMC's management team tended to be more comfortable with highly controlled internal flows of information."[13]

While any change effort is difficult, Hollis had an advantage. Most people at EMC knew that the status quo was untenable and had a niggling sense that there was a better way. Hollis writes:

- As our company had grown in complexity, simple processes such as communication, interaction and collaboration across many dozens of business units were becoming increasingly difficult. As a result, most people in the organization didn't exactly know what the rest of the business was doing. A sense of isolation and frustration was growing quickly within the company.
- Most people's calendars were filling up with meetings, concalls, remote presentations and inordinate amounts of email traffic. More and more important business activities required large teams to participate, and getting everyone to synchronize was slowing business progress.
- More progressive users of external social platforms were frustrated that EMC didn't understand what these new tools and capabilities could offer in a business setting.[14]

The problem of revitalizing employee engagement would require a new solution, but one that wouldn't be rejected as alien to its culture. Hollis and his team realized the emerging approaches, technologies, and attitudes of social media, Web 2.0, and Enterprise 2.0 could provide a useful frame.

"During 2004 to 2006, it was clear that something transformational was happening in our culture and our economy:

- Social sites and tools such as LinkedIn, MySpace and Facebook were exploding in popularity. These platforms were increasingly finding their way into business discussions.
- A few companies had discovered that communicating through blogging and discussion forums could be far more effective than traditional mechanisms.

- A new generation of internet-literate employees was entering the workforce, expecting the same kind of open access to information and conversation that they had become accustomed to outside of the workplace.
- More and more businesses were establishing online communities of aligned parties; these were proving to be incredibly effective engagement tools."[15]

Perhaps the social networking movement's mindset could promote strategic conversations and help them scale.

Hollis' insights about using social media as a frame for stimulating scalable strategic conversations proved highly fruitful and have been used by several of the organizations we've observed. The following enterprise social networking characteristics are especially germane for promoting dialog between senior managers and employees:

1. **Inclusivity and transparency**. Strategic conversations can only thrive when participants can share relevant knowledge. Some organizations have legitimate questions about such increased openness. PwC (and other professional services firms like it) must protect the confidentiality of client information and their financials, and they operate in regulatory environments that require complete segregation of certain practice areas. Hollis also noted that some managers at EMC had issues, fearing openness would lead to their revealing technical secrets in EMC's highly competitive environment. Nonetheless, both of these organizations, and especially EMC, have adopted a bias towards openness, and withhold information on an exception basis rather than the other way around.

2. **An open meritocracy**. In a social media world participants self-select based on their passion and time constraints. No one is forced to contribute. Hollis writes, "We did not use 1.0 nomenclature and terms such as teams, meetings, schedules and task forces. As a result, we discovered and engaged several dozen employees from around the globe who contributed significantly to

our initial thinking. Simply put: we used social media techniques to solve social media problems whenever possible."[16] Employees are rightly dubious of leaders when they are selected by management, especially when management isn't close enough to the situation to know who the real leaders are. It is common practice in organizations with successful strategic conversations to emphasize the word 'leaders' (employees who lead through influence over a network of people) over 'managers' (who have authority vested in them from their position in the hierarchy and are more concerned with control than supporting employee efforts).

3. **An enterprise, conversational focus.** Even though they are large, global organizations, EMC, Best Buy, the World Bank, and PricewaterhouseCoopers have all taken an enterprise view for promoting strategic conversations. They tend to avoid local solutions like eRooms and stand-alone SharePoint sites, which tend to proliferate but more often than not become "dumping grounds for someone's files." Social media platforms allow organizations to take advantage of scale and diversity of thought for crowdsourcing of new ideas and for creating teams on the fly. Best Buy's WOLF Packs, PwC's PowerPitch competition, the World Bank's concept of developing the science of delivery for poverty work, are all enterprise-wide initiatives. At EMC it is not uncommon for innovators from Shanghai, Mumbai, St. Petersburg and Tel Aviv to collaborate. Hollis calls this "the big conversation." EMC's platform for supporting strategic conversations, EMC|One, was purposely designed to be "conversation-centric vs. document-centric." Hollis writes, "Many people tend to think in terms of collaboration and information sharing in terms of documents and files. While it's clear that document-centric collaboration has its role within most organizations, we felt that there was a higher-order (and higher-value) collaboration model that focused on people: their interests and their dialogue."[17]

4. **Hierarchy-free, self-policing expression.** For strategic conversations to thrive and scale, they need to be direct, directed, and immediate. They can't wait for permission to traverse the chain of command. And it's impractical, and undesirable, to throttle conversations by assigning policing teams to ensure that rules of confidentiality and speech etiquette are followed. But this doesn't mean that successful strategic conversations are ungoverned. This means that individuals, and the community, need to self-police. We've already seen in Chapter 7 how Red Hat reined in harsh and inappropriate speech through community action (what we call 'soft governance'). At EMC, Chuck Hollis and his group steadfastly refused to adjudicate disputes involving people being offended by remarks or communities forming around topics "owned" by functional areas and who didn't want people invading their turf. "The natural reaction from the aggrieved individual would be to tell their manager, who would call that person's manager, and complain about the posting, with the expectation that the other manager would 'fix' the situation. We thought this sort of up-and-down behavior was a complete waste of everyone's time."[18] While Hollis and his team would coach the aggrieved parties, for instance on "learning how to disagree without being disagreeable," they have been largely successful in avoiding interventions. "We consider the ability to identify and resolve conflict – without appealing to authority – a key social media skill."[19]

5. **Even at scale, face time is essential.** As scholar and friend of the authors Laurence Prusak says, "the planes are still full for a reason." While strategic conversations can (and must in large, global organizations) occur via phone calls, emails, chats, posts to intranets, etc., their warmth and depth increase substantially when people connect in person. PwC's PowerPitch events involve teams working together with a mentor to prepare, and finalists all get together with the senior partners to share ideas. Best Buy's WOLF Pack gatherings were legendary for creating lasting bonds, and thousands attended. And EMC systematically flies its natural

leaders from all of its Centers of Excellence across the globe so that they can connect faces to names and deepen their relationships.

In practice, using a social networking approach has resulted in some pleasant surprises, as well as a few bumps in the road for the organizations using it. One surprise has been the ease of uptake with older employees. Generations X and especially Y have grown up with these concepts and naturally question the command and control model of management. What has surprised the intrapreneurs we've spoken to is how baby boomers have also joined in these conversations enthusiastically as well. Given an outlet, employees in their 40s, 50s, and 60s have participated in innovation communities and other types of strategic conversations, have blogged and posted, and have been happy to mentor younger colleagues.

One constituency often naturally averse to a social media approach is middle management. Used to being the conduit for knowledge between senior managers and employees, with the power that that position gains them, the social media approach can bypass them and threaten that power. Gilbert suffered taunts and even had her car vandalized by middle managers who perceived threats to their authority from her WOLF Pack activities. Hollis writes, "we were quite surprised at how important – and how reluctant – middle management was to our overall initiative. Individual contributors will only go so far in embracing new ways of doing things unless their management team is 'on board.' And middle managers can be categorically risk-adverse [sic]."[20]

The answer has been to redefine middle management roles to be more focused on providing mentoring and guidance and less on "management" and "control" (much along the lines suggested by Google's Project Oxygen, mentioned earlier). This is a radical change of role and organizational aesthetic for middle managers.[21] It falls in line with the powerful notion of "servant leadership"[22] – the focus on what leaders do for those they lead. Our book argues that the core function of middle managers, just like that of senior managers, is to select and shape the uncertainties that are met by those whose activities actually add value – the workers at the coal face.

The social networking approach for promoting strategic conversations across the organization is transformational – and takes a while. But the potential is massive. In our conversation with Chuck Hollis he noted that it took about five years for EMC to move from a top-down culture to one in which "the new normal is that every employee is expected to contribute to innovation. It's fundamental to how we train our 'leaders.'"[23] When we spoke to employees in Massachusetts, St. Petersburg and Shanghai, their engagement was palpable. They were all convinced that they could have impact in their respective areas far beyond what they were accustomed to in other firms. But healthy strategic conversations can't be taken for granted. As the Best Buy case illustrates, when senior management loses interest in them, they can quickly deteriorate.

For EMC, the engendering of enterprise-wide strategic conversations using a social media approach has spurred a deep cultural change with far-ranging implications. Not only have these conversations created a much more engaged and capable workforce, they have also significantly deepened relationships with customers – who find the organization listening to them in new ways. The topic of how strategic conversations can be used externally is the focus of the next chapter.

Who are your social media pioneers?

In most organizations today, at least one part of the organization has already been exposed to social media principles. Perhaps marketing is working to establish brand awareness and buzz with Facebook and Twitter. Maybe HR is already using LinkedIn to source and vet employee candidates? Oftentimes information technologists are interacting with open source organizations, which were perhaps the first to consistently use and embody the social media ethos.

- How can you make these social media pioneers examples to the rest of your organization?
- EMC and our other cases had specific problems they were trying to solve. How, specifically, could your organization benefit from using social media principles to enhance strategic conversations?
- What inhibits your organization making social media principles more pervasive?

9 Engaging the world outside in the conversation

> No man is an island entire of itself; every man
> is a piece of the continent, a part of the main;
> if a clod be washed away by the sea, Europe
> is the less, as well as if a promontory were, as
> well as any manner of thy friends or of thine
> own were; any man's death diminishes me,
> because I am involved in mankind.
> And therefore never send to know for whom
> the bell tolls; it tolls for thee.
>
> *John Donne, MEDITATION XVII, "No Man is an Island"*[1]

Almost every modern organization finds itself playing on a global stage, even if it never intended to. Today, as perhaps never before, it's critical to pay attention to the outside world because the speed of change has accelerated, bringing new threats and opportunities at an often bewildering pace. To be able to avoid danger and seize advantage in this sped-up environment, good ideas for bolstering and evolving the business model can and should come from everywhere, including players outside the firm.

As Peter J. Williamson points out, many of the assumptions about the way organizations compete, assumptions that have been with us for more than a generation, are rapidly losing their validity:

- It used to be that high-end technology could capture a price premium. Now, sophisticated GPS systems, once a technocratic luxury, are a me-too feature in many smart phones. Another example; the Chinese firm Dawning now embeds supercomputer capability – once only available to a few governments and very large corporations – into low-cost computer servers.

- Just a few years ago companies could expect to earn more for customization. Today offering bespoke products and services is no longer a sure-fire path to profits. 3D printing appears to be on the verge of allowing for the mass customization of just about any physical object – even handguns. And global giants like China and India are brute-forcing this advantage away. Williamson illustrates this point with the example of the Shanghai Zhenhua Port Machinery Company. It hired 800 design engineers, who earn salaries much lower than their western counterparts, to massively increase the number and types of products it offered to serve the custom needs of its port customers. Its German and Italian competitors typically have forty in-house design engineers.

- Companies used to be able to gain selling power by catering to niche markets. But by driving down the prices of luxury goods, new market entrants are popularizing what used to be the territory of the well-to-do. Williamson notes that wine chillers were once only owned by oenophiles, but became cheap and easily available to a broad consumer base. With business and technical acumen, Chinese appliance company Haier has captured 60 percent of the United States wine chiller market, selling its products through mass outlets like Sam's Club in the United States.[2]

These examples of the types of changes facing businesses today just skim the surface of the challenges facing businesses worldwide. But there is opportunity as well. As Williamson points out, emerging markets are growing two to three times faster than those in the developed world. Companies that can learn to serve these markets can reap significant rewards.

As powerful as strategic conversations are between senior managers and employees, for most companies working in a global context this communication channel will be necessary but insufficient. To prosper, businesses will need to extend their strategic conversations to customers, partners, and even competitors. By harnessing the knowledge and imagination of these constituents, organizations can significantly increase their understanding of the competitive landscape.

Extending strategic conversations to embrace customers and partners shouldn't be confused with the practice of making external strategy consultants the drivers of business model innovation. Recall our fourth Iron Law of Value Creation: "The benefits of business model innovation are best realized when the innovation is done internally." For innovations to be optimized for an organization's opportunity space, those who inhabit it need to contribute their understanding to the innovation's development. And for the innovation to stick and flourish, those who implement it must have skin in the game. Consultants can't have the same deep understanding of, or commitment to, the business as those who work within it every day. This is not to say that strategy consultants can't make valuable contributions. They can offer perspectives, frameworks, concepts, market data and analysis that would otherwise be unavailable to the firm. But they can do little more than point to the constraints to the employees' capacity for innovation. Our caution is that organizations ultimately falter when senior managers abdicate their mandate to be the drivers of innovation.

This chapter focuses primarily on the needs of the first two of our strategizing modes, Discovery and Judgment, the object being to reduce the knowledge absences the organization has chosen to engage – its strategy. We'll explore some of the ways that organizations have successfully engaged the outside world. We'll also offer some cautions about some of the pitfalls to avoid when working with those outside of the firm.

A powerful technique that's especially useful for organizations in sectors involving science and technology uses sensing and operationalizing strategic conversations to cultivate relationships with colleges and universities. Mid-sized Japanese pharmaceutical Eisai realized that in order to compete with larger companies it needed to do at least as well, if not better, at anticipating trends in health care. It could not afford to be caught flat-footed. To give it visibility into its environment, it has established small-dollar research agreements with schools in Boston, Massachusetts and Cambridge, England to help the firm keep abreast of new developments in science and regulatory affairs. Eisai scientists (who both teach and take courses) interact with top researchers and students from the schools. The payoff is rich: at very low cost Eisai is able to tap some of the best minds in their fields while also vetting and recruiting local talent. It has given Eisai the opportunity to start rich strategic conversations with candidates before they are even hired.[3]

Steve Todd, Director of EMC's Global Innovation Network, has used a similar approach. Each of EMC's seven Centers of Excellence (CoEs) – located in India, China, Egypt, Israel, Ireland, Russia, and North Carolina – has explicit end-to-end processes for establishing relationships with local universities and students. Engagement starts with high school students visiting the CoE on field trips. Sustained engagement starts in the first year of university with scholarships and continues with an internship program and mentorship until the most promising students are ready for conversion to a permanent position. Simultaneously, EMC participates in joint collaboration activities with academics.

To get a more granular view of how EMC's CoEs work, we spoke with Inga Petryaevskaya, New Business Development Manager for EMC in St. Petersburg. She told us that EMC was careful to shape their outreach efforts to match EMC's strategy with Russian strengths – in this case cloud and big data technologies. They created collaborative research programs within seven universities in St. Petersburg and four in Moscow. They have a high conversion rate of interns to employees – over 90 percent. The research programs are leading to potential start-up spin-offs as well as new directions for EMC products. Petryaevskaya sees these efforts leading to EMC being able to effectively participate in the rapidly growing Russian venture ecosystem.

Another effective way to stimulate external strategic conversations is to bring lead customers into the strategizing process. Engaging lead customers in business model innovation more effectively can help ensure that the company's direction satisfies customer needs while increasing switching costs and enhancing brand loyalty. EMC's St. Petersburg CoE has started down this path with RZhD, the huge Russian Railways company and a large EMC customer with unique needs. In a business model innovation instituted by Russian EMC salespeople, EMC engineers are now collocated with RZhD engineers in a joint lab where they are customizing EMC enterprise storage systems to RZhD needs.

Global information technology services firm Infosys also engages lead clients in their strategy-making process. They meet with clients individually and in groups to test strategy ideas and hear client suggestions for new directions. One of the results was that Infosys decided to increase its commitment to being a software developer as opposed to being just a service provider. It had already been developing basic operational software for Indian banks. Following client recommendations, it expanded the product line to include modules like consumer finance, wealth management, and Islamic banking, and in so doing has become a major player in the global market.[4]

During Julie Gilbert's tenure at Best Buy, the company had one of the most profound strategic conversations at the retail level that we're aware of. We covered some of the WOLF Pack story in Chapter 6. In early 2007, Gilbert began engaging the outside world in the strategic conversation by expanding the WOLF Pack concept to include female consumers, calling these Omega WOLF Packs. These teams worked with Best Buy's female employees, and were charged with nothing less than helping to reinvent the company. The teams generally consisted of ten to fourteen members from outside the company who, along with Best Buy employees and a subject matter expert or other innovation leader, would work together on a specific topic or project for ninety days, meeting for ten to twelve hours each month. The entire Omega WOLF Pack would meet periodically with the Best Buy business owner accountable for their topic, providing progress reports, getting feedback, and refining plans.

Besides being given a specific business topic on which to focus, Omega pack members were also given specific corporate roles to play, such as finance, marketing, or sales. This provided an exciting opportunity for the women participants, many of whom were stay-at-home mothers interested in rejoining the workforce, to learn new skills. The role-playing also helped to ground the Pack's work in business realities.

Over the course of eighteen months, Omega WOLF Packs expanded to ten cities in the US and UK, with twenty chapters of thirty to fifty female consumers each. The Omega teams were built in a grassroots fashion, with members recruiting other women over dinner or coffee by inviting them to an upcoming WOLF networking event. Gilbert focused on attracting influential women leaders in each community, in the belief that they would in turn bring their networks. In New York City, Gilbert even hired a female leader with an extensive network of personal connections to recruit women to the Omega network full-time.

Omega members benefited by building a network with other women leaders in their local community, gaining exposure to Best Buy executives and culture, and opening up possible new career opportunities because of these networks. In addition to the Innovation Teams, Omega members also got to participate in WOLF networking events, held once a month in their city, as well as quarterly WOLF GiveBack events designed to benefit local women and girls.

Gilbert knew that if Best Buy's women employees and customers were given a voice, they would bring their passion, and their networks, to the table. By actively soliciting the opinions and recommendations of female consumers, these Omega Packs enabled Best Buy to benefit from their insights and unbiased ideas and recommendations. We know the WOLF Packs resulted in increased purchasing from women, and greater brand loyalty. Internal Best Buy research showed that after participation in an Omega network, the percentage of women indicating Best Buy as their primary shopping destination increased from 13 to 60 percent.

But perhaps the best illustration of the success of the Omega WOLF Packs is the story of the Parker, Colorado Best Buy store. One of Gilbert's more ambitious experiments was to have female consumers have a major hand in designing a Best Buy store – optimized for women shoppers. In Parker, Colorado, the local Omega WOLF team worked with Best Buy corporate designers to do just that. The store opened in October of 2008.

Gilbert attended the first large event there and was surprised by the nearly 100 people who also attended. The thirty women who worked on the innovation team had told friends, co-workers and fellow church members, who in turn told women in their networks, about the Omega experience. One of these told Gilbert that they were excited by the prospect of a company that wanted to hear their ideas for how it could better serve women, and were eager to be heard. The passion and networks Gilbert expected were fully in evidence.

The store was successful, its business outcomes and overall customer experience metrics were fantastic. Even more telling, it outperformed a comparable Best Buy store less than two miles away.

All told, over the duration of the Omega WOLF Pack projects, over 1,500 members completed a ninety-day innovation project, and even more participated in networking events and GiveBacks. The Omega teams demonstrated the truth of Gilbert's hypothesis that, to be a great place for women to shop, you must first create a great place for women to work.[5]

Since leaving Best Buy, Gilbert has shown that this type of strategic conversation with female customers is generalizable. In 2012 she was approached by Chuck Cohen, the Managing Director of Benco Dental. Benco is the largest privately owned dental supply company in the United States, with revenues in 2012 of $389 million and a workforce of over 1,100 employees. Cohen, who is the grandson of the company's founder, noted that the gender makeup of the dental field was rapidly changing; today over 50 percent of dentists are women, with the percentage continuing to rise. Yet of his seventy-five dental hardware sales representatives, only two were women.

And the equipment they were selling was designed for men's taller frames and bigger hands. It was clear to Cohen that his company, and his competitors, were underserving what was becoming the largest segment of his market.

Gilbert recommended setting up an innovation community, which was named Lucy Hobbs (after the first woman to graduate from a dental school in America). The community included female dentists, Benco employees, and female consumers. The goal is to innovate the way dental care is delivered, including product design as well as dentistry offices' physical layout and processes. Like Best Buy's WOLF Packs, there was also an element of community service, 'give back events' designed to help those who have difficulties affording dental services. As of this writing, the Lucy Hobbs innovation community is just kicking off, but Cohen is optimistic. The events held so far have exceeded his expectations – over 5,000 people have signed up as participants. If this community can help Benco co-create the future of dentistry with his customers, Cohen expects his company to benefit greatly. Cohen told us that "even if this effort only translates to 200 basis points more in growth" it would be a great success.

Collaboration with partners is a type of business model innovation often used to gain access to markets, technologies, or capabilities at lower overall cost than would be possible without the partner. Such conversations can be especially rich when they engage actual or potential competitors. Partnerships provide the opportunity to learn more about the capabilities of partners and how they view the market.

Special care needs to be taken, though, when working with partners. As business writers Gary Hamel, Yves L. Doz, and C. K. Prahalad have pointed out, conversations with partners who may very well morph into competitors need to be carefully managed. Employees collaborating with competitors need to be instructed on how to be both humble and diligent. Japanese electronics manufacturers in the 1980s were particularly astute at learning from their partners (as are many Chinese organizations today). One senior Japanese executive told researchers that "Our Western partners approach us with the attitude of teachers. We are quite happy with this because we have the attitude of students." Alas for the teachers, the students learned all too well.[6]

Employee interlocutors should be instructed by senior management on how to converse with competitors so they don't give away the store. This illustrates how strategic conversations are not simply about what to say, they are also about what NOT to say – which is where the leaders' inputs can be pivotal. Some organizations in especially sensitive competitive situations smartly insist that important conversations with partners should be threaded through a single senior point-of-contact so that outbound information can be controlled and information about the competitor disseminated internally.

Nonetheless, strategic conversations with partners, even in competitive situations, can be immensely valuable. The adage 'keep your friends close and your enemies closer' applies to strategic conversations as well. External strategic conversations are useful for sensing serious threats to the organization. They provide a framework for looking at the world that employees and management can share, an effective mechanism for raising alarms. For instance, Toyota opened the NUMMI joint car manufacturing venture with General Motors in Fremont, California in 1984 partly because it wanted to ascertain if its partner would be capable of bridging the quality and production gap with Japan.

When they are informed and guided by management's agenda, these strategic conversations with partners can provide competitive intelligence with a high signal-to-noise ratio.

Involving partners can also be a powerful way to introduce new thinking into the strategizing process and to help vet strategy directions. Red Hat provides us another innovative example. Red Hat actively involves the open source community – the people largely responsible for developing the product that it sells and services – in helping it think about its strategy. The technology strategy team was able to tap into existing networks within the open source community, and in a valuable give-and-take, run strategy ideas by the community at large, while also continuing to expose themselves to new ideas and perspectives. Members of the external community were able to weigh in on ideas, which helped those in the open source development community better understand and appreciate Red Hat's strategic direction. It also helped Red Hat stay on top of market trends and directions, identifying next-generation technologies at very early stages. The whole process was very effective at distilling insights from customers and the market, as well as identifying opportunities.

Involving the larger community provided a viability testing ground for strategies (from Practice, the fourth mode of the Strategizing Cycle). Red Hat had the opportunity to observe community reactions to, and see potential unanticipated ramifications of, particular strategic decisions. Red Hat executives even went so far as to discuss strategy with leaders of other organizations, to ensure that it could achieve its goals without undermining the larger community. This open dialog with external stakeholders has helped Red Hat be nimble in responding to market changes, and remains a key component of their success. From February of 2008, when they instituted their new approach to strategic planning, to February of 2011, Red Hat's total net income increased nearly 40 percent, and their stock price more than doubled.[7]

The World Bank is coming to see their collaboration with in-country partners as vital to shaping their strategy for achieving poverty reduction. In Chapter 3 we described a 'chaordic strategic conversation' where the Bank successfully introduced a development model from Mexico City, conditional cash transfers, to Brazil. The program provided families with cash, which they could spend in any way they wanted, as long as their children attended school regularly and received the vaccinations the program required. The implementation of this program amounted to a profound modification of the Bank's business model. The Bank has shifted from being the possessor and arbiter of development know-how to acting in a humbler, more facilitative role, supporting, advising and convening, and increasing its focus on south-to-south knowledge transfers. And the Bank is increasingly focusing its funding at a more granular level, on projects that directly impact beneficiaries. The conditional cash transfers concept is now promoted by the Bank in over thirty countries with positive effect.[8]

The program was initially introduced locally by the Bank's Latin America office and, like many other innovations done at the local level, would probably not have been propagated across the Bank if it had not been so enthusiastically adopted by a huge Bank client, in this case the country of Brazil. Rather than leave innovation diffusion to chance, the Bank is now working to systematize learning from partners, both governmental and non-governmental. And it is finding it especially fruitful to interact with partners closer to beneficiaries – the poor whose lives the Bank is seeking to improve.

We spoke with Jan Weetjens, the Bank's Indonesia Social Development Sector Manager. Weetjens has oversight responsibility for a $1.5 billion a year development program meant to reduce poverty in over 70,000 villages and improve local governance. He also manages a nearly $500 million multi-donor Trust Fund that provides block grants directly to local groups at the district and village level for small-scale infrastructure, social, and economic activities.[9] One of the issues facing the Government of Indonesia, the World Bank, and the donors was how to make sure that marginalized people – such as street children, landless farmers, former sex workers, victims of domestic violence – really benefited from these funds. The World Bank agreed to work with national partners to address the issue. The Indonesian government had connections with community services organizations and had them administer the programs at the local level.[10] Serving these marginalized populations has always been especially challenging in a development environment. By partnering with local organizations, Weetjens and the World Bank fostered two-way learning: The Bank learned how to reduce red tape by relying on the procurement systems of the local organizations that work with these marginalized groups. At the same time, the local organizations working with the Bank learned how to scale up their existing efforts and strengthen their capacity to reach more people.

Another example where the Bank is actively working with partners in ways that will directly and indirectly affect its strategy is through its support of the Open Development Technology Alliance. The idea is to give partners and beneficiaries access to data, and the ability to contribute data, using simple mobile technology available to many, even in poor areas. (For instance, in Kenya nearly 30 percent of Kenyans use the internet and more than 80 percent have mobile phones.) With better data, both the partners and the poor can make better decisions, help monitor development programs, and be more in charge of shaping their own destinies. There are four areas of focus:

1. Citizen feedback for public service delivery. Connecting citizens and service providers in a collaborative partnership by establishing mechanisms that help citizens provide direct feedback on public services received and help support the suppliers of these services as they publicize and respond to this information.
2. Participatory decision-making. Harnessing information technology to help local governments or public service delivery agents involve citizens in key decision-making activities such as budgeting, prioritization, and allocation of service delivery.
3. Participatory monitoring. Facilitating the ability of citizens and/or independent third parties such as civil society organizations to use information technology to conduct monitoring of local public services (e.g., supervise projects, validate services, etc.) in order to increase transparency and support accountability.
4. Open data/open government. Making the currently available datasets about government and/or organizational activities, such as financial data, freely and openly accessible to the general public via technology-enabled platforms.[11]

The Open Development Technology Alliance facilitates the development of these types of applications. The Alliance helped to sponsor a "Water Hackathon," where partner and indigenous developers worked with experts to design and build water-related applications in Nairobi, Bangalore, London, and Washington, DC. Though these efforts are just getting traction, they are already helping government and civil society to monitor the functionality of water access points better with entry-level smart phones. Handheld applications include tools for remote activation of irrigation pumps, utility bill payment and flood warning.[12]

These efforts, where beneficiaries and local groups more actively participate in their own development activities, are already changing the way the World Bank thinks about its business model in new and exciting ways.

Some organizations have turned the external strategic conversations concept on its head. Rather than using strategic conversations to improve strategy, designing and supporting external strategic conversations *is* their strategy. One such organization is the Clean Air Task Force (CATF), a non-profit organization dedicated to decarbonizing the world's energy system to address global warming.

Before its attention shifted to climate change, CATF was a traditional public advocacy organization focusing on reducing air pollution and its negative effects through legislative and policy action, primarily in the United States. CATF prides itself on its fact-based and intellectually honest approach, supported by rigorous scientific research and analysis. For instance, it helped shepherd the development of rules under the Clinton and Bush administrations to cut smog and soot pollution from coal-fired power plants. The result has been a 70 percent reduction in smog and soot pollution from American power plants, which the Environmental Protection Agency has shown prevents thousands of premature deaths each year.[13]

With the advent of climate change and the threats it represents, CATF turned much of its attention to reducing global warming caused by rising levels of green-house gases in the atmosphere. It quickly became apparent that CATF's traditional approach wouldn't be sufficient. CATF's Executive Director Armond Cohen is fond of saying that the sum of the efforts to correct the climate problem will dwarf efforts like the Manhattan Project and the Apollo Moon missions, both in complexity and scale. Energy policy affects every human and government on the planet, thousands if not millions of energy-related enterprises, and is one of the foundations of all modern economies. Even though it has a massive installed infrastructure, the energy market is almost bewilderingly dynamic, with prices, fuel availability, and technologies constantly changing. At the same time, 87 percent of the planet's energy comes from burning fossil fuels such as coal, oil, and gas – which account for most of the world's warming emissions. Mature economies have seen demand level off; developing economies like those in China and India are rapidly adding coal capacity – as much as one United Kingdom's worth of coal-fired energy per year.

On one hand CATF's analysis of the situation was optimistic. It was becoming increasingly clear that there would be no need to completely replace fossil fuels like coal that presently generate much of the world's electricity – leading to today's utilities industry with its huge infrastructure – in order to significantly reduce green-house gases. Technologies already exist that can sequester the harmful gases these facilities emit. Other potentially affordable carbon-free technologies that can operate at market scale are being discussed to address increases in energy demand and to replace aging capacity, such as advanced smaller and safer nuclear sources, energy storage that could help wind and solar technologies provide power even when the wind wasn't blowing or the sun shining, and carbon-free liquid fuels. In China – the country whose energy-generating capacity is growing faster than any other – there is considerable interest in these technologies and a rapidly growing know-how to adopt them.

On the other hand, the exploration and development of these new, climate-friendly technologies was at best sporadic. For many energy companies the financial risk was simply too great. The time frames for proving and deploying new technologies, even if they worked, were long, while most energy company divisional managers were concerned with quarterly profits. Managers were incentivized to pay principal attention to their profit centers. Climate-friendly innovations would require embracing several different divisions within any one utility company, and would likely require partnerships with other companies. In addition, the costs were generally too high for any one divisional leader to shoulder alone.

Corporate-level energy company executives were likewise not motivated to pursue these new technologies. The value of early-stage R&D is generally difficult to appropriate; once the investment in perfecting a technology has been made others can often copy it at considerably less expense.[14] Finally, many executives weren't aware of opportunities because discovering them required crossing geographies, finding and vetting numerous small start-ups, and identifying still ill-defined opportunities lodged in academic and governmental institutions. The end result has been that many promising technologies either never make it beyond the concept stage or languish in 'the valley of death' between being successful in the lab or tested in pilots at scale, and build-out at commercial scale. The business model and technical innovations required to halt, and potentially reverse, climate change frequently fall into a massive, global 'white space' where no one feels compelled or enabled to act.

This situation is typical of the problems of innovating an organization's business model, and is one of the main reasons for employing innovation communities. Effective innovation communities can identify and act upon white space opportunities that depend on cross-functional thinking and cooperation, as we've already seen with telehealth at Boston Children's Hospital, the Hyde Space's new ability to engage clients at KBS+, or significantly increasing the size of Best Buy's share of the women's market.

We defined an innovation community as:

> A diverse team of employee leaders, empowered by and in constant communication with senior management, who collaborate on specific issues outside of their normal operational duties to promote cross-organizational business model innovation critical to the organization.

CATF created an innovation community dedicated to promoting early-stage technology that could address the white space and create business models that could shepherd viable ideas out of the 'valley of death.' They believed that once technologies were piloted at scale, the market, supplemented where appropriate by supporting policy, could then take worthy models to full-blown implementation. In effect their notion of an innovation community modified our definition to become:

> A diverse team of energy industry leaders, informed and assisted by CATF, who collaborate on specific issues outside of their normal business operations to promote cross-organizational business model innovation critical to creating a global energy economy that doesn't contribute to global warming.

CATF spins the strategy wheel used by companies to create their own strategies, but at the industry level – their strategizing helps create a low-carbon energy strategy for their entire business sector. CATF aims to influence the sector's actors through leadership that is derived from the strength of its ideas, the impeccability of its motives, and its persuasive powers. In the Discovery mode it is responsible for understanding the energy sector terrain profoundly through strategic conversations with industry players, academics, environmental groups, and governments. It was especially diligent understanding the fast-developing, sophisticated, and highly dynamic Chinese energy market. CATF then uses its Judgment, the second strategizing mode, to select the business models most likely to be successful. It then uses Persuasion to change the industry calculus to get industry players to act; to pilot these new models by 'putting steel in ground.' Its strategizing is then tested in Practice and is readjusted in Learning.

No question, CATF's innovation community model has been a challenge to implement; energy sector companies aren't used to this type of collaboration. Nonetheless it is producing results. Take the Texas Clean Energy Project (TCEP). Slated to be built near Odessa, Texas, and, as of this writing, awaiting financial close, it will be a

400 mega-watt coal-fired facility that will capture approximately 90 percent of the carbon it produces. The captured gases – as they are being sequestered – will be used in a process called enhanced oil recovery to extract crude from wells that otherwise would be too expensive to exploit. This is cutting-edge technology that, if widely adopted, could significantly impact green-house gas emissions.

Perhaps even more remarkable than the technology was the deal-making effort required to make the project happen. CATF first introduced the concept to Summit Power, a company with significant project management experience as a natural gas and wind developer, but without a track record in coal. CATF helped overcome this gap by introducing Summit Power to Future Fuels, a company that had a novel technology for turning coal into synthetic gas. Due to Summit's connections, Future Fuels was later acquired by Siemens, which benefited all parties. But in the design stage the project hit a serious snag as it became clear that the energy produced would be too expensive to be viable economically. To overcome this challenge CATF introduced the notion of making the plant "polygenic": besides electricity it could be designed to produce sulfuric acid and fertilizer as well, and so gain additional revenue. To further enhance the financial picture, CATF successfully advocated to the US Department of Energy to provide $450 million of funding for the carbon reduction technology implementation (thus reducing the risk for this first-mover). To increase the project's viability even more, CATF used its extensive Asian connections to secure partnerships with Chinese companies to help construct the plant and provide potential investments for follow-on projects. Finally, CATF worked with environmental groups to help them understand the benefits of the project and to head off the widespread resistance that often results when new coal-fired plants are proposed. Summit's surprise at the result of this intervention is evident in a presentation it gave at an energy industry meeting. Summit crowed that TCEP has received "ardent support from national environmental groups NRDC, EDF" with "no environmental opposition – not even Sierra Club" and has "received air permit without opposition in record time."[15]

CATF has taken a leadership role in the clean energy space in classic strategic conversation fashion. It has substantially expanded the opportunity space for low- and zero-carbon energy technology. The only difference from any other strategic conversation is that it is almost 100 percent externally directed, demonstrating the extensibility of the strategic conversation framework.

External strategic conversations create collateral benefits. For instance, they foster purposeful external networking by taking people out of their normal circle of colleagues and exposing them to new and valuable connections outside of the firm. The resulting networks, accessing both competitive intelligence and innovative ideas, are just one of strategic conversation's collateral benefits – the subject of the next chapter.

How well does your company exploit opportunities to learn from the world?

Does your company have the attitude of a student when it interacts with the outside? Identify changes to your business model over the past one to three years that have directly resulted from interactions with people outside of the firm. Do employees believe that it is their job to bring outside ideas to management's attention? Is there a well-understood process for doing this?

10 Creating a self-reinforcing innovation platform – collateral benefits

> Knowledge is more a matter of learning than of the exercise of absolute judgment. Learning requires time, and in time the situation dealt with, as well as the learner, undergoes change.
>
> Frank H. Knight, *Risk, uncertainty and profit*[1]

If the only advantage to strategic conversations were better strategies and more useful business models, that alone would be justification for using them. But strategic conversations confer other substantial benefits. Employee engagement, organizational alignment, learning, organizational agility, leadership development, talent management, and brand are all enhanced when strategic conversations are practiced consistently. Effective strategic conversations, and the strategizing process they engender, can become the business' central organizing principle. Activities that once seemed distinct – creating strategy, people management, change management, learning – converge into a seamless value-creating dynamic of managing and value-seeking under uncertainty.

EMC provides a prime example. We spoke at length with Jon Fay, EMC's Vice President for Executive Development. Fay, who holds a degree in economics from Harvard, originally came to EMC as a consultant to help with executive development. Fay recalls that CEO Joe Tucci figured out "before us mere mortals" that the tech industry works on an approximately fifteen-year cycle: first mainframes were dominant, then desktops, then the internet, and now cloud computing. Tucci's *coup d'oeil* has serious implications. The transition between cycles is often hard on incumbents. When mainframe dominance ended, IBM stumbled for a while and other

mainframe-oriented businesses were either absorbed into other companies or failed altogether.[2] Tucci was under no illusions that he, or
his EMC colleagues, could predict the future, but if the company could
get better at just peeking around the corner it could at least have a shot
at shaping events rather than being completely at their mercy.

As an avid business historian, Fay was intrigued by the challenge laid out by Tucci, and became a full time employee. Under his
direction, they took the lead in designing and developing EMC's
Executive Program. The first session was held in 2003. Fay wryly calls
the Executive Program "a wolf in sheep's clothing." It's an activity
that lives in a gray space because it's not just traditional executive
development (e.g., sending managers to an expensive executive education course), but also involves getting executives, directors, and
managers to think about the direction of the economy and the future
of the company and its markets. It was meant to be a forum for the
free expression of ideas and analyses. According to Fay, Tucci's
vague and bland name for the program was purposeful and in reality
quite clever. If he had called it a strategy forum, then executives
would have viewed it from the point of view of hierarchy and power
as they jockeyed for position. If he had called it a change management
initiative then the participants would have viewed their task as
constructing the change story for employees, developing the FAQs
and then the communication plan. The deliberate vagueness helped to
make participants less programmed and guarded.

Fay says that the program's topics have been very broad and
"hard." Tucci doesn't believe that past is prologue to the future, or at
least a future that would make EMC successful. The program held in
2006 was code-named "Mars Invades!" It focused on potentially dis-
ruptive competitors, like Amazon, Google, and Apple, companies that
didn't even appear on most data storage industry strategy maps at that
time. (The iTunes store had only been introduced in 2003.) EMC
invited retired Marine Lieutenant General Paul Van Riper to stir their
thinking. Riper had gained fame when, in a simulated war game set in
the Persian Gulf, his team used swarms of small, inexpensive speed

boats complemented by a barrage of land-based missiles to sink six-teen major warships belonging to the team representing the United States Navy.[3] Tucci didn't want his large company to be an aircraft carrier that ended up on the ocean floor. The war game was a good analogy to the type of asymmetric threats that Tucci felt EMC was facing. Stimulated by Tucci's insights and Van Riper's war stories, EMC executives were able to loosen their operational mindsets and the easy conviction that battling against current competitors would be sufficient. They began to think about the future with new openness and vigor.[4]

Each year the EMC program addresses a different theme: big data, the cloud, etc. To set it up Fay's team does extensive pre-session preparation over six months (Discovery as its strategizing mode), collecting data, and trying to identify trends. But after all this work the resulting framework remains relatively inchoate. EMC business unit leaders are a hard-driven bunch and generally not comfortable with uncertainty; but that is the point. It is up to these leaders to deal with uncertainty and the knowledge absences that impede their progress towards the organization's goals, to arrive at consistent and compelling direction (Judgment in our model).

The Executive Program starts with the most senior executives. Their job is to come up with the broad outlines of what "World War IV," as Fay described it, is going to look like and the potential object-ives that EMC should pursue. The second session is larger, with about thirty executives in the room. This group drills down on the broad outline and a picture of the strategy begins to emerge. The third session refines the vision. By the fourth session a tight picture of industry direction emerges, with value migration flows and market control points clarified.

At this stage approximately 160 of EMC's top people – the CEO team, EVPs, and VPs – have contributed to the now-gelling strategy. The next stage of the process involves discussing the strategy map with directors, teasing out how they will pitch the new direction to customers, and the resourcing choices that will be required in order to

implement it. The conversation is still two-way, but has become more focused. Senior management learns what it will mean to implement the strategy at the coal face. Directors are exposed to senior management's view of the industry and forced to think about how it applies to how they run their operations. Overall, Fay's group puts on about 50 2-day sessions around the world, reaching about 1,200 directors. Finally, they reach out to another 1,000 managers in condensed, 1-day programs. Executive Judgment is then put into practice as 'organizational fractals' – localized versions of the executives' strategic intent.

Fay says that it has taken about ten years to make this model work well. A meticulous planner, Fay remains uncomfortable with the process because the concepts are so vague and messy at the start. He is also candid about the personal challenges: "it's a bit of a tight wire act because we really don't have all the answers. As an academic and consultant – it's unnerving, it's unlike anything I've ever done before."[5] He notes strategy making and changing requires personal courage. If you're being honest, you have to tell others you don't know all the answers and have to make judgment calls. Helping executives be comfortable with situational uncertainty has been, and remains, a struggle. The 'old' EMC was a bare-knuckle culture where admitting to not knowing was viewed as a sign of weakness. From the beginning, Tucci and Fay emphasized 'Vegas Rules': what happened in the Executive Program stayed in the Executive Program. It took years, not months, to get the executives to loosen up. But now the program has generated some comfort with indeterminateness and the culture has undergone a fundamental shift. Much like Chuck Hollis' effort to loosen EMC's command and control culture from below with a social media way of thinking, the Executive Program has fostered T-shaped strategic conversations that have transformed EMC from an almost purely command and control culture to a more collaborative and reflective one. According to Fay, these changes are now baked into the business' processes and sustainable.

When we asked Fay whether leadership, strategy, and learning have converged at EMC, he answered in the affirmative – emphatically.

Without this kind of open leadership, there isn't the experience and courage to make decisions and the skill to persuade others to follow, which are essential for strategizing. Executive training that is not tightly tied into the business' strategy is just too low-octane to be useful. Through the Executive Program, thousands of managers have learned about EMC's industry and about management, about communicating effectively, and, most importantly, about what it really means to be a leader, all in real time while doing real work. It is their own business school wherein their teachers are their own managers, and their peers, enriched with selected outsiders like General Paul Van Riper.

Do the financial and opportunity costs of the Executive Program make for good investments? On the one hand the Executive Program is expensive in terms of time and travel. On the other, it is more or less paid for out of everyday operating expenses. As our third Iron Law of Value Creation states, "[c]ompanies must continually update their business models, so management must be perpetually entrepreneurial." The Executive Program is an ongoing cost of doing business, not an incremental discretionary expense. Not doing it could prove to be a crippling underinvestment in a core business function; like deciding not to pay for accounting.

As we've seen, organizational learning is a key collateral benefit of strategic conversations. So is alignment – the rich conversations engendered by the Executive Program create buy-in and understanding across management levels. All this has led to "strategic acceleration," which Fay calls the real business payoff. Today, EMC is able to find its strategic direction, align staff, and implement strategy faster than ever before, even as it has grown greatly in headcount and revenue.

The connection between strategic conversations, especially T-shaped ones, and executive learning, organizational learning, and alignment exists because strategic conversations are a form of work-based learning. Both GE's and SUPERVALU's programs fit the profile of T-shaped strategic conversations with strong work-based learning roots. General Electric created its Business Manager and Executive Development Courses at its Crotonville training center in Connecticut to help its top managers think about how to improve the business. For instance, a session in the late 1990s focused on how to approach the Russian and Mexican markets. The business decisions made were important, but the participants reported that it also served to teach managers what was really meant by business model innovation within the context of GE values and culture.[6] At food retail giant SUPERVALU, thirty mid-level and director-level managers each year – representing all major corporate functions – were assigned key strategic issues selected by executive staff. Teams met 'virtually' at least weekly, and in person four to five times during the span of the program as they worked out a strategic challenge.[7]

An early adopter of this work-based learning model was ARAMARK, whose story we detailed in Chapter 3 to illustrate the T-shaped model of strategic conversations. ARAMARK employs approximately 260,000 people worldwide and since 1998 has consistently ranked in the top three in its industry (diversified outsourcing services) on Fortune Magazine's list of the "World's Most Admired Companies." Its Executive Leadership Institute (ELI) was established to create the kind of mental spaces where managers could think about strategy and interact with senior management. In its ten years of existence, ELI involved hundreds of ARAMARK's managers in "action projects": time-limited assignments given to a cross-functional group of managers. Managers compared notes about what they had seen while serving customers and while working with suppliers and partners. They explored new ideas for making improvements (or addressing threats) to existing businesses and creating new businesses. These T-shaped strategic conversations established continuous cycles of learning that have significantly increased ARAMARK's adaptability and flexibility.

Another important collateral benefit of strategic conversations is raised employee passion. This may seem like an indefinable metric for creating value, but it's not. Whether we were speaking with employees from huge technology firm EMC in St. Petersburg, Russia, or cutting-edge advertising firm KBS+ in New York City, or a YMCA in a small town in Eastern Canada, or boutique software development firm Rite-Solutions in Rhode Island, the energy and engagement is the same. The passion of Best Buy's WOLF Pack members was legendary. Strategic conversations have given these employees an understanding of the broader context of their work and the opportunity to shape their own work, and the larger company.

Deloitte's Center for the Edge has surveyed other corporation's employees across a wide set of industries globally to see what percentage classified themselves as passionate, engaged, passive, or disengaged at work. The percentages vary across industries – the energy sector had the highest percentage of passionate employees at 27 percent, insurance was the lowest at 18 percent – with an average of about 23 percent in 2010. These numbers matter, because passionate employees are much more likely to exhibit two important behaviors than are disengaged employees: "questing" and "connecting." Questing employees appreciate challenges, seeking them out, and actively look for ways to improve their own performance. They see the unexpected as an opportunity to grow and learn, to surprise themselves and the business. Disengaged or dispassionate workers, lacking a questing disposition, are more likely to experience challenge or pressure as stressful, and this can lead to burnout. The connecting characteristic represents a desire to network with others whose experience and insight is relevant to the employee's work, and will aid their efforts to meet challenges and improve their own performance. For example, connecting may show up as conference attendance, reading trade journals and blogs, or social media activity with other professionals. Being connected involves the employee in an increased number of knowledge flows. This is directly relevant to our second Iron Law, which stresses the importance of more and better knowledge flows. Passionate workers are naturally eager to quest and connect, as much as twice the level other workers do. These behaviors create value, both for the individual and the organization as a whole, as they promote organizational agility and the ability to innovate the business model.[8]

But how, in an era when employee loyalty is at all-time lows, can organizations retain these invaluable passionate employees, those that will quest for business model innovation and connect to the concepts and people that will bring the necessary knowledge to bear? Here, the answer is a bit circular, yet hopefully encouraging: passionate employees, those engaged by strategic conversations, are much less likely to leave than the passive and disengaged. Recall Mitra Best, PricewaterhouseCoopers' US Innovation Leader. When she first joined the firm, she had only planned to stay two or three years. Now she is into her second decade with PwC precisely because of her passion for her work. At Best Buy, within eighteen months of introducing WOLF Packs to the company, female employee turnover declined by 5.7 percent – a significant change, because employee turnover costs the firm real money in training and lost productivity. According to Gilbert, this reduction saved the company about $5 million in training and recruitment costs, which was more than the entire WOLF budget.[9] Data from Deloitte's Center for the Edge supports these anecdotes. Disengaged and passive employees are far more likely to want to leave their jobs than passionate ones.[10]

One way to keep employees passionate is to coach them. In Chapter 7 we referred to Google's Project Oxygen, which used advanced data analysis tools to identify their best managers and distill the traits and practices they had in common. Of Google's eight guidelines for good management that resulted from this study, the one ranked first was "be a good coach." Many of the organizations which practice strategic conversations bake coaching into their process. PwC's PowerPitch competition includes significant coaching of the young contestants by firm partners. WOLF Pack participants received significant mentoring on how to do presentations to senior management, how to think strategically, and how to take on business roles that would have not have been part of their normal duties. Innovators at Boston Children's Hospital are coached on business language and how to pitch their ideas in business terms. Participants with promising innovations receive help with working on the complex web of constituents – finance, regulations, insurance companies, physicians, vendors, partner institutions – so that they can negotiate the hurdles to success.

Likewise, in the innovation competition initiated by KBS+ CEO Lori Senecal the participants received coaching on their presentations. The competition winners also receive significant guidance as senior management help them bring their ideas to fruition. For instance, Mark Jensen and Nick Vidovich's Hyde Project received advice directly from President Ed Brojerdi and Co-Chief Creative Officer Izzy DeBellis. KBS+'s supercharged culture has created an almost insatiable desire to learn more about how innovation works. Based on this, Darren Herman, President of KBS+ Ventures, collaborated with other venture capitalists, including heavies like Tim O'Reilly, to write *kbs+ Ventures: Creative Entrepreneurship*, a book he uses as a text for teaching KBS+ 'fellows,' self-identified employees who want to learn about the theory and practice of start-ups.

Strategic conversations, by fostering dialog among innovators irrespective of an organization's hierarchy, expose talent that otherwise might not have been visible to management. Warren Buffet famously wrote that "you only find out who is swimming naked when the tide goes out."[11] Strategic conversations lower the tide on hierarchy, and as the waters recede senior management often finds that it is unfamiliar with the business' innovative, passionate, and best-dressed bathers. Innovation leadership is remarkably emergent. General Electric gives managers stretch assignments, and they team up with other managers from different areas of the organization to address business challenges. Their progress is carefully monitored and their ideas are presented to senior management, often to the CEO.[12] Similarly, SUPERVALU's management teams are vetted. Because their assignments are so intense and can last months, managers at both GE and SUPERVALU give more responsibility to their subordinates, helping to prepare them as potential successors.

Thus talent management is often an important collateral benefit to strategic conversations.

We've seen how strategic conversations, as cross-organizational problem-solving crucibles, can build enduring social networks that facilitate knowledge exchange and promote organizational learning. EMC's Centers of Excellence, Best Buy's WOLF Packs, and KBS+'s Hyde Space were designed to spawn connections, both internally and with customers and partners. For instance, based on the WOLF Pack work, Best Buy established direct connections with customers like their "moms on the run" through social media like Twitter.

Sometimes the network-enhancing properties of strategic conversations become their primary goal. In 1999, the pharmaceutical company AstraZeneca, following the merger of Astra AB of Sweden and Zeneca Group PLC of the UK, created innovation communities to tackle the huge challenge of realizing the merger's benefits. Angela Hyde, then Vice President for Global Learning and Development, initiated the Growing Our AstraZeneca Leaders (GOAL) program to help integrate the newly formed company's 600 top managers. Each of these managers – most of whom were running significant businesses – participated in innovation communities of approximately twenty members each, that purposely combined managers from Astra and Zeneca. The program spanned four to six months and focused on the issues of integration, organizational effectiveness, and leading across borders. Even after the program was officially ended, many of the groups continued to meet because the bonds formed, and the value created, were strong and personally valued.[13]

We've been touting strategic conversation's power to accelerate growth by facilitating change. But how do strategic conversations and the strategizing techniques relate to change management? The difficulty of effecting and managing change – a critical issue in a world that constantly demands it – is deeply frustrating for senior leaders who don't use strategic conversations. Creating strategy at the senior management level, while comfortably cloistered with bright and amenable consultants, can seem a pleasure. But after intense and passionate sessions with "people who get it," enthusiasm often turns into grim discouragement as they begin the long march to convince the remaining employees. Many associate the emergence of change management with the business reengineering processes spearheaded by gurus like Michael Hammer back in the 1980s. Consultants would come in, develop a new strategy, and then it fell to senior management to convince the employees to work with them to implement the changes chosen. Given the lack of employee involvement in the process, it's not surprising that management's efforts were often met with indifference at best, sometimes with outright resistance. Reacting to the high failure rate of strategic change efforts, the change management discipline was reborn in the mid-1990s.

Unfortunately, such change management still didn't see the top-down nature of these strategy decisions as a problem. Rather, the problem was 'resistance', employees' recalcitrance, and their reluctance to accept their managers' superior judgments. Descriptions and definitions of change management reflect this mentality: "minimize resistance,"[14] "shift people from a current state to a desired one," "keep the effort under control."[15] None of this sounds like fun; and it wasn't successful. When change management was reintroduced twenty years ago success rates were low – about 30 percent. The rates today – as if reflecting some universal constant – remain at 30 percent.[16] Change management has become business strategy's catalytic converter. Nobody likes it. It's an expensive, energy-wasting, end-of-pipe solution to a problem that in a perfect world wouldn't exist.

So, is change management really a necessary evil? From our interviews and observations, it is clear that organizations that use strategic conversations have effectively eliminated, or considerably reduced, their need for such change management. They are achieving change faster, with better decision-making under uncertainty, and with greater staff engagement. When we asked Red Hat CEO Jim Whitehurst whether he used change management he answered with a flat "no." Red Hat's strategizing process was so inclusive that by the time decisions were ready to be implemented employees already understood the new direction and the reasons why it had been chosen. Not everyone agreed with the decision, but most agreed the process had been open and fair. Implementation is then able to move forward.

When Lori Senecal became CEO of KBS+, her vision was to transform it into a market-creating social media powerhouse. She soon tweeted the quote we used at the beginning of Chapter 3, "Change what works and change everything else."[17] But she didn't use change management. Like a gardener cultivating her plot, she cultivated change, using her leadership to shape and enrich the KBS+ environment for staff-driven innovation. Her technology group became "Spies and Assassins," and quickly evolved from being a support group to being a driver of innovation. She blessed a venture capital fund that tracks early to mid-stage social media stocks, to create real options from KBS+'s knowledge of the area while growing that knowledge for the benefit of KBS+'s clients. As we described in Chapter 6, she held a competition for ideas, and awarded two of her most junior staff the opportunity to create the Hyde Space. She also supported the creation of KBS+ Action Sports, whose mission was to infiltrate the world of skateboarding and surfing. Her list goes on, all accomplished in three years. All without change management.

Innovation can be fraught with challenge for institutions like the Boston Children's Hospital that operate in a complex and often risk-averse business environment. Change threatens established practices, and comes with serious risks to reputation in an industry where reputation matters greatly. Nonetheless, the hospital has created a matrix of support to foster change. Potential innovators have been given access to mentorship, grants, IT resources, and ultimately, decision-makers. As we've seen, the hospital has been rewarded with innovators like Dr. David Hunter seizing the opportunity. The complex telehealth program to treat eye disease in premature babies is now in pilot. Its success will profoundly reduce the risk for affected babies and will lower system costs. Even though the changes are profound, the rollout plan doesn't include a complex change management regimen because there's no need: the insurers, nurses, financial people, and local hospitals are already on board.

How about at a giant company like EMC? Is change management still needed? Here the answer is mixed. Their Centers of Excellence, located across the globe, are generators of business model innovation and as such, these changes don't require much, if any, formal change management. And these innovations are finding their way back to EMC's headquarters in Hopkinton, MA in a process some have called "reverse innovation."[18] But when we asked Jon Fay, EMC's VP for Executive Development, whether EMC was ready to jettison change management altogether, his answer was more guarded than Red Hat CEO Jim Whitehurst's. Certainly the Executive Program and Centers of Excellence reduce the need for change management, but in a company as huge, complex, and geographically dispersed as EMC, Fay believes that change still needs oversight.

The last collateral benefit we offer is that strategic conversations help sell your brand. For instance, research has shown that an organization's reputation for innovation enhances the prospects of new offerings. As marketing guru David Aaker has remarked, "Customers reduce their natural skepticism about a new offering when it comes from a firm that has a perceived track record of innovation. Customers have a bias to working with firms they respect. At the end of the day, buyers don't want to analyze attributes of offerings and usually go with their gut."[19] Consumers are less apt to buy products and services from a company where innovation is held in check, where employees are supposed to do just what they're told, or are cynical about management's ability to lead, and feel trapped in a job where no one is interested in their ideas. On the other hand, turned-on employees create turned-on consumers. In a survey of 300,000 businesses, Gallup found that when employees were enthusiastic about their jobs businesses garnered 70 percent higher customer loyalty and 40 percent higher profits than when employee passion was low.[20]

We've observed organizations purposefully expose the workings of their strategic conversations to enhance their brands. KBS+'s Hyde

Space is a showcase for clients and prospects to observe the employee creativity and passion being displayed. EMC likewise showcases its employees when it embeds them with customers and interacts with potential employees through its mentorship programs with universities. EMC's 'social media' culture has encouraged growing numbers of employees to express their knowledge and passion to the world through blogs. (Unlike in many organizations where external communications are tightly controlled by a corporate function, EMC employees are free to express their ideas. This has led to a flourishing of blogging activity. We would argue that it's only because EMC has strong strategic conversations that it can trust its bloggers to stay on message.) Rite-Solutions, the 200-person software development firm in Rhode Island, has parlayed its bet on employee engagement into a branding bonanza. It's been written up in dozens of articles, including in the Harvard Business Review, and several books. This recognition plays a huge part in how Rite-Solutions sells to prospects.

Strategic conversations are their own reward. Nonetheless, the collateral benefits they impart to organizations that use them are significant, and should be actively exploited.

HOW TO ENJOY THE COLLATERAL BENEFITS OF STRATEGIC CONVERSATIONS

If, like most companies, you have more initiatives than you know what to do with, then don't add to the list. Indeed we sometimes define strategizing as learning when to say 'no!' Instead, deepen and enrich the initiatives already chosen with strategic conversations. These can become part of your always-running learning program, providing action learning opportunities that have a real impact. Likewise, strategy development processes like the Balanced Scorecard promote and benefit from strategic conversations for they powerfully inform its non-financial perspectives – the measures of learning and innovation, internal processes, and customer attitude.

11 Measuring the future

> I don't care how big and fast computers are, they're not as big and fast as the world.
>
> Herbert Simon[1]

Business model innovation isn't chemistry. Add two parts management attention, five parts employee participation, and three parts customer involvement today, repeat the next day – and the results are likely to be different. One day you make millions from pet rocks. The next day you flop with New Coke. A few months later you reintroduce the old formula and make many more millions with Coke Classic. Who knew?

As maddening as it may be, entrepreneurs depend on this type of uncertainty. Economist Frank Knight famously stated that without uncertainty, there would be no opportunity to make a profit. No uncertainty, no entrepreneurs (or entrepreneurial workforce). Perfect markets (in which economists argue there could be no profits) rely upon perfect information. Not to worry, entrepreneurs, there is no such thing. Markets are not perfect, and uncertainty abounds. But uncertainty often makes measuring the inputs, outputs, and, most importantly, outcomes of strategic conversations more art than science. Given this fundamental difficulty, what managerial measures are appropriate? Is it enough to believe in the irrefutable benefits of strategic conversations – perhaps based on a book you've been reading – and throw up one's hands and say it's not worth the effort to measure what is most likely un-measurable?

As tickled as we'd be that we had engendered such trust in the intrinsic value of strategic conversations, we would still caution with the well-worn adage that "you can't manage what you can't measure." A recent study of 30,000 US businesses by the US Census Bureau's Center for Economic Studies showed that those that had structured management practices focused on performance monitoring and targets had significantly better financial results than companies that didn't apply these types of measures.[2] Aptly, this study confirms statistically that, in fact, you can't manage what you can't measure, at least not well. So it wouldn't be prudent to just throw up our hands because the problem of measuring strategic conversations is thorny.

We've observed that four types of measurement have been applied to evaluate the strength, source, and value of strategic conversations. They are all valid, with different levels of precision and varying purposes:

1. Impressionistic and anecdotal
2. Experiments, natural and otherwise
3. Social network and textual analysis
4. Strategic conversation mapping

Impressionistic and anecdotal. For some, the benefits of strategic conversations are almost self-evident, even for the most hard-bitten. ARAMARK's Joe Neubauer has said that he believes his company wouldn't have had its profitable growth without the innovation communities sponsored by the Executive Leadership Institute (as described in Chapter 6). Chuck Hollis, EMC's Global Marketing CTO and the person who spearheaded his company's effort to adapt a non-hierarchical social media framework to promote strategic conversations, was sometimes asked to provide a return on investment (ROI) for his work, even though the incremental costs – his salary, a small staff, and the intranet software – were quite modest, especially for a company as large as EMC. Hollis told us "we learned to treat this as an understandable defensive reaction in response to a new situation, rather than a de facto demand for a business case."[3] Recall that when Hollis first began his efforts, EMC was becoming increasingly command-and-control-oriented, with all the attendant slowness and risk aversion. To many it seemed unlikely that it could scale further. So, Hollis argued for a different ROI: what was the 'Risk of Ignoring' the situation?

However, once EMC|One and its social media ethos started to take off, Hollis noted that even though they never "got a good handle on hard metrics," people didn't really show much interest in the numbers. Hollis puts it this way: "Why work to better understand numbers that weren't really needed or wanted?" (Though he cautions others that they probably won't be as lucky as he was. And as we'll shortly see, his colleague at EMC, Steve Todd, did take strategic conversation measurement *very* seriously.) How did EMC's social media approach to facilitating strategic conversations, bolstered by the EMC|One intranet, impact the business? Hollis noted several significant achievements in his farewell blog on the topic. He included faster realization of value from product launches, customer campaigns and more, due to improved engagement and dissemination of information; greater efficiency of communication and collaboration, such as by replacing conference calls and emails; an efficient social network (or "social computer," in Hollis' words) that could be tapped to answer questions or find resources; the ability to quickly coalesce engaged employees around topics of interest; and substantial changes in EMC's corporate culture.[4] Like Hollis, many at organizations using strategic conversations note important differences, albeit impressionistic, after their implementation. These conclusions rely upon managerial judgment – which isn't to criticize using judgment – just the opposite: it's what managers get paid for.

Experiments, natural and otherwise. In his book, *How to Measure Anything: Finding the Value of Intangibles in Business*, Douglas W. Hubbard provides a wealth of advice on how to assess phenomena that have generally been considered immeasurable – like the value of strategic conversations – and to do so at reasonable cost. Using his techniques, one can answer subjective questions like "Is 'strategic alignment' higher if the profit went up by 10% but the 'total quality index' went down by 5%?"[5] His techniques aren't for the faint of heart, especially if that college statistics course is a distant memory, but his suggestions may help strategic conversation advocates make their case to doubters.

The techniques used to measure intangibles are improving, and the ability to do so will only grow in importance as the economy becomes even more service-oriented, and thus less amenable to easily measured outputs. One example especially germane to strategic conversations is "what is the value of managing pathos?" In a particularly elegant experiment, Adam Grant, a professor at the Wharton School of Business, looked to see exactly how intrinsic motivation would add value to a business process. In particular, when applied to a call center at a college soliciting money for scholarships. Call centers are stressful places to work (rejection and verbal abuse are commonplace), and typically suffer from low employee engagement. The manager of the college's call center had already tried incentives like prizes and competitions, without much improvement in motivation or fundraising performance. Grant suggested a straightforward and inexpensive experiment. A student who had received one of the scholarships raised by the call center was brought in and the call center workers were given a ten-minute break to listen to the student talk about what the scholarship had meant to him.

Grant had, of course, hypothesized this intervention would have a positive impact on the call center employees. But even he was surprised by the magnitude of the results. A month after this visit, even though their call scripts remained unchanged, the student workers were spending more time on the phone and bringing in 171 percent more revenue. In a later study the increase in revenue reached 400 percent, and in other studies, merely reading letters from scholarship recipients led to an increase in the workers' fundraising performance. Making that emotional connection to someone who would benefit from their work significantly increased the call center employees' motivation and success.[6]

To our knowledge, none of our strategic conversation case-companies have experimented greatly with measuring the value of their conversations. Nonetheless, the weight of empirical data can be convincing even if cause and effect can't be established with scientific rigor. Many organizations that use strategic conversations note important differences in key indicators after their implementation. SUPERVALU reported 50 percent of their innovation community innovations were implemented. (They also noted that participant retention rates were higher than for those who didn't take part.) Japanese pharmaceutical Eisai has tracked how innovation communities significantly reduced the time it takes to put new ideas into practice.

Best Buy's WOLF Pack program, as we saw in Chapter 6, has a wealth of such data, showing increases in revenue generated by women, increased female market share, more female employees with lower female employee turnover, even improved brand perception. Obviously this data would be taken seriously by Best Buy's executives, even those not naturally disposed to the idea of strategic conversations.

The WOLF Pack case also provides some more scientifically valid data through natural experiments. For instance, female recruits increased by more than 37 percent in areas where WOLF Packs existed, compared to stores where there were none. Recall the example from Chapter 9 of the Best Buy store in Parker, Colorado, which provided a great illustration of a natural experiment. The store was redesigned by female consumers – Omega Wolves – in partnership with the corporate design team, and it outperformed a store just a mile and a half away, on both financial and customer experience measures. These types of natural experiments are generally more feasible in organizations with multiple comparable units of analysis, like Best Buy's stores. For many organizations this isn't possible, but other measurement methods are available. For example, companies with significant collections of textual and social network data can use it to understand the effectiveness of their strategic conversations better and, for large companies with global work forces, to find out who may be best to lead them.

Social network and textual analysis. One of the advantages of working for a large organization is the opportunity to be exposed to an enriching diversity of thought. Even though Chuck Hollis, who spearheaded the development of EMC's social media culture and its intranet infrastructure EMC|One, has not felt the need to apply metrics to his work, his colleague and sometime collaborator Steve Todd, Director of Global Innovation, has been dedicated to developing hard measures. As Hollis told us, "Steve Todd is formalizing the innovation culture and making it measurable."

Strategic conversations are inherently a network-change phenomenon, bypassing hierarchies and organizational boundaries to explore and bring into existence innovative business models. For this reason, Todd has used big data and social network analysis to understand the nature of EMC's strategic conversations better, and in a number of different ways.

Discovering the hot topics that currently figure in the employees' discussions has been one area of interest. Since employees are often closest to client needs, this data can be invaluable in signaling emerging market opportunities to senior management – a type of sensing and operationalizing strategic conversation. Todd has used a tool called the Stanford Topic Modeling Toolkit to visualize topic trends over time, applying it to analyze the thousands of entries in EMC's Innovation Showcase. He has also been tracking the top twenty-four topics under discussion for several years.[7] Analysis revealed that employment engagement was hot in 2011 – with a focus on benefits and productivity. As Todd put it, "EMC employees had quite a bit of interest in their relationship to their corporation."[8] Since then, big data and the cloud have come to dominate the employees' innovation submissions.

How can EMC take advantage of this window into the thoughts of its global innovators? Todd has worked with others to initiate innovation events and communications focusing on idea trends that weren't already being addressed in other forums. He used the names of the submitters to the innovation database and called upon them to speak or start innovation communities.

Another of his investigation areas has been how to improve the quality and impact of idea submissions. He had EMC Distinguished Engineer and Data Scientist John Cardente analyze a variety of parameters related to the submission of employee ideas. Some of the factors that went into the analysis of idea contest success were:

- How many people were on the submitting team?
- How many words were used to describe the idea?
- How many people external to the team commented on the idea and over what time period?
- How many sponsors (people posting specific challenges) were on the submission?
- How long before the deadline was the idea submitted?

These factors were then correlated with the success of the idea: was it selected as a finalist, was it a winner, and what resources were given to it? Cardente's analysis produced clear results. Successful contest ideas had the following characteristics:

- More detailed problem descriptions.
- More comments (indicating greater interest and perhaps better networks of collaborators).
- Later submissions (perhaps because they built upon the ideas of early submissions).

Large teams didn't make any difference. Based on this analysis Todd changed the instructions for visitors to the idea portal, stressing the importance of having a detailed problem description and of having colleagues comment on submissions to tap into the wisdom of the crowd. He also is considering running analytics on individual submissions in real time and then sending helpful suggestions like this one: "Successful entries have descriptions of 500 words or more. Your description may be too short. The contest ends in 30 days. Consider adding additional detail."[9]

A key problem for EMC was to identify, and promote, emergent leaders. If EMC was really to become a meritocracy where strategic conversations could flourish, then it had to be able to identify real leaders, those with the ability to influence networks of employees to innovate. Given its immense size and geographical dispersion, finding these people would be an enormous challenge. Todd decided to use social network analysis tools, powered by big data software, to find patterns in the thousands of presentations, intranet entries, meeting attendance, and other textual data produced by EMC employees. Using these techniques, patterns emerged, as did leaders. One such leader was Jidong (Roby) Chen from EMC's Shanghai office. The software identified Chen as being a key connector in two key research areas – big data and the cloud – with influence spanning Russia, Egypt, Ireland, India, the US, and Israel. Employees like Chen, once identified, are vetted and then often receive training as "innovation facilitators" and are given more prominent positions to recognize their contributions but also to further amplify their abilities to promote innovation.[10]

Strategic conversation mapping. Even under such uncertainty, some things *are* certain: nothing ventured, nothing gained. Unless your organization is placing bets, and doing so by involving a diverse set of perspectives, it can't innovate, grow, and be profitable. Which is why Strategic Conversation Mapping – the last technique for "measuring the future" that we shall describe – can be useful. It can help identify where business model innovation is, or could come from. Gaps can be addressed proactively.

Rosabeth Moss Kanter writes that successful innovators use an "innovation pyramid," with several big bets at the top that get most of the investment; a portfolio of promising mid-range ideas in test stage; and a broad base of early-stage ideas or incremental innovations.[11] This portfolio approach is common, and companies like Best Buy use it every day. We agree with the portfolio approach, but believe companies might do better by adding a couple of other measures to their toolbox. For instance, they can monitor the degree of cognitive diversity they are bringing to the business model innovation process. As our fourth Iron Law of profitability states, "the more relevant perspectives brought to bear, the more opportunity there is for innovation." Ensure a variety of people are looking at how to innovate your business model and you reduce the risk of mistakes and missed opportunities.

With this in mind, we've developed a diagnostic, Strategic conversation contribution map. Its purpose is simple; to highlight innovation sources and to identify key stakeholders who aren't contributing. Innovative business model initiatives are mapped from left to right, with the largest on the left (in this example, Business Model Innovation (1)) to the smallest (5). The wider the column, the larger the impact of the business model innovation (this could be captured as potential value, cost to implement, or some other metric). For each project, those driving it are noted, as are contributors. Hierarchy, area, or geography (not shown here) can be used as perspectives.

In the hypothetical example shown in Table 11.1, the hierarchical view shows that top leadership is driving most business model innovation. By function, R&D and the lead customer are the main groups driving business model innovations. The map shows that other important constituents – including staff, business units and areas like marketing, legal, customers, and information technology – aren't actively engaged in the process. This suggests a leadership issue that should be addressed using strategic conversation techniques such as innovation communities.

One variation of this mapping technique we've seen was how Steve Todd at EMC mapped key topics (ideas that could lead to business model or product innovations) onto geographies and onto individuals acting as "network connectors." Even if you don't have access to tools like the Stanford Topic Modeling Toolkit or Hadoop (a program Todd also uses for analyzing massive amounts of textual data), you can learn a lot by mapping different groups' involvement in strategic conversations, for the map quickly reveals gaps and under-participation, and can suggest new approaches.

The second measure we introduce is the Innovation attention map (see Figure 11.1). Its purpose is to reduce the risk that management is overly focused on maintaining current processes and products and ignoring future growth. The map shows how much of the organization's attention and efforts – at the enterprise, divisional, and functional levels – are dedicated to advancing the business model. It can

Table 11.1 *Strategic conversation contribution map*

		Business model innovations				
		1	2	3	4	5
Hierarchy	Staff		▨			▨
	Management					▮
	Leadership	▮	▮	▮	▮	
	Consultants	▨		▮	▮	
Function	R&D		▮			▮
	Marketing					
	Sales	▨				
	Legal					
	IT					
	B-Unit A		▨			
	B-Unit B					
	B-Unit C					
	University					▨
	Supplier					
	Lead Customer	▮				
▮			= Driver			
▨			= Contributor			

also help to identify underexploited opportunities. It looks at each funded business activity along two dimensions:

1. how much of the activity is 'maintenance' versus 'innovation';
2. the degree to which the activity has senior management's attention and is part of a strategic conversation, or is a 'local' or 'administrative' conversation unknown to senior management.

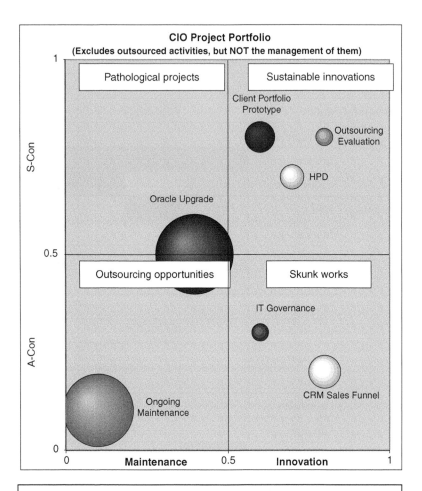

In Q1 13% of the cost of the CIO's portfolio is projects that are innovative *and* have senior management attention. Two projects are 'skunk works' (IT Governance and CRM Sales Funnel) – innovative projects that don't have senior management's attention and support, and may be ignored by the rest of the organization. The remainder are maintenance projects attracting little or no management attention.

FIGURE 11.1 Innovation attention map

In Figure 11.1 (a simplified version of a chart created by a CIO we worked with), each bubble represents an information technology project; the larger the bubble, the greater its budget. The CIO made this map to help ensure his IT department was a real partner to the business and not merely a cost center for keeping the firm's computers running and up-to-date.

The Sustainable innovations quadrant (top right) shows the project dollars being spent on innovations that have a high chance of benefiting the organization and which should therefore have senior management's attention. In Figure 11.1, 13 percent of the cost of the CIO's total project portfolio fits this description. The bottom right quadrant shows skunk works, innovative activities that take place out of sight, under the senior management's radar. As a result, these activities are rarely promoted to become sustainable innovations in organizations with divisional structures. Without a mechanism, such as innovation communities, for presenting them to senior leaders, their funding will be insecure, visibility will be low, and the innovation will have little chance of benefiting the organization as a whole. Equally, without support and recognition for the innovations, employees involved in them move on or lose interest.

We call the top left quadrant Pathological because it represents 'maintenance' projects that have attracted senior management attention even though they are not strategically relevant. This either means that the oversight, assessment, and funding processes are out of control and senior management doesn't trust the business unit to perform effectively, or that the processes are working fine but senior managers don't understand that their principal role is to focus on creating new value and not merely to obsess about administration. The Outsourcing opportunities in the bottom left quadrant are routine operations that don't offer much opportunity for innovation, have little downside risk, and don't require management's ongoing attention. Ultimately, these projects should be outsourced and moved off the map altogether to ensure that they don't take up much management attention at any level of the organization. (This may involve creating another, smaller and ongoing Outsourcing maintenance project in the lower left quadrant.)

The Innovation attention map, like the Strategic conversation contribution map, need not take long to put together and the results can be very revealing. Goals can be established, e.g., to reduce expenditure on maintenance activities by 50 percent and increase expenditures on skunk works and sustainable innovation. Changes can be tracked through time. The analysis helps indicate when existing projects should be repurposed. In this example the Oracle upgrade (now hovering between the Outsourcing and Pathological quadrants) could be used to introduce business model innovation – for instance, to allow suppliers to do automatic restocking – and in so doing move the project rightwards.

The Innovation attention map (Figure 11.1) is powerful because it can be compared across functional areas, and so provides incentives for all departments to innovate more systematically by participating in strategic conversations. And of course, it is itself a form of strategic conversation, helping to communicate management's intent and, through dialog, giving employees the opportunity to visualize, and envision, the organization's future.

How strong are your strategic conversations?

Determining the strength of strategic conversations can normally be done in a couple of hours.

Just take the top initiatives for the current or next year, for instance those that together constitute 80 percent of your spend related to changing the business model for your company or division (generally there will be fewer than ten). Plot out the Strategic conversation contribution and the Innovation attention maps. Are strategic conversations widespread or is the locus of innovation centered on a few? If you want to see yearly trends, look at the maps of one and then two years back. In short order, you should have a clear sense of how engaged your employees are, and how much you're learning from the outside world.

12 Epilogue – on managing

On its surface our book outlines a novel management tool – the design and implementation of strategic conversations – a tool relevant to complex organizations competing in dynamic global markets roiled by rapid technological change. But the reader has seen it is also about something subtler and deeper – the managerial role, how modern managers might best think about their work, responsibilities, and relationships.

To get at this we presented managing as a profoundly creative activity, perhaps our society's most crucial, for without the economic value managers help create there would be no funds, nor time nor place for the arts or social improvements such as health care or education. Managers deal with people, their dreams and fears, their efforts to learn and desires to participate, not simply with investors' funds and the market's demands for goods and services. They make work happen, and work is where many people find a significant part of their identity and place in the world.

Thus, from our book's start, we presented strategizing as a uniquely human activity, fired by our imagination and informed by our social and personal values. Managing people is not managing transactions. Properly done, both the manager and the managed are transformed and shaped to help achieve the organization's goals. And as people are systematically changed, the strategy process becomes inescapably ethically burdened.

Managing, and managers, matter. Unfortunately, too often we hear yesterday's impersonal view of managing – rational data collection and analysis as if numbers alone could or should drive our actions. They cannot; never have, never will. Strategic conversations make managing personal. Human contact, listening and persuading, is central. In today's turbulent times, hiding behind the organization's rules to be administered impersonally without regard to their human consequences is no longer tenable. Inevitably, we humans have gaps in our knowledge and deficiencies in our wisdom. Managers can't afford to be alone, unsupported by the skilled professionals working around them who can help the organization move ahead by filling in for their manager's shortcomings.

We see our society's challenges as calling for more skills, more collaboration, more consciousness of our responsibilities to others, more awareness that we cannot and need not address serious challenges alone. This kind of managing calls for patience and respectfulness towards others, reflection, and self-knowledge. We have borrowed from rhetoric because it has a long history and engages all of these issues. Even though few of the leaders we interviewed had training in rhetoric, all had developed their own sense of how effective human communication works through respectful listening and patient persuasion, with judicious resort to non-factual discourse, and by raising others' passions.

In the end we hope our book helps readers feel the importance of managing and influencing the imagination of others and, even more importantly, the centrality of self-knowledge and personal preparation for managing. Strategic conversations aren't just an improved communication technique. Humility is crucial. Realizing one's own shortcomings is the surest way to appreciate the need for others' help. Resolution too is vital. The leader's greatest contribution lies in embodying a clear and compelling vision that helps others to realize the best in themselves. At their subtlest, strategic conversations are a training ground wherein managers and managed alike discover that the disciplined application of their imagination leads to ethically rich forms of fulfillment – as well as economic success.

Further reading

There is a surfeit of writing describing frameworks for developing strategy, but little about the conversations needed for effective strategizing. While rhetorical techniques have been de-emphasized for quite some time now, that doesn't mean that their importance has been forgotten by all. This is a list of some of our favorite works on the subject – some of which tackle rhetoric head on, and others which illustrate the points through stories – that may be helpful in elevating your strategic conversations.

Amabile, Theresa M., "How to kill creativity," *Harvard Business Review* 76(5) (September–October 1998), 76–88.

Argyris, Chris, "Empowerment: the emperor's new clothes," *Harvard Business Review* 76(3) (May 1998), 98–105.

Beer, Michael and Eisenstat, Russell A., "How to have an honest conversation about your business strategy," *Harvard Business Review* 82(2) (February, 2004), 82–89. ⚹

Cain, Susan, *Quiet: the power of introverts in a world that can't stop talking* (New York, NY: Crown Publishers, 2012).

Conaty, Bill and Charan, Ram, *The talent masters: why smart leaders put people before numbers* (New York, NY: Crown Business, 2010).

Heath, Chip and Heath, Dan, *Made to stick: why some ideas survive and others die* (New York, NY: Random House, 2007).

Heinrichs, Jay, *Thank you for arguing: what Aristotle, Lincoln, and Homer Simpson can teach us about the art of persuasion* (New York, NY: Three Rivers Press, 2007).

Kidder, Tracy, *The soul of a new machine*, first Back Bay paperback edn. (Boston, MA: Little, Brown and Company, 2000).

Leith, S., *Words like loaded pistols: rhetoric from Aristotle to Obama* (New York, NY: Basic Books, 2012).

Manville, Brook and Ober, Josiah, *A company of citizens: what the world's first democracy teaches leaders about creating great organizations* (Boston, MA: Harvard Business School Press, 2003).

Pascale, Richard Tanner, and Sternin, Jerry, "Your company's secret change agents," *Harvard Business Review* 83(5) (May 2005), 72–81. ⚹

Spender, J.-C., *Business strategy: managing uncertainty, opportunity, and enterprise* (Oxford University Press, in press). ⚹

Notes

I INTRODUCTION – WHAT ARE STRATEGIC CONVERSATIONS?

1 Adam Smith, *An inquiry into the nature and causes of the wealth of nations* (London: W. Strahan and T. Cadell, 1776).

2 CLC Human Resources, "The disengaged star: four imperatives to reengage high-potential employees" (Corporate Executive Board Company, 2011).

3 Peter F. Drucker, *The essential Drucker: selections from the management works of Peter F. Drucker*, Classic Drucker Collection edn. (Oxford: Butterworth-Heinemann, 2007).

4 Evidently a term coined by Clay Shirky.

5 J.-C. Spender, *Business strategy: managing uncertainty, opportunity, and enterprise* (Oxford University Press, in press).

2 THE STRATEGIC CONVERSATIONS IMPERATIVE

1 Sheldon Laube, conversation with author (October 17, 2012).

2 These trends are nicely explained in John Hagel III, John Seely Brown, Duleesha Kulasooriya, and Dan Elbert, "Measuring the forces of long-term change: the 2010 Shift Index" (Deloitte Center for the Edge, 2010).

3 Ramon Casadesus-Masanell and Joan E. Ricart, "How to design a winning business model," *Harvard Business Review* 89(1–2) (January–February 2011), 100–107.

4 David J. Teece, "Business models, business strategy and innovation," *Long Range Planning* 43(2) (2010), 172–194.

5 These notions are discussed at greater length in Spender, *Business strategy.*

6 J.-C. Spender, *Industry recipes: the nature and sources of managerial judgement* (Oxford: Basil Blackwell, 1989).

7 Charles Baden-Fuller and Mary S. Morgan, "Business models as models," *Long Range Planning* 43(2) (2010), 156–71. See also Spender, *Industry recipes.*

8 Reena Jana, "Innovation: the biggest bang for the buck," *BusinessWeek* (September 22, 2008).

9 David Owen, *Copies in seconds: how a lone inventor and an unknown company created the biggest communication breakthrough since Gutenberg – Chester Carlson and the birth of the Xerox Machine* (New York, NY: Simon & Schuster, 2004).

10 B. Van Isacker, "iTunes has become the biggest music retailer worldwide," *SideLine Music Magazine* (October 9, 2009), www.side-line.com/news_comments.php?id=43561_0_2_0_C.

11 Steve Lohr, "Sure, big data is great. But so is intuition," *The New York Times* (December 30, 2012), BU3.

12 Frank J. Knight, *Risk, uncertainty and profit* (Boston, MA: Houghton Mifflin Co, 1921).

13 Teece, "Business models."

14 Don Tapscott and Anthony D. Williams, *Wikinomics: how mass collaboration changes everything* (New York, NY: Portfolio, 2006), 77–86.

15 Scott E. Page, *The difference: how the power of diversity creates better groups, firms, schools, and societies* (Princeton, NJ: Princeton University Press, 2007).

16 Booz Allen Hamilton, "No relationship between R&D spending and sales growth, earnings, or shareholder returns" (October 11, 2005), www.businesswire.com/news/home/20051011005323/en/Money-Doesnt-Buy-Results---Innovation-Study#,Uwhøj4VWrKd.

17 Kenneth J. Arrow, *Collected papers of Kenneth J. Arrow: production and capital*, first edn. (Boston, MA: Belknap Press, 1985), vol. 5, 144.

18 See, e.g., Carmine Ornaghi, "Mergers and innovation in big pharma," *International Journal of Industrial Organization* 27(1) (2009), 70–79. The author observed that innovation performance was consistently worse among merged companies compared to non-merging companies. In addition, being highly technologically related did not improve the performance of the merged parties.

19 See, e.g., David Witt, "Only 14% of employees understand their company's strategy and direction," Blanchard Leader Chat (May 21, 2012), leaderchat. org/2012/05/21/only-14-of-employees-understand-their-companys-strategy-and-direction/; and Arne Gast and Michele Zanini, "The social side of strategy," *McKinsey Quarterly* (May 2012).

20 This view is most forcefully argued in Michael E. Raynor, *The strategy paradox: why committing to success leads to failure (and what to do about it)* (New York, NY: Doubleday, 2007). (And while we disagree with the author on who has ownership of strategy, we do admire his brilliant take on what strategy is.)

21 See, e.g., James P. Womack and Daniel T. Jones, *Lean thinking: banish waste and create wealth in your corporation*, second edn. (New York, NY: The Free Press, 2003); or Donald G. Reinertsen, *Managing the design factory: a product developer's toolkit* (New York, NY: The Free Press, 1997).

22 Jim Whitehurst, interview with author (November 20, 2012).

3   STRATEGIC CONVERSATIONS IN THE WILD

1 Lori Senecal, @digitalori, tweeted June 5, 2012.

2 Osvald M. Bjelland and Robert Chapman Wood, "An inside view of IBM's 'Innovation Jam'," *MIT Sloan Management Review* 50(1) (Fall 2008).

3 Matthias Kaiserswerth, "IBM Jams: spurring innovation from within," IBM Research – Zurich, presentation at University of Zurich (March 30, 2009), 17, www.slideshare.net/IBMResearchZurich/uni-zurich-20090330-6019341.

4 *Ibid.* at 19.

5 *Ibid.* at 24.

6 Dr. Naomi Fried, interview with author (October 30, 2012).

7 Which doubles as professional development for the employee, an added perk.

8 See Susan Cain, *Quiet: the power of introverts in a world that can't stop talking* (New York, NY: Crown Publishers, 2012). See also the perspective of Rite-Solutions CEO Jim Lavoie, as detailed in Chapter 6.

9 Steve Todd, "Innovation and topic modeling," Information Playground [blog] (February 16, 2012), stevetodd.typepad.com/my_weblog/2012/02/innovation-and-topic-modeling.html.

10 Morten T. Hansen, *Collaboration: how leaders avoid the traps, create unity, and reap big results* (Boston, MA: Harvard Business School Press, 2009).

11 Edith Penrose, in her classic book, *The theory of the growth of the firm*, argued that an innovator within a firm formed an "image" based on his or her imagining what the firm could achieve. For this act of imagination to occur, and to be acted upon, innovators had to be given time away from their operational duties. Edith Penrose, *The theory of the growth of the firm*, fourth edn. (Oxford University Press, 1959).

12 Dr. Al Vicere, Professor of Business Administration, Smeal College of Business, Penn State, interview with author (August 20, 2009).

13 Tom Hayes, "Conversation with a change agent: Al Vicere on Aramark," *Human Resource Planning* 27(2) (2004), 5–8.

14 HCL ISD, "My Blueprint & my analysis: applying the latest leadership management innovation to create a front-line driven growth plan" [video] (May 31, 2010), www.youtube.com/watch?v=XcsWUW_We5w.

15 Gary Hamel, "HCL's CEO on its 'management makeover'," WSJ Blogs, The Wall Street Journal (August 24, 2010), blogs.wsj.com/management/2010/08/24/hcls-ceo-on-its-management-makeover/.

16 Jim Whitehurst, interview with author (October 30, 2012).

17 Steve Todd, interview with author (October 22, 2012).

18 Dee Hock, "The chaordic organization: out of control and into order," *World Business Academy Perspectives* 9(1) (1995), 1.

19 Until 2008, Visa was a private membership corporation, owned by the financial institutions that created its products. In 2008, it converted most of its member organizations to a publicly-traded company, moving further from Hock's chaordic ideal.

20 For more on chaordic thought, see Dee Hock, *Birth of the chaordic age*, first edn. (San Francisco, CA: Berrett-Koehler Publishers, Inc., 1999).

21 "How to get children out of jobs and into school," *The Economist* (July 31, 2010).

22 The World Bank, "Bolsa Familia: changing the lives of millions in Brazil," go.worldbank.org/DOMFU4AYO0.

23 The World Bank, "Brazil – Bolsa Familia project" (June 28, 2010), 19, documents.worldbank.org/curated/en/2010/06/12568141/brazil-bolsa-familia-project.

24 The World Bank, "FAQs: projects and lending," (June 2012), go.worldbank.org/5FP6CH1BL0.

25 Prudence Ho, "Chinese bank takes great leap forward," *The Wall Street Journal* (May 9, 2012), C1.

26 Jim Yong Kim, "Delivering on development: harnessing knowledge to build prosperity and end poverty," keynote speech to World Knowledge Forum, Seoul, Republic of Korea (World Bank Group, October 8, 2012).

4 ENGAGING EMPLOYEES IN MANAGEMENT'S AGENDA

1 Carl von Clausewitz, *On war*, ed. and trans. Michael Howard and Peter Paret (Princeton, NJ: Princeton University Press, 1976), 112.

2 Lori Senecal, interview with author (November 29, 2012).

3 These observations are confirmed by research. See Theresa M. Amabile, "How to kill creativity," *Harvard Business Review* 76(5) (September–October 1998), 76–88.

4 Michael Beer and Russell A. Eisenstat, "How to have an honest conversation about your business strategy," *Harvard Business Review* 82 (2) (February 2004), 82–89.

5 Julian Birkinshaw, Cyril Bouquet, and J.-L. Barsoux, "The 5 myths of innovation," *MIT Sloan Management Review* 52(2) (Winter 2011), 43–50.

6 This example comes from Chip and Dan Heath's wonderful book, *Made to stick: why some ideas survive and others die* (New York, NY: Random House, 2007), 166–168.

7 Tina Rosenberg, *Join the club: how peer pressure can transform the world* (New York, NY: W. W. Norton & Company, 2011).

8 It's important to note that Athenian society was by no means an ideal place. Slavery was institutionalized and women were denied political participation. The authors believe that strategic conversations tend to unleash human potential (no small thing). They are, however, not the solution to all of humanity's ills.

9 Brook Manville and Josiah Ober, *A company of citizens: what the world's first democracy teaches leaders about creating great organizations* (Boston, MA: Harvard Business School Press, 2003).

10 Jim Whitehurst, "How Red Hat found its mission-the open source way," *Management Innovation eXchange* (August 16, 2011), www.managementexchange.com/blog/how-red-hat-used-open-source-way-develop-company-mission.

11 The concept of "positive deviants" is borrowed from Richard Tanner Pascale and Jerry Sternin, "Your company's secret change agents," *Harvard Business Review* 83(5) (May 2005), 72–81.

12 Joseph A. Raelin, *Work-based learning: bridging knowledge and action in the workplace* (San Francisco, CA: Jossey-Bass, 2008), 278–279.

13 Saul Hansell, "Daring to dream of a resurgent AOL," *The New York Times* (July 23, 2009), B1.

14 Alex Osborn, *Your creative power: how to use imagination* (New York, NY: Charles Scribner's Sons, 1948).

15 Andrew Armour, "Why we need more conversation and less brainstorming," *TrinityP3* (October 1, 2012), www.trinityp3.com/2012/10/why-we-need-more-conversation-and-less-brainstorming/.

16 Jonah Lehrer, "Groupthink: the brainstorming myth," *The New Yorker* (January 30, 2012).

17 Steven Johnson, *Where good ideas come from: the natural history of innovation* (New York, NY: Riverhead Books, 2010).

18 Columbia Ideas at Work, "Strategic intuition: the key to innovation," Columbia Business School (June 27, 2006), www4.gsb.columbia.edu/ ideasatwork/feature/70123/Strategic Intuition: The Key to Innovation.

19 The concept of business strategy is even younger, first emerging with the writings of Alfred Sloan and Chester Barnard in the 1920s and 1930s. See Pankaj Ghemawat, "Competition and business strategy in historical perspective," *Business History Review* 76(1) (Spring 2002), 37–74.

20 Von Clausewitz, *On war*, 21.

21 William Duggan, "Coup d'oeil: strategic intuition in Army planning," *Strategic Studies Institute* (November 2005).

22 Charles S. Jacobs, *Management rewired: why feedback doesn't work and other surprising lessons from the latest brain science* (New York, NY: Portfolio, 2009), 10–12.

23 Von Clausewitz, *On war*.

24 Hansell, "Resurgent AOL."

25 YMCA of Greater Moncton, "2011 Annual Report," www.ymcamoncton. com/temp/Annual%20Report%20Final%202012.pdf.

26 Christopher Bassford, "Clausewitz and his works," Clausewitz.com (2013), www.clausewitz.com/readings/Bassford/Cworks/Works.htm.

5 STRATEGIZING AND THE LEADERS' ROLE

1 Edith Penrose, *The theory of the growth of the firm*, fourth edn. (Oxford University Press, 2009), 32, by permission of Oxford University Press.

2 See, e.g., Amitai Etzioni, *A comparative analysis of complex organizations: on power, involvement, and their correlates* (New York, NY: Free Press, 1961).

3 David Barboza, "Despite a decade of criticism, worker abuse persists in China," *The New York Times* (January 4, 2008).

4 Etzioni, *Complex organizations*.

5 CEB Corporate Leadership Council, "Global workforce insights quarterly report: your resource for the latest Q4 2012-Q1 2013 trends impacting your workforce plan" (Corporate Executive Board Company, 2013).

6 Chris Argyris, "Empowerment: the emperor's new clothes," *Harvard Business Review* 76(3) (May 1998), 98–105.

7 Fred Kofman, *Conscious business: how to build value through values*, annotated edn. (Boulder, CO: Sounds True, Incorporated, 2006).

8 The notion that there's been an inflection point away from heroic leadership was introduced to the authors by strategy consultant and executive coach Sudhir Chadalavada.

9 Julie Wulf, "The flattened firm – not as advertised," Working Paper 12–087, Harvard Business School (April 9, 2012).

10 Jim Yong Kim, "Delivering on development".

11 Not everything William Wrigley, Jr. touched worked out so well. His Chicago Cubs haven't won the World Series since he bought them over 100 years ago.

12 A well-crafted phrase we borrow from Henry Mintzberg's book of the same title. Henry Mintzberg, *Strategy safari: a guided tour through the wilds of strategic management* (New York, NY: The Free Press, 1998).

13 Some of the material that follows is abridged from Spender, *Business strategy*.

14 Alfred Chandler, *Strategy and structure: chapters in the history of the American industrial enterprise* (Cambridge, MA: MIT Press, 1962).

15 R. P. Rumelt, D. Schendel, and D. J. Teece, "Strategic management and economics," *Strategic Management Journal* 12 (Winter Special Issue, 1991), 5–29, reprinted with permission from Elsevier.

16 J. Kraaijenbrink, J.-C. Spender, and A. Groen, "The resource-based view: a review and assessment of its critiques," *Journal of Management* 36(1) (2010), 349–372.

17 Henry Mintzberg, "Strategy formation: schools of thought," in J. W. Fredrickson (ed.), *Perspectives on strategic management* (New York, NY: Harper & Row, 1990), 105–235.

18 Vaclav Smil, *Energy at the crossroads: global perspectives and uncertainties* (Cambridge, MA: The MIT Press, 2003).

19 Dana O'Donovan and Noah Rimland Flower, "The strategic plan is dead. Long live strategy," *Stanford Social Innovation Review*, Blog (January 10, 2013), www.ssireview.org/blog/entry/the_strategic_plan_is_dead._long_live_strategy.

20 Roger Martin, "Strategy and the uncertainty excuse," *Harvard Business Review*, HBR Blog Network (January 8, 2013), blogs.hbr.org/cs/2013/01/the_uncertainty_excuse.html.

21 Lohr, "Sure, big data is great."

22 David Brooks, "What data can't do," *The New York Times* (February 18, 2013).

23 Spender, *Industry recipes*.

24 Charles Baden-Fuller and Mary S. Morgan, "Business models as models," *Long Range Planning* 43(2) (2010), 156–171.

25 John P. Kotter, "Accelerate!," *Harvard Business Review* 90(11) (November 2012), 44–58.

6 PUTTING STRATEGIC CONVERSATIONS INTO PRACTICE – INNOVATION COMMUNITIES

1 Michael E. Raynor, *The strategy paradox: why committing to success leads to failure (and what to do about it)* (New York, NY: Doubleday, 2007).

2 Tracy Kidder, *The soul of a new machine*, first Back Bay paperback edn. (Boston, MA: Little, Brown and Company, 2000).

3 Mary Poppendieck and Tom Poppendieck, *Lean software development: an agile toolkit*, Kindle edn. (Boston, MA: Addison-Wesley Professional, 2003).

4 John Shook, "The remarkable chief engineer," Lean Enterprise Institute (February 3, 2009), www.lean.org/shook/displayobject.cfm?o=906.

5 Lindsey Hoshaw, "Sources", Vector: Boston Children's Hospital's science and clinical innovation blog (September 10, 2010), vectorblog.org/2010/09/sources/.

6 C. B. Mahnke, C. P. Jordan, E. Bergvall, D. A. Person, and J. E. Pinsker, "The Pacific Asynchronous TeleHealth (PATH) system: review of 1,000 pediatric teleconsultations," *Telemed J E Health* 17(1) (February 6, 2011), 35–9.

7 *Ibid.*

8 Broadband Expanded, "Broadband & telemedicine: stats, data & observations" (July 2010) www.nyls.edu/advanced-communications-law-and-policy-institute/wp-content/uploads/sites/169/2013/08/Telemedicine_StatsData.pdf.

9 Howard Anderson, "Survey: consumers keen on telemedicine," *HealthData Management* (July 23, 2009), http://archive.is/8OJfy.

10 Ken Terry, "Telehealth market to hit $6.28 billion by 2020," *InformationWeek* (September 20, 2011), www.informationweek.com/healthcare/mobile-wireless/telehealth-market-to-hit-628-billion-by/231601670.

11 Matthew A. Hein, "Telemedicine: an important force in the transformation of healthcare," US Department of Commerce, International Trade Administration (June 25, 2009), ita.doc.gov/td/health/telemedicine_2009.pdf.

12 Stuart Elliott, "An ad agency crowdsources its own employees' morale," *The New York Times* (September 7, 2012), B3.

13 Jonah Lehrer, "Groupthink: the brainstorming myth," *The New Yorker* (January 30, 2012).

14 Rite-Solutions' logo is a rowing shell, hence the "bow."

15 Jim Lavoie, "Nobody's as smart as everybody: unleashing individual brilliance and aligning collective genius," *Management Innovation eXchange* (September 14, 2011), www.managementexchange.com/story/nobody%E2%80%99s-smart-everybody-unleashing-quiet-genius-inside-organization.

16 "Rite-Solutions: using collective intelligence to accelerate the future," *Business Digest* 236 (May 2013), www.business-digest.eu/en/2013/05/15/the-signal-and-the-noise/. Business Digest is a Paris-based observatory for new ideas and trends in management and business.

17 Jim Lavoie, interview with author (June 1, 2013).

18 Lavoie, "Nobody's as smart as everybody."

19 *Ibid.*

20 Matthew Boyle, "Best Buy's giant gamble," *Fortune* (April 3, 2006), money.cnn.com/magazines/fortune/fortune_archive/2006/04/03/8373034/index.htm.

21 *Ibid.*

22 Audrey Gray, "An exit interview with Best Buy's Brad Anderson," *Dealerscope* (June 2009), www.dealerscope.com/article/interview-brad-anderson-ceo-best-buy-406025/1.

23 John Wolpert, "Kal Patel – tapping the best of Best Buy" (June 26, 2007), thethreepercent.com/2007/06/26/kal-patel-tapping-the-best-of-best-buy/.

24 Bettina Buechel, "Developing WOLF: driving results through the women's movement at Best Buy," International Institute for Management Development, IMD-3–2098 (May 20, 2009).

25 *Ibid.*

26 *Ibid.*

27 *Ibid.*

28 All bulleted statistics are from Buechel, "Developing WOLF," except for final bullet point.

29 Ronald Heifetz, Alexander Grashow, and Marty Linsky, "Leadership in a (permanent) crisis," *Harvard Business Review* 87(7/8) (July–August 2009).

30 Buechel, "Developing WOLF."

7 CONVERSATION TRUMPS STRUCTURE – NEW NORMS FOR DIALOG

1 See Chris Argyris, *Reasons and rationalizations: the limits to organizational knowledge* (Oxford University Press, 2004). In it he describes Intel's struggle with moving from DRAM to microprocessors and the ultimate failure of a large joint venture in medical equipment, both because of poor communication patterns.

2 These notions are not new, even if often forgotten. This chapter pays some attention to the research done over the years on conversations in organizations and their impact on strategizing and corporate performance. While this research is extensive and ongoing, and we have no intention of forcing the reader to engage too much of it, it is clear that little of it appears in the popular management literature or on the financial pages where it truly belongs if we are to understand how senior managers actually shape their firm's performance. Organizations comprise people and their interactions, not just the resources that appear on the balance sheet. Conversations are the most fundamental of human interactions, trumping instructions and the exercise of power. See, e.g., David Barry and Michael Elmes, "Strategy retold: towards a narrative view of strategic discourse," *Academy of Management Review* 22(2) (1997), 429–452.

3 Teresa M. Amabile, "How to kill creativity," *Harvard Business Review* 76 (5) (September–October, 1998), 76–88.

4 See James D. Thompson, *Organizations in action: social science bases of administrative theory* (New Brunswick, NJ: Transaction Publishers, 2003).

5 Spencer E. Ante, "Starwood Hotels: rubbing customers the right way," *BusinessWeek* (October 7, 2007), www.businessweek.com/stories/2007-10-07/starwood-hotels-rubbing-customers-the-right-way.

6 Uri Hasson, "Defend your research: I can make your brain look like mine," *Harvard Business Review* (December 2010), hbr.org/2010/12/defend-your-research-i-can-make-your-brain-look-like-mine/ar/1.

7 See Spender, *Business strategy.*

8 "Enjoyment appears at the boundary between boredom and anxiety, when the challenges are just balanced with the person's capacity to act." Mihaly

Csikszentmihalyi, *Flow: the psychology of optimal experience* (New York, NY: HarperCollins Publishers Inc., 1990).

9 Christopher Chabris and Daniel Simons, *The invisible gorilla: and other ways our intuitions deceive us*, Kindle edn. (New York, NY: Crown Publishers, 2010).

10 Fabrizio Ferraro, Jeffrey Pfeffer, and Robert I. Sutton, "Economics language and assumptions: how theories can become self-fulfilling," *Academy of Management Review* 30(1) (2005), 8–24.

11 Kirsten Grind, *The lost bank: the story of Washington Mutual – the biggest bank failure in American history* (New York, NY: Simon & Schuster, 2012).

12 Chris Argyris and Donald A. Schon, *Organizational learning: a theory of action perspective*, Addison-Wesley series on organizational development (Boston, MA: Addison-Wesley Publishing Co., 1978).

13 Fred Kofman, *Conscious business: how to build value through values*, annotated edn. (Boulder, CO: Sounds True, Incorporated, 2006).

14 Eddie Obeng, "Smart failure for a fast-changing world," TEDGlobal (June 2012), www.ted.com/talks/ eddie_obeng_smart_failure_for_a_fast_changing_world.html.

15 Laurence G. Weinzimmer and Jim McConoughey, *The wisdom of failure: how to learn the tough leadership lessons without paying the price* (San Francisco, CA: John Wiley & Sons, 2012).

16 Richard Pascale, Mark Millemann, and Linda Gioja, "Changing the way we change," *Harvard Business Review* 75(6) (November 1997), 126–139.

17 David A Garvin, *Learning in action: a guide to putting the learning organization to work* (Boston, MA: Harvard Business School Press, 2000), 106–116.

18 Pascale, et al., "Changing the way we change."

19 Adapted from Pascale, et al., "Changing the way we change."

20 Jim Yong Kim, "Delivering on development."

21 Scott Keller and Carolyn Aiken, "The inconvenient truth about change management: why it isn't working and what to do about it," McKinsey & Company (2008), www.mckinsey.com/App_Media/Reports/ Financial_Services/ The_Inconvenient_Truth_About_Change_Management.pdf.

22 See, e.g., Fredric M. Jablin, "Superior-subordinate communication: the state of the art," *Psychological Bulletin* 86(6) (November 1979), 1201–1222,

and Rudi Klauss and Bernard M. Bass, *Interpersonal communication in organizations* (Waltham, MA: Academic Press, Inc, 1982).

23 Adam Bryant, "Google's quest to build a better boss," *The New York Times* (March 12, 2011).

24 Kofman, *Conscious business.*

25 Michael Beer and Russell A. Eisenstat, "How to have an honest conversation about your business strategy," *Harvard Business Review* 82 (2) (February 1, 2004), 82–89.

26 Interestingly for such a high-tech company, Red Hat memo-list is based on listserv, a technology that's been around since the 1980s.

27 DeLisa Alexander, "Fueling passion: the employee-led evolution of memo-list at Red Hat," *Management Innovation eXchange* (August 24, 2011), www.managementexchange.com/story/employee-led-evolution-memo-list-red-hat.

28 *Ibid.*

29 Lavoie, "Nobody's as smart as everybody."

30 Beer and Eisenstat, "Honest conversation."

31 Jay Heinrichs, *Thank you for arguing: what Aristotle, Lincoln, and Homer Simpson can teach us about the art of persuasion* (New York, NY: Three Rivers Press, 2007).

32 Sam Leith, *You talkin' to me? Rhetoric from Aristotle to Obama* (London: Profile Books, 2011).

8 STRATEGIC CONVERSATIONS ACROSS GEOGRAPHIES, GENERATIONS, AND THE MULTITUDE

1 Joseph Schumpeter, "Economic theory and entrepreneurial history," in *Change and the entrepreneur: postulates and the patterns for entrepreneurial history* (Boston, MA: Harvard University Press, 1949), 71–72.

2 Don Tapscott and Anthony D. Williams, *Wikinomics: how mass collaboration changes everything* (New York, NY: Penguin Group, 2006).

3 Alison Overholt, "American Idol: the PwC accounting edition," *Fortune* (October 17, 2011).

4 See Chapter 5 for the full story.

5 Vijay Govindarajan and Chris Trimble, "The CEO's role in business model reinvention," *Harvard Business Review* 89(1–2) (January 2011), 108–114.

6 Herminia Ibarra and Morten T. Hansen, "Are you a collaborative leader? How great CEOs keep their teams connected," *Harvard Business Review* 89(7–8) (July 2011), 68–74.

7 *Ibid.*

8 Vijay Govindarajan and Chris Trimble, *Reverse innovation: create far from home, win everywhere*, Kindle edn. (Boston, MA: Harvard Business Review Press, 2012).

9 Bernard T. Ferrari and Jessica Goethals, "Using rivalry to spur innovation," *McKinsey Quarterly* (May 2010).

10 Mitra Best, interview with author, September 17, 2012.

11 *Ibid.*

12 Buechel, "Developing WOLF."

13 Chuck Hollis, "EMC|ONE: A journey in social media," EMC Corporation (December 2008), chucksblog.emc.com/content/ social_media_at_EMC_draft.pdf.

14 *Ibid.*

15 *Ibid.*

16 *Ibid.*

17 *Ibid.*

18 *Ibid.*

19 *Ibid.*

20 *Ibid.*

21 Ikujiro Nonaka, "Toward middle-up-down management: accelerating information creation," *MIT Sloan Management Review*, 29(3) (Spring 1988), 9–18.

22 Robert K. Greenleaf, *Servant leadership: a journey into the nature of legitimate power and greatness*, 25th anniversary edn. (Mahwah, NJ: Paulist Press, 2002).

23 Chuck Hollis, interview with author (October 8, 2012).

9 ENGAGING THE WORLD OUTSIDE IN THE CONVERSATION

1 John Donne, *Devotions upon emergent occasions* (1624).

2 Peter J. Williamson, "Cost innovation: preparing for a 'value-for-money' revolution," *Long Range Planning* 43(2–3) (2010), 343–353.

3 Ikujiro Nonaka, Ryoko Toyama, and Toru Hirata, *Managing flow: a process theory of the knowledge-based firm* (New York, NY: Palgrave Macmillan, 2008), 70–87.

4 Vijay Govindarajan and Chris Trimble, "The CEO's role in business model reinvention," *Harvard Business Review* 89(1–2) (January–February 2011), 108–114.

5 Buechel, "Developing WOLF."

6 Gary Hamel, Yves L. Doz, and C. K. Prahalad, "Collaborate with your competitors—and win," *Harvard Business Review* 67(1) (January 1989), 133–139.

7 Jackie Yeaney, "Democratizing the corporate strategy process at Red Hat," *Management Innovation Exchange* (November 10, 2011).

8 The World Bank, "Conditional cash transfers," go.worldbank.org/BWUC1CMXM0.

9 The World Bank, "Community driven development," go.worldbank.org/0L7YALE031.

10 The World Bank, "Agreement signed to help the marginalized population in Indonesia" (June 30, 2011), www.worldbank.org/en/news/feature/2011/06/30/agreement-signed-help-marginalized-population-indonesia-feature-story.

11 Open Development Technology Alliance, "About," odta.net/2976/about.

12 Open Development Technology Alliance, "WaterHackathon" (November 2011), www.opendta.org/Pages/Initiatives/initiative-water-hackaton.aspx.

13 United States Environmental Protection Agency, "Cross-state air pollution rule (CSAPR)," www.epa.gov/airtransport/CSAPR/index.html.

14 As Nobel Laureate economist Kenneth J. Arrow put it, "we expect a free enterprise system to underinvest in invention and research because it is risky and because the product can be appropriated only to a limited extent. This underinvestment will be greater for more basic research." Kenneth J. Arrow, *Collected papers of Kenneth J. Arrow: production and capital*, first edn. (Boston, MA: Belknap Press, 1985), vol. 5, 114.

15 Summit Power, "Texas clean energy project: a progress report," presentation at the 2011 NETL CO_2 Capture Technology Meeting (August 25, 2011), www.netl.doe.gov/publications/proceedings/11/co2capture/presentations/4-Thursday/25Aug11-Kirksey-Summit-Carbon%20Capture%20using%20Rectisol.pdf.

10 CREATING A SELF-REINFORCING INNOVATION PLATFORM — COLLATERAL BENEFITS

1 Frank J. Knight, *Risk, uncertainty and profit* (Boston, MA: Hart, Houghton Mifflin Co, 1921).

2 David E. Sanger, "Bailing out of the mainframe industry," *The New York Times* (February 5, 1984), A1.

3 Thom Shanker, "Iran encounter grimly echoes '02 war game'," *The New York Times* (January 12, 2008), A1.

4 This kind of thinking pays off. In an act of business jujitsu, instead of being a competitor, Apple is a major customer of EMC storage solutions. See Rik Mislewski, "Apple 'orders 12 petabytes of storage' from EMC," *The Register* (April 6, 2011), www.theregister.co.uk/2011/04/06/ apple_isilon_order/.

5 John Fay, interview with author.

6 Bill Conaty and Ram Charan, *The talent masters: why smart leaders put people before numbers* (New York, NY: Crown Business, 2010), 56–57.

7 Joseph A. Raelin, *Work-based learning: bridging knowledge and action in the workplace*, new and revised edn. (San Francisco, CA: Jossey-Bass, 2008).

8 Hagel, et al., "2010 Shift Index."

9 Jackie Crosby, "Women's warrior at Best Buy," *Star Tribune* (December 18, 2007), www.startribune.com/business/11980251.html.

10 Hagel, et al., "2010 Shift Index."

11 Warren Buffet, "Berkshire Hathaway 2001 Chairman's letter to shareholders" (2001), www.berkshirehathaway.com/letters/2001pdf.pdf.

12 Conaty and Charan, *The talent masters*.

13 Raelin, *Work-based learning*, 289.

14 BusinessDictionary.com, "change management," www. businessdictionary.com/definition/change-management.html.

15 John Kotter, "Change management vs. change leadership – what's the difference?," *Forbes* (July 12, 2011).

16 Scott Keller and Carolyn Aiken, "The inconvenient truth about change management: why it isn't working and what to do about it," McKinsey & Company (2008), www.mckinsey.com/App_Media/Reports/ Financial_Services/ The_Inconvenient_Truth_About_Change_Management.pdf.

17 Lori Senecal, @digitalori tweet (June 5, 2012).

18 See Vijay Govindarajan and Chris Trimble, *Reverse innovation: create far from home, win everywhere*, Kindle edn. (Boston, MA: Harvard Business Review Press, 2012).

19 David A. Aaker, "Innovation: brand it or lose it," *California Management Review* 50(1) (Fall 2007), 8–24.

20 Harry Hoover, "Why passionate employees matter," MarketingProfs.com (November 5, 2002), www.marketingprofs.com/2/hoover1.asp.

II MEASURING THE FUTURE

1 Byron Spice, "CMU's Simon reflects on how computers will continue to shape the world," *Pittsburg Post-Gazette* (October 16, 2000), old.post-gazette.com/regionstate/20001016simon2.asp.

2 Nicholas Bloom, Erik Brynjolfsson, Lucia Foster, Ron Jarmin, Itay Saporta-Eksten, and John Van Reenen, "Management in America," Center for Economic Studies, US Census Bureau CES 13–01 (January 2013).

3 Chuck Hollis, interview with author (October 8, 2012).

4 Chuck Hollis, "EMC|One: a journey in social media," white paper, EMC Corporation (December 2008), chucksblog.emc.com/content/social_media_at_EMC_draft.pdf.

5 Douglas W. Hubbard, *How to measure anything: finding the value of 'intangibles' in business*, second edn., Kindle edn., (Hoboken, NJ: John Wiley & Sons, 2010), 215.

6 Adam Grant, "Is giving the secret to getting ahead?," *New York Times Magazine* (March 27, 2013), www.nytimes.com/2013/03/31/magazine/is-giving-the-secret-to-getting-ahead.html.

7 Steve Todd, "Evolutionary topic modeling," Information Playground [blog] (February 23, 2012), stevetodd.typepad.com/my_weblog/2012/02/evolutionary-topic-modeling.html.

8 Steve Todd, "Innovation and topic modeling," Information Playground [blog] (February 16, 2012), stevetodd.typepad.com/my_weblog/2012/02/innovation-and-topic-modeling.html.

9 Steve Todd, "Idea contests: an exhaustive look," Information Playground [blog] (September 5, 2012), stevetodd.typepad.com/my_weblog/2012/09/idea-contests-an-exhaustive-look.html.

10 Steve Todd, "Phase 4 innovation analytics: boundary spanner validation," Information Playground [blog] (June 7, 2012), stevetodd.typepad.com/my_weblog/2012/06/phase-4-innovation-analytics-boundary-spanner-validation.html.

11 Rosabeth Moss Kanter, "Innovation: the classic traps," *Harvard Business Review* 84(11) (November 2006), 72–83.

Index

3D printing, 165
3M, 101

Aaker, David, 194
acquisitions
    as source of business model innovation,
      17
AirAsia, 77
Alexander, DeLisa, 143
Amazon, 12, 117, 183
American Idol, 28, 110, 149
ancient Athens, 149
    forums for structured conversations,
      55–56
    use of rhetoric, 55–56
Anderson, Brad, 117–120, 122, 155–156
anecdotal type of measurement, 197–198
Angell, Chuck, 115
anonymity
    avoidance in strategic conversations,
      145–146
Ansoff matrix, 78
antitrust legislation, 79
AOL, 61, 64
Apple, 12, 74, 79, 98, 129, 183
    concerns about secrecy, 21
    employee implementation of the
      business model, 148
    iPod, 14, 82, 100
    iTunes store, 14, 21, 82
ARAMARK, 187, 197
    T-shaped strategic conversations,
      33–34
Argyris, Chris, 73, 136
Aristotle, 126
Armstrong, Tim, 61, 64
AstraZeneca, 191
Augustus, Mike, 115

Balanced Scorecard tool, 80, 88
Bassford, Christopher, 70

Benco Dental
    Lucy Hobbs innovation community,
      170–171
Best Buy, 159, 203
    Geek Squad, 12, 118–119
    Geek Squad problem-solving approach,
      149
    Omega WOLF Pack projects, 168–170
    WOLF Pack innovation community,
      117–219
    WOLF Pack members' passion, 188
Best, Mitra, 28–29, 149–150, 154–155, 189
big data
    uses and limitations, 85–86
Bloom, Jonah, 110
Boeing 787 Dreamliner, 13
Bonaparte, Napoleon, 62
Boston Children's Hospital
    celebration-type innovation days, 26
    dealing with innovation and change, 194
    support for innovators, 190
    telehealth innovation community, 42,
      102–108, 128–129
Boston Consulting Group
    Growth-Share Matrix, 78
bounded rationality, 84
    decision-making under, 84–85
brainstorming, 4, 61–62
brand enhancement
    benefits of strategic conversations, 194–195
Brojerdi, Ed, 111, 190
Brooks, David, 86
Buffet, Warren, 190
business
    challenges in a changing world, 164–165
    strategic conversations in real situations,
      2–3
business growth
    benefit of strategic conversations, 2
business model innovation
    barriers to, 100–101

benefits of internal innovation, 16
by effective knowledge flows, 16
compared to technical innovation, 14
for value creation, 14
generating innovative ideas, 61–62
innovation communities, 100–102
M&A as sources of, 17
managing strategic conversations, 127–128
R&D as source of, 17
recruitment of top leaders (white knights)
    to innovate, 17
uncertainty in, 196
business models
    adapting to opportunities and threats, 13
    as thought exercises, 12
    assessment and adjustment, 133
    creating new opportunity spaces, 12
    definition and scope, 8–9
    exploiting the opportunity space, 10–12
    factors which shape choices, 10–12
    leadership accountability for, 13
    leap of faith required, 15, 137
    modeling the organization, 12
    need for continual updating, 15
    relationship to strategy, 18–19
    risk of failure, 137–139
    role in organizational learning, 12–13
    variety of possible configurations, 9–10
    ways of providing value, 12
business reengineering, 192
business strategy. See strategy

Cardente, John, 201–202
Cathcart, Ron, 136
celebration-type innovation days, 26
challenges
    combining types of strategic
        conversation, 42–46
    impact on business growth, 42
    level of inclusivity, 42
    type of strategic conversation, 28–30
Chandler, Alfred, 78–79
change management
    benefits of strategic conversations,
        191–194
chaordic strategic conversations, 37–41
    combining types of strategic
        conversation, 42–46
    impact on business growth, 42
    level of inclusivity, 42

chaos
    concern about strategic conversations,
        19–20
Chen, Jidong (Roby), 203
Chen, Tao, 31
Clausewitz, Carl von, 48, 62–64, 70, 90, 132
Clean Air Task Force (CATF)
    external strategic conversations, 176–181
Coca-Cola, 79
coercive leadership styles, 72
Cohen, Armond, 176
Cohen, Chuck
    Lucy Hobbs innovation community,
        170–171
collateral benefits of strategic conversations
    brand enhancement, 194–195
    building social networks, 191
    change management, 191–194
    EMC Executive Program, 182–186
    executive learning, 182–187
    external networks, 181
    how to enjoy, 195
    organizational alignment, 182–187
    organizational learning, 182–187
    raised employee passion, 187–189
    range of benefits, 182
    talent management, 189–191
communities of practice (CoPs)
    distinction from innovation
        communities, 108–109
competitions
    combining types of strategic
        conversation, 42–46
    impact on business growth, 42
    KBS+ Hyde Experiment, 109–113
    level of inclusivity, 42
    type of strategic conversation, 27–28
Competitive Strategy (Porter), 79
competitors
    strategic conversations with, 171–172
consultants, 16
    limitations of contribution to strategy,
        166
    role in strategic change, 191–192
    strategic tools, 80
controller style of management, 73–74
conversational health
    conversational norms of an organization,
        146
    influence on quality of strategy, 140–146

conversational leadership style, 73–75
conversations
    and the strategizing model, 133
    business model assessment and
      adjustment, 133
    creating a learning social apparatus,
      132–133
    creating new knowledge and value,
      132–133
    fostering knowledge exchanges,
      128–129
    functions in large organizations, 5
    language management by leaders, 134
    persuading employees to pursue a
      specific strategy, 132
    reducing knowledge absences, 128–129
    roles in supporting the strategizing
      process, 128–133
    shaping to make them productive,
      129–132
    use of framing, 134
    See also strategic conversations
Cook, Tim, 74
corporate culture
    effects of strategic conversations, 22
Costco, 118
coup d'oeil (flash of strategic insight), 63–64
Crazy Eddie, 117
crowdsourcing, 28–29
cultures
    bridging with strategic conversations,
      152–154
customers
    involving in the strategizing process,
      167–171
customization
    limitations of profitability, 165

Dahl, Allison, 30
Danone, 151
Data General Corporation, 101
Dawning (Chinese computer firm), 164
DeBellis, Izzy, 111, 190
decision-making
    under uncertainty, 2, 84–85
delivery knowledge
    embedding in strategy, 75–76
Dell, 118
Deloitte
    survey of employee engagement, 188–189

dialog. See conversations, strategic
    conversations
Digital Equipment Corporation, 101
Discovery mode, 87–89
diversity
    celebration in strategic conversations,
      152–153
Donne, John, 224
Doz, Yves L., 172
Drucker, Peter, 1
Duggan, William, 63
Dunn, Brian, 117, 122, 124
dynamic capabilities, 80

Eisai, 166–167, 200
EMC, 146, 188, 204
    analysis of intranet topics, 30–31
    brand enhancement, 195
    bridging geographical distance, 152–153
    celebration of diversity, 152–153
    change management, 194
    cultural change, 22
    Executive Program, 182–186
    Global Innovation Network, 167–168
    leadership presence of Joe Tucci, 51
    measurement of effects of strategic
      conversations, 197–198
    social network analysis, 200–203
    social networking proficiency initiative,
      156–162
    strategy reviews, 36–37
employee engagement
    agenda for strategic conversations, 60–62
    appeals to passion and personal
      commitment (pathos), 52–55
    appeals to character and higher interest
      (ethos), 52–55
    assessment of, 70
    context of actionable meaning, 51–52
    drivers within the business environment,
      7–8
    encouragement by leaders, 127
    encouraging employee participation,
      59–60
    engaging younger employees, 149–151
    entrepreneurial potential of employees,
      49–50
    financial incentives, 50
    finding innovation team leaders, 59–60
    generating innovative ideas, 60–62

impact of transactional leadership, 72–73
insights from military strategy, 62–64
Kirshenbaum Bond Senecal (KBS+),
    48–49, 65–66
leading with personal presence, 50–51
limitations of appeals to logic (logos),
    52–55
making sure all voices are heard, 143–146
motivational factors, 52–55
not brainstorming, 61–62
Red Hat Software, 56–59
Rite-Solutions, 48–49, 64–65
shaping of conversations by leaders,
    62–64
suggestion boxes, 24
untapped source of advantage, 1–2
use of rhetoric by leaders, 52–55
use of social media, 149–151
using strategic conversations, 2
ways to engage employees, 50–60
YMCA Canada, 66–69
employee passion
    influence of strategic conversations,
        187–189
employees
    debate about role in strategizing, 20
    disconnection from strategy
        development, 49
    entrepreneurial potential, 49–50
    lack of involvement in the strategizing
        process, 93–95
    motivation of social rewards, 137
    objections to their involvement in
        strategy, 19–22
entrepreneurial potential of employees,
    49–50
entrepreneurial workforce, 2
entrepreneurs, 9
    opportunities from uncertainty, 196
ethical burden of strategic conversations, 97
ethos
    appeals to character and higher interest,
        52–55
executive learning
    benefit of strategic conversations,
        182–187
experimental types of measurement, 198–200
External-Internal-Fit paradigm, 78–79
external strategic conversations
    as strategy for CATF, 176–181

assessing outside interactions, 181
challenges in a changing business world,
    164–165
collaboration with partners, 171–176
collateral benefits, 181
influences from the outside world, 164
involving customers, 167–171
need to engage with the outside world,
    165–166
sensing and operationalizing platforms,
    166–168
with competitors, 171–172

Facebook, 157, 162
failure
    managing, 137–140
    risk in business models, 137–139
Fay, Jon, 182–186, 194
financial incentives for employee
    engagement, 50
five forces framework (Porter), 79
Five Iron Laws of Value Creation, 14–18
    Law 1 (innovating the business model),
        14, 17, 83
    Law 2 (business models require a leap of
        faith), 15, 89, 137
    Law 3 (continual updating of the business
        model), 15, 17, 75, 140
    Law 4 (knowledge flows enhance
        strategizing and innovation), 16–17,
        45, 75, 188
    Law 5 (benefits of internal innovation),
        16–17, 92, 166
flash-crashes, 85
flash of strategic insight (coup d'oeil),
    63–64
flat organizational structures, 74–75
Ford, Henry, 61
fractals metaphor
    approaches to program implementation,
        68–69
framing
    in conversations, 134
    transactional framing, 134–135
Fried, Naomi, 103–105, 107, 129

Gains, Al, 115
GE/McKinsey matrix, 78
General Electric (GE), 14, 33, 60, 74, 187,
    190

General Motors (GM), 16
  NUMMI joint venture with Toyota, 172
generation gap
  using strategic conversations to bridge,
    153–154
  ways to bridge, 149–151
geographical distance
  using strategic conversations to bridge,
    152–154
Gilbert, Julie
  Lucy Hobbs innovation community,
    170–171
  Omega WOLF Pack projects, 168–170
  WOLF Pack innovation community,
    119–219
global context. *See* external strategic
    conversations
goal of strategy, 83–85
Google, 183
  Project Oxygen, 141, 189
Grant, Adam, 199
Great Recession, 136
Grind, Kirsten, 135
groupthink, 12
Grove, Andy, 74
Growth-Share Matrix, 78

Hadoop program, 204
Haier, 165
Haldane, Scott, 66–69
Haloid (later Xerox), 14
Hamel, Gary, 172
Hammer, Michael, 192
Hansen, Morten, 32, 152
HCL Technologies, 35–36
hedge fund failures, 85
helicopter view of a business, 9
Herman, Darren, 110, 190
heroic leaders, 73–74
hierarchies, 66
  effects of flattening, 74–75
history of business strategy, 77–81
Hock, Dee, 38
Hollis, Chuck, 146, 185, 197–198, 201
  social networking proficiency initiative,
    156–162
Honda, 60
horizontal integration, 78
Hubbard, Douglas W., 198
Hubbell, John, 115

human relationships
  importance of managing, 209–210
Hunter, David G., 105–108, 128–129, 193
Hyde, Angela, 191

Ibarra, Herminia, 152
IBM, 14
  business model innovation, 15
  Innovation Jams, 25–26
  ideation-type innovation days, 24–27
Immelt, Jeffrey, 33, 74
impressionistic type of measurement,
    197–198
industrial organization economics, 79
Infosys, 151, 168
innovation
  benefits of internal innovation, 16
  See also business model innovation
Innovation attention map, 204–208
innovation communities, 41–42, 199–200
  Benco Dental, 170–171
  combining types of strategic
    conversation, 42–46
  definition, 99
  distinction from communities of practice
    (CoPs), 108–109
  distinction from Tiger Teams, 124–219
  fostering business model innovation,
    100–102
  impact on business growth, 42
  innovation team members, 99–100
  level of inclusivity, 42
  Rite-Solutions Rite-Track innovation
    community, 114–117
  See also Best Buy, Boston Children's
    Hospital, Kirshenbaum Bond Senecal
innovation days
  celebration-type, 26
  combining types of strategic
    conversation, 42–46
  ideation-type, 24–27
  impact on business growth, 42
  level of inclusivity, 42
  type of strategic conversation, 24–27
innovation pyramid approach, 203
Intel, 74

Japan
  nemawashi process, 56
Jensen, Mark, 109–111, 137, 190

Jobs, Steve, 21, 51, 74, 77, 98, 129, 148
Johnson, Stephen, 61
Judgment mode, 89–90

Kanter, Rosabeth Moss, 203
Kidder, Tracy, 101
Killinger, Kerry, 136
Kim, Jim Yong, 40, 75–76, 139–140
Kirshenbaum Bond Senecal (KBS+), 188
    accomplishing change, 193
    employee engagement, 48–49
    employee innovation, 65–66
    engaging younger employees, 151
    Hyde Experiment innovation
        community, 109–113, 137
    Hyde Space, 194
    innovation competition, 190
    vision of Lori Senecal, 130
Knight, Frank H., 15, 84, 90, 182, 196
knowledge absences
    and business decision-making, 15
    and strategists' judgment, 84–85
    fostering knowledge exchanges, 128–129
Knowledge-Based view, 80
knowledge flows
    importance in strategizing and
        innovation, 16
knowledge gained by employees
    embedding in strategy, 75–76
Kodak, 14
Kofman, Fred, 73, 142
Korytko, Zane, 69

Laker, Freddie, 77
language management in conversations, 134
Laube, Sheldon, 7
Lavoie, Jim, 48–49, 52, 64–65, 114–117,
    144–145
leader's values
    influence on strategic judgment, 85
leaders
    coup d'oeil (flash of strategic insight),
        63–64
    encouraging employee participation, 127
    experience used to ground strategic
        conversations, 63
    language management in conversations,
        134
    making sure all voices are heard, 143–146
    managing strategic conversations, 127–128

openness to new possibilities, 63
    recruitment to innovate business models,
        17
    role in strategic conversations, 71–72
    shaping strategic conversations, 62–64,
        129–132
leadership
    accountability for business models, 13
    creating meaning for employees, 51–52
    differences in strategic conversations,
        71–72
    identifying opportunities and threats, 13
    implications of strategic conversations
        approach, 209–210
    importance of human relationships,
        209–210
    scaling up strategic conversations, 55–56
    under strategic conversations, 95–97
    use of rhetoric to engage employees,
        52–55
leadership styles
    coercive, 72
    controller, 73–74
    conversational, 73–75
    heroic leaders, 73–74
    learner, 73–74
    transactional, 72–73
leading with personal presence, 50–51
learner style of management, 73–74
Learning mode, 93
LinkedIn, 157, 162
logic (logos)
    limitations in changing behaviors, 52–55
Lohr, Steve, 85
Long Term Capital, 85
Lucy Hobbs innovation community, 170–171
Lula da Silva, Luiz Inácio, 39

Madany, Peter, 152–153
Mahdy, Medhat, 69
management
    value-creating dynamic, 182
managerial role
    implications of strategic conversations
        approach, 209–210
    importance of human relationships,
        209–210
managers
    aesthetic associated with strategic
        conversations, 18

managers (cont.)
    changing role of, 161–162
    espoused theory versus theory-in-use, 136
managing failure, 137–140
Manville, Brook, 55
Martin, Roger, 82
McKinsey & Company, 140
measurement
    anecdotal type, 197–198
    by experiments, 198–200
    importance for effective management,
        197
    impressionistic type, 197–198
    social network analysis, 200–203
    strategic conversation mapping, 203–208
    textual analysis, 200–203
    types of, 197–208
    uncertainty in business model
        innovation, 196
meetings, 4
mergers and acquisitions (M&A)
    as sources of business model innovation,
        17
Microsoft, 15, 89
middle managers
    changing role of, 161–162
    perceived threat from social networking
        approach, 161–162
military applications of strategy, 78
Mintzberg, Henry, 80
monopoly theory, 79
Moritz, Bob, 150
motivation of employees
    intrinsic and extrinsic factors, 52–55
    social rewards, 137
Murthy, N. R. Narayana, 151
MySpace, 157

Nayar, Vineet, 35–36
nemawashi process (Japan), 56
Netflix, 12
networks
    enhancing effects of strategic
        conversations, 191
    See also social media, social networking
        approach
Neubauer, Joe, 33–34, 197
niche markets
    limitations of profitability, 165
Nike, 112

opportunities
    identifying and responding to, 13
opportunity costs of strategic conversations,
    20–21
opportunity space, 10–12
    use of strategy to expand, 83–85
O'Reilly, Tim, 190
organizational alignment
    benefit of strategic conversations,
        182–187
organizational culture
    effects of strategic conversations, 22
organizational learning, 80
    benefit of strategic conversations,
        182–187
    role of business models, 12–13
organizational secrets
    potential risk from strategic
        conversations, 21
organizational structure
    flattening hierarchies, 74–75
    secondary to good strategic
        conversations, 126
Osborn, Alex, 61
Otellini, Paul, 74
outside world. *See* external strategic
    conversations

partners
    strategic conversations with, 171–176
Patel, Kal, 119
pathos
    appeals to personal commitment and
        passion, 52–55
Penrose, Edith, 71
Pericles, 55–56
persuading employees to pursue a specific
    strategy, 132
Persuasion mode, 90–92
Petryaevskaya, Inga, 167
Pitney Bowes, 30, 60
Porter, Michael
    five forces framework, 79
Post-it® Notes, 77
Practice mode, 92–93
Prahalad, C. K., 172
PricewaterhouseCoopers (PwC), 7, 60,
    159–160, 189
    employee engagement, 8
    iChallenge initiative, 28–29

PowerPitch competition, 28, 149–150, 189
promoting ideas and innovation, 154–155
productive inquiry, 141–143
Prusak, Laurence, 33, 160
purpose of strategy, 76–78

R&D (research and development)
    as source of business model innovation, 17
Reagan, Ronald, 79
Red Hat Software, 22, 38, 52, 160
    employee engagement, 92
    leadership style, 74
    making sure all voices are heard, 143–144
    strategic conversations on the company mission, 56–59
    strategic conversations with partners, 172–173
    strategizing process, 193
Resource-Based View, 79–80
rhetoric, 126
    appeals to character and higher interest (ethos), 52–55
    appeals to personal commitment and passion (pathos), 52–55
    aspects of effective communication, 210
    limitations of appeals to logic (logos), 52–55
    persuading employees to pursue a specific strategy, 132
    persuasive powers, 91–92
Riboud, Franck, 152
Rigobon, Roberto, 85
Rite-Solutions, 48, 188
    brand enhancement, 195
    employee engagement, 48–49
    employee innovation, 64–65
    introverts as an underutilized resource, 144–145
    Rite-Track innovation community, 114–117
Rosenberg, Tina, 54
Ryanair, 77
RZhD (Russian railways company), 168

Sam's Club, 165
Schon, Donald, 136
Schulze, Dick, 117

Schumpeter, Joseph, 148
self-reinforcing innovation platform.
    See collateral benefits of strategic conversations
Senecal, Lori, 23, 48–49, 52, 65–66, 109–113, 130, 137, 193
sensing and operationalizing platforms, 30–31, 93, 119
    combining types of strategic conversation, 42–46
    Eisai, 166–167
    EMC, 167–168
    impact on business growth, 42
    level of inclusivity, 42
Shanghai Zhenhua Port Machinery Company, 165
Shirky, Clay, 1, 109
silo thinking, 32
Simon, Herbert, 81, 87, 90, 196
Six Sigma programs, 127–128
small thinking
    concern about strategic conversations, 19–20
smart failure
    need for organizations to manage, 137
Smith, Adam, 1, 20
social media
    engaging younger employees, 149–151
    identifying pioneers within the organization, 162–223
social network analysis, 200–203
social networking approach
    identifying pioneers within the organization, 162–223
    responses across generations, 161
    strategic conversations, 156–162
    threat perceived by middle managers, 161–162
    transformational potential for organizations, 162
social networks
    enhancing effects of strategic conversations, 191
social rewards
    motivation of employees, 137
Southwest Airlines, 21, 77
Stanford Topic Modeling Toolkit, 30, 201, 204
Starbucks, 82
Starwood Hotels, 128

Strategic conversation contribution map, 204, 208
strategic conversation mapping, 203–208
  determining the strength of strategic conversations, 208
strategic conversations
  application in real business situations, 2–3
  bridging cultures, 152
  bridging generation gaps, 149–151
  concern about producing chaos, 19–20
  concern about small-thinking, 19–20
  concern about time and effort involved, 20–21
  concern that strategy is not the role of employees, 20
  contradictory messages from management, 136
  definition, 2
  demands on corporate cultures, 22
  effects on the strategy development process, 22
  employee contributions, 2
  espoused theory versus theory-in-use, 136
  ethical burden, 97
  importance of conversational health, 140–146
  informing leadership decisions, 13
  making sure all voices are heard, 143–146
  management aesthetic, 18
  managing role of leaders, 127–128
  nature of good conversations, 127–128
  not brainstorming, 61–62
  objections to involving employees in strategy, 19–22
  potential benefits for organizations, 2
  potential risk to organizational secrets, 21
  productive inquiry, 141–143
  resisting anonymity among participants, 145–146
  rules for candid, respectful dialogue, 134–135
  scaling up, 55–56
  shaping of conversations by leaders, 62–64
  shutting down by management, 135–136
  social nature, 69–70
  social networking approach, 156–162
  social rewards, 137
  starting in your organization, 46–47
  techniques to span geographies, generations, and cultures, 153–154
  technology-free, 148–149
  See also conversations
strategic conversations typology, 23–24
  challenges, 28–30
  chaordic strategic conversations, 37–41
  combining different types, 42–46
  comparison of levels of inclusivity, 42
  competitions, 27–28
  impact on business growth, 42
  innovation communities, 41–42
  innovation days, 24–27
  sensing and operationalizing platforms, 30–31
  strategy reviews, 34–37
  T-shaped strategic conversations, 32–34
strategic planning approach, 81–82
strategic tools, 80
strategizing modes, 86–94
  Discovery mode, 87–89
  Judgment mode, 89–90
  Learning mode, 93
  Persuasion mode, 90–92
  Practice mode, 92–93
strategizing process, 86–97
  decision-making, 76
  Discovery mode, 87–89
  effects of strategic conversations, 22
  employee disconnection from, 49
  ethical burden, 97
  fostering knowledge exchanges, 128–129
  influence of the leader's values, 85
  Judgment mode, 89–90
  lack of employee involvement, 93–95
  leadership under strategic conversations, 95–97
  Learning mode, 93
  limitations of big data, 85–86
  Persuasion mode, 90–92
  Practice mode, 92–93
  questions leaders need to address, 97–98
  relation to conversation, 133
  role of strategic conversations, 95–97
  strategizing modes, 86–94
  supporting roles of conversation, 128–133

strategy
    definition, 18–19
    difficulty of defining, 76–78
    expanding opportunity space, 83–85
    form of social intercourse, 69–70
    goal of, 83–85
    influence of quality of conversations,
        140–146
    purpose of, 76–78
    relationship to business models, 18–19
strategy nihilists' approach, 81–82
strategy reviews
    combining types of strategic
        conversation, 42–46
    impact on business growth, 42
    level of inclusivity, 42
    type of strategic conversation, 34–37
strategy theory
    dynamic capabilities, 80
    External-Internal-Fit paradigm, 78–79
    history of business strategy, 77–81
    Knowledge-Based View, 80
    military analogies, 78
    organizational learning, 80
    Porter's five forces framework, 79
    profusion and variety of initiatives,
        80–81
    Resource-Based View, 79–80
suggestion boxes, 24
Sullivan, Gordon R., 137
Sun Microsystems, 15
SUPERVALU, 60, 187, 191, 200
SWOT analysis, 78, 88
systems theory, 20

T-shaped strategic conversations, 32–34, 185
    combining types of strategic
        conversation, 42–46
    encouraging employee participation, 60
    impact on business growth, 42
    level of inclusivity, 42
Taleb, Nassim, 81
talent management
    benefits of strategic conversations,
        189–191
technical innovation
    compared to business model innovation,
        14
technology
    limitations of competitive advantage, 164

not essential for strategic conversations,
        148–149
Teece, David, 8–9
textual analysis form of measurement,
        200–203
Thatcher, Margaret, 79
The Apprentice, 149
threats to business
    identifying and responding to, 13
Tiger Teams
    distinction from innovation
        communities, 124–219
tobacco companies
    anti-smoking advertising, 54
Todd, Steve, 36–37, 167, 198, 204
    social network analysis, 200–203
Toyota, 101
    NUMMI joint venture with GM, 172
Toyota Production System, 16, 21, 79
transactional framing
    effects on strategic conversations,
        134–135
transactional leadership style, 72–73
Tucci, Joe, 51, 182–184
Twitter, 162, 191

uncertainty
    and business opportunities, 15
    decision-making under, 2, 84–85, 90
    in business model innovation, 196
    link with profit, 84–85
    value-seeking under, 182
United States Army
    after action reviews (AARs), 137–139
    managing failure, 137–139

value creation. See Five Iron Laws of Value
        Creation
value-seeking under uncertainty, 182
Van Riper, Paul, 183–184, 186
vertical integration, 78
Vidovich, Nick, 109–111, 137, 190
Visa, 38

Wallace, William S., 138
Walmart, 118
war games
    business analogies, 183–184
Washington Mutual bank, 135–136
Wealth of nations (Smith, 1776), 1, 20

Weetjens, Jan, 174–175
Welch, Jack, 33, 74
West, Tom, 101
white knights
    recruitment to innovate business models, 17
Whitehurst, Jim, 22, 56–59, 74, 193
Williamson, Peter J., 164–165
women
    empowerment of. *See* Best Buy WOLF Pack innovation community
World Bank, 71, 75–76, 139–140, 159
    chaordic strategic conversations, 38–40

collaboration with partners, 173–176
Open Development Technology Alliance, 175–176
Wrigley's chewing gum, 77, 82
Wulf, Julie, 74

Xerox (formerly Haloid), 14
Xerox PARC, 77

Yeaney, Jackie, 59
YMCA Canada, 188
    participation in strategy development, 66–69